OUT OF THE BASEMENT

Out of the Basement

Youth Cultural Production in Practice and in Policy

MIRANDA CAMPBELL

McGill-Queen's University Press
Montreal & Kingston • London • Ithaca

ISBN 978-0-7735-4152-8 (cloth)
ISBN 978-0-7735-4153-5 (paper)

Legal deposit second quarter 2013
Bibliothèque nationale du Québec

Printed in Canada on acid-free paper that is 100% ancient forest free
(100% post-consumer recycled), processed chlorine free

This book has been published with the help of a grant from the Canadian
Federation for the Humanities and Social Sciences, through the Awards to
Scholarly Publications Program, using funds provided by the Social Sciences
and Humanities Research Council of Canada.

McGill-Queen's University Press acknowledges the support of the Canada
Council for the Arts for our publishing program. We also acknowledge the
financial support of the Government of Canada through the Canada Book
Fund for our publishing activities.

Library and Archives Canada Cataloguing in Publication

Campbell, Miranda, 1981–
    Out of the basement: youth cultural production in practice
    and in policy / Miranda Campbell.

    Includes bibliographical references and index.
    ISBN 978-0-7735-4152-8 (bound). – ISBN 978-0-7735-4153-5 (pbk.)

    1. Cultural industries – Canada – Case studies. 2. Youth – Canada –
    Case studies. 3. Popular culture – Canada – Case studies. 4. Cultural
    policy – Canada – Case studies. I. Title.

    HD9999.C9473C3 2013   306.0971   C2012-908581-2

This book was typeset by Interscript in 10.5/13 Sabon.

Contents

Acknowledgments

This book began as my doctoral dissertation in the Department of Integrated Studies in Education at McGill University and was enabled by financial support from the Fonds de recherche sur la societé et la culture as well as the McGill University Recruitment Excellence Fellowship. I would like to thank my doctoral supervisor, Bronwen Low, who provided direction and mentorship from the earliest stages of this project, and helped me clarify my research focus and questions. My PhD committee members, Michael Hoechsmann and Will Straw, are also to be thanked for their assistance in refining my areas of research through their suggestions. Will's encouragement initiated the process of revising the disseration and seeking out publication, and I thank him for his continued support and expertise in the areas of cultural policy and creative economies. As the external examiner of my dissertation, Ruben Gaztambide-Fernandez helped provide direction for the revision process through his useful comments.

I am grateful to Pat Tobin in the Department of Canadian Heritage, who helpfully provided me with an overivew of the current cultural policy and youth policy landscapes in Canada. I wish to thank three anonymous peer reviewers whose valuable feedback shaped the structure, scope, and argumentation of this book. I'd also like to thank my acquisition editor Jonathan Crago at McGill-Queen's University Press for his interest in the project, and his support, patience, and guidance through the publication process. As managing editor, Ryan Van Huijstee at MQUP has also provided valuable assistance in the publication process of this book: thank you, Ryan. I'm thankful to Joanne Muzak for copy editing, Elena Goranescu for production managing, David Drummond for designing the cover, and Rob Mackie for overseeing typesetting.

My partner, Adam Waito, has been an unflagging source of support through every stage of this project. Though he is not formally interviewed in this project, his experiences as an emerging musician form the backdrop of my understanding of the issues that I set out to tackle in this book and underride many of my assumptions about trends in youth cultural production. My interview subjects also sparked new ideas and avenues of research through their comments about their experiences; I thank them for their time, patience, and willingness to share their stories.

Many friends and family members have cheerleaded me through this project. My parents, Kathy and Peter Campbell, have always supported me and my academic endeavours, and I'd like to thank them for their unwavering faith in my abilities. Through their example, I credit them with instilling in me both a strong work ethic and a belief in the importance of education itself. Without this, this project would have never come to fruition.

PART ONE

Practices

Mapping Youth Cultural Production

From bedrooms, to classrooms, to studios, dark rooms, and green rooms, youth are increasingly producing creative works. More than a passing hobby, this surge in youth cultural production represents a significant employment trend that has yet to be grappled with at the policy level. With a quick glance, it may seem like it is aging boomers, not youth, who have the real clout in the creative industries. In the music industry, seasoned performers like The Rolling Stones, U2, Madonna, Bon Jovi, and Bruce Springsteen had the highest grossing concert tours in the 2000s. But figures other than concert revenues, such as digital downloads and ringtone sales, paint a different picture – both of where the music industry may be heading and of who is leading it there. Youth are changing the parameters of how money is (and is not) made not only in the music industry but in the creative industries at large. These changing parameters of the creative industries in the new millennium need to be mapped in order to get a better sense of new economic directions in these industries and to take better notice of the emerging routes that youth develop to make careers for themselves in creative fields. While examining prior forces that have shaped contemporary youth realities, *Out of the Basement: Youth Cultural Production in Practice and in Policy* takes up youth cultural production in the twenty-first century, and asks what has – or has not – changed as youth attempt to make a living from creative works.

No longer exclusively working in silo-specific fields like visual arts, music, dance, and film, youth are exploring new modes of cultural production. Angela McRobbie suggests that for youth, cultural practice may now include activities such as "cooking, gardening, sports, rambling, 'internetting,' producing fanzines, etc."[1] Although this definition may be overly broad, it is suggestive of the ways in which cultural production has exploded, in part due to the digitization of various forms of media, and is no longer necessarily tied to "the arts" as they have been traditionally understood. This explosion necessitates a redefinition of culture; for McRobbie, "culture in this specific context refers to the creative, expressive, and symbolic activities in media, arts and communicative practices which demonstrate, in this instance, potential for gainful activity."[2] Working with McRobbie's two articulations of cultural practice, this book looks at youth small-scale and self-generated creative employment. Activities that may have once been considered hobbies, or that may not have formerly been considered cultural, are now forming the basis for youth cultural employment. In this book, I set out to map these new characteristics of youth involvement in the creative industries and ask what the relationship between these activities and educational and cultural policies could be. Along the way, the book tracks structures that youth encounter as they attempt to create careers in the creative industries, including federal, provincial, and municipal policies, and also looks at initiatives that youth create themselves to facilitate their entries into the realm of work in this field.

BEEFS AND BILLBOARD CHARTS, GENERATIONAL DIVIDES, AND DIGITAL YOUTH: WHAT SOULJA BOY CAN TEACH US ABOUT CONTEMPORARY YOUTH CULTURAL PRODUCTION

Youth cultural production does not only happen quietly at home, in basements and bedrooms. By examining some youth creative workers who have broken through to mainstream success, the opening section of this Introduction highlights some themes and experiences that set the tone for later profiles of emerging young Canadian cultural producers. In 2007, at the age of seventeen, Soulja Boy home-recorded and self-produced the Grammy-nominated single, "Crank That (Soulja Boy)," more commonly known as "Superman," which spawned the "Superman" dance craze, became a number 1 single on the Billboard charts and also set records in digital download and ringtone sales as well as YouTube hits. Detractors criticized the vapidity of Soulja Boy's lyrics and accused him of writing for the highly lucrative but blatantly commercial and sonically simplistic ringtone market; nonetheless, his career sheds light on emerging trends in contemporary youth cultural production.

Amongst Soulja Boy's detractors was veteran rapper Ice-T. On a mixtape that was released in June 2008, Ice-T recorded a rant in which he decried the "garbage" quality of Soulja Boy's "Crank That (Soulja Boy)" single and suggested that Soulja Boy "single-handedly killed hip hop" by destroying the importance that has been given to lyrics by hip hop icons Rakim, Das EFX, Big Daddy Kane, and Ice Cube.[3] While Ice-T framed his criticism of Soulja Boy around the parameters of authenticity that have long been so central to hip hop culture, Soulja Boy was quick to reframe the terms of the debate from authenticity to generation. Soulja Boy responded to Ice-T through a YouTube video, and opened by stating, "This nigga Ice-T is old as fuck! This nigga is old enough to be my great-grandfather. We wikipedia'd this nigga. This nigga was born in 1958."[4] Soulja Boy evokes a generational (or hyperbolic multigenerational) divide not only between himself and Ice-T, but also implicitly between contemporary and seminal hip hop, emerging and established artists. This divide is not only evoked in terms of age, but also in terms of different modes of accessing and publishing information. Wikipedia is Soulja Boy's go-to reference for background knowledge to discredit Ice-T's ability to comment on youth cultural production, and YouTube is the vehicle to publish these opinions, rather than Ice-T's more traditional medium of a recorded and distributed musical release.

For Soulja Boy and many youth like him, the Internet and other digital technologies are not only a source of information, but are integral to the development of a creative career. Soulja Boy originally self-published his music on the Internet, and the Internet was also the source of the growth of his fame; his debut album is entitled *souljaboytellem.com*, which is also the name of his website. The music video for "Crank That (Soulja Boy)" depicts Soulja Boy's record contract being signed by instant messaging and shows fans watching his famed "Superman" dance online and on cell phones. It also features its own generational divide between parents and children, the latter having fully tuned in to Soulja Boy via various platforms, and the former scratching their heads at this seemingly unknown Internet star but then running to cash in by signing him to a record deal. In the beef with Ice-T, Soulja Boy positions Ice-T in a similar way to the clueless parent who is seen in his video. That Ice-T was born before the age of the Internet is a great source of amusement to Soulja Boy, and he highlights the rapid cycles of stardom that the Internet creates and that Ice-T is seemingly unable to grasp. He states: "I looked you up. This is a new day and age ... You was born before the Internet was created! How the fuck did you even find me? 'Superman,' that was last year, you late! Get with the times, you old-ass nigga."[5] Soulja Boy does not refute his Internet-based flash-in-the-pan status, but rather dismisses Ice-T for being so attached to something that has now become passé, even if what is passé is his own hit record. He instructs Ice-T that he "must understand. Shit is different." Hyperaware of his Internet phenomenon status, Soulja Boy comments on the video that he is making for YouTube saying, "this is going to have a million views in like, three days." After repeatedly stating that Ice-T's age voids his ability to comment on new trends in hip hop, Soulja Boy works his way into a more engaged response to Ice-T's criticisms and asserts that if Ice-T is dissatisfied with the state of hip hop, he should take action to improve it. Soulja Boy suggests that Ice-T "go to the hood. Start a hip hop school."[6]

This beef may have been Ice-T's stab at garnering media attention and selling records that Soulja Boy happily participated in, but Soulja Boy's story also illuminates new means of cultural production and distribution. For Soulja Boy, these new means are overlain on a generational divide and generationally divergent routes of cultural production. If this is the case, what does this beef have to tell us about youth involvement in the creative industries? The Canadian Youth Arts Network has noted the "lack of communication between established and emerging artists, which prevents a transfer of information across generations."[7] Is this beef one type of "communication" – or lack thereof – between established and emerging artists, one that illuminates not a lack of transferred information, but a lack of transferred values and priorities behind cultural production between generations? If Soulja Boy suggests that starting a "hip hop school" is a way to improve the state of contemporary hip hop, is this the role that systems of education might play vis-à-vis trends in youth cultural production? While Soulja Boy may be sometimes ridiculed for his approach to songwriting and his public persona, the questions that his oeuvre raises are important ones to grapple with if we do not want to perpetuate the divide that his "Superman" video presents of clueless parents and tuned-in youth. In many cases, this divide is seen in current cultural and educational policies that bear little relevance to contemporary youth cultural work, but this does not need to be the case. To this end, this book asks what the role of policy could be in relation to youth cultural production and suggests the need for more awareness and support of contemporary youth realities.

FOREVER YOUNG? EXTENDED YOUTH AND THE CREATIVE INDUSTRIES

Teen phenomena like Soulja Boy are hardly new, but the greater access to the means of cultural production that the digitization of media has brought means that younger youth are becoming involved in creative industries work. For some youth, like Justin Bieber, this means a new kind of Cinderella story: from local talent show to world tours via Usher playing the fairy godmother and YouTube playing the magic wand. This Bieber/Soulja Boy model of being discovered and subsequently shot to megastardom by initially building a following online is hardly representative of the average youth's experiences, but is suggestive of some of the characteristics of youth engagement with the creative industries, minus the megastardom. Access to digitized means of production and distribution means a changing landscape of creative industries work that can involve youth at younger and younger ages, as well as a broadening of definitions of creative industries work.

Take, for example, Tavi Gevinson, who in 2008 started a fashion blog, *The Style Rookie*, at age eleven. Though she has only recently begun high school, Gevinson is firmly entrenched in the world of fashion commentary and journalism due to her blogging experience. Known for her clever observations and the witty prose on her blog, Gevinson has been an invited speaker at panels such as "The Future of Fashion Blogging" and the "Generation Next Forum," which examined Generation Y's consumer habits. She's been a guest stylist for a fashion spread in *Black Book*, has guest-hosted *Fashion Television*, appears at high fashion events like New York Fashion Week, and is the youngest writer to have published an article in *Harper's Bazaar*. Discussing the importance of the Internet, Gevinson touches not on her Internet-based rise to stardom, but the role of the Internet in her self-education. The Internet "has given her an endless supply of music, fashion and other types of art. At her keyboard, she has developed expertise on a wide range of subjects – from Bob Dylan, her favorite singer, to Japan's Rei Kawakubo, one of her fashion design heroes."[8] That the Internet is the source of this knowledge raises questions about the relationship between youth and the formal education system. Gevinson has both tapped into her personal interests and developed these interests through writing via the Internet, not through any form of schooling. Gevinson also cites a disconnect between the formal education system and her blogging practice – a venture that has allowed her to develop her writing skills in ways that were not possible in school. Describing her posts as "not really articles," but rather "more just journal entries,"[9] Gevinson comments, "I never really liked writing before because at school I never got to write about what I like … With my blog, it's my thoughts, like my brain is being translated onto the computer."[10] This pattern of a divide between schooling and creative industries pursuits is found in many of the life stories of youth in this book. Soulja Boy's "hip hop school" may be a simplified shortcut to address this problem, but rather than perpetuate this divide between schooling and self-development, I examine what role education systems could play in youth's participation in the creative industries and if they could be more responsive to the needs of contemporary youth as they face these industries.

Though her life trajectory may end up being shaped by what her blog spawns rather than any form of schooling, Gevinson remains committed to attending high school and college. Her early career has been launched by her blog, but *The Style Rookie* is not a direct source of financial gain for her. Asked if she will monetize her blog and make it a source of income, Gevinson states, "No, but that might change. A college fund could be helpful."[11] Megan Twohey reports that Gevinson has "declined reality show pitches and book deals."[12] Still, Gevinson has suggested that she may want a career in fashion as an adult, and her youthful experiences have certainly primed her to make this a reality if she chooses it. Gevinson's story illuminates the ways in which new kinds of creative pursuits, like blogging, can lead into creative industries work in indirect ways. Due to her age and situation, Gevinson's creative practice is currently not hindered by the need to earn a living, but the question of income is a pressing concern for many youth creative workers.

The models that Soulja Boy, Justin Bieber, and Tavi Gevinson provide are hardly representative of typical youth experiences, but they elucidate new points of entry into creative industries work at young ages. Though any youngster with a laptop might have greater means to make music, films, or publish writing than in the past, the navigation and negotiation of the logistics of creative industries careers necessitates skills that are not always intuitive or taught in schools. The access to the tools of creation that many youth have does not in itself enable success in the creative industries or suggest that the creative industries are outpacing other career options altogether. The changing parameters of the creative industries might mean new types of access for younger youth, and the instability of work in the creative industries might also mean the prolongation of a youthful lifestyle for those on the older end of the youth spectrum. Quebec's 2001 youth policy document, *Bringing Youth into Québec's Mainstream*, grapples with this extension of youth on both ends. It states that it is primarily directed towards youth aged 15–29, but extends to youth aged 30–35 and aged 12–14 in cases where issues would be pertinent to older and younger youth, such as work and civil service, and adolescence, respectively.

Much has been made of the ever-lengthening transition from youth to adulthood. In 1991, we saw aging slackers in Douglas Coupland's novel *Generation X* check out of careers and families, opting instead to pursue self-discovery in the desert. Through the 1990s, with films like *Clerks* and *Mallrats*, director Kevin Smith depicted driftless twenty-somethings with no serious career or family ambitions. Even Sonic Youth aren't so young anymore, as the band members have reached their fifties, with Thurston Moore still sporting the baggy jeans/T-shirt/sneakers style that was emblematic of the '90s grunge era. These aging youth are not just a phenomenon of the '90s; the 2000s have seen the continuation of this trend. In 2010, CBS debuted the sitcom *$#*! My Dad Says*, adapted from Justin Halpern's bestselling book, based on the Twitter feed he began to record his father's inane comments after moving back in with his parents at age twenty-nine. Halpern remarks that his father is "like one of [his] best friends,"[13] suggesting a new type of relationship between parents and adult children, as these children increasingly delay reaching full independence and autonomy but are not dependent on their parents as they were as minors.

For some analysts, this extended period of youth is a result of changing economic and social conditions. Foremost amongst these conditions is the changing reality of securing stable full-time employment. Sylvain Bourdon and Mircea Vultur note the trend towards temporary, contract, and part-time work, as well as multiple jobs

and self-employment for youth, which marks a shift away from the
permanent full-time work that has been associated with reaching
adulthood.[14] When noting the trend towards the extension of youth,
Quebec's youth policy suggests that the shift in employment patterns
away from permanent full-time work prolongs youth because life
paths are no longer linear.[15] Instead of moving steadily and progressively towards adulthood, youth move back and forth between starting new careers, returning to school, living independently, and living
with their parents, which results in a lengthier term of obtaining the
traditional markers of adulthood – marriage, house, career, children,
etc. This means that the transition to adulthood is not only delayed,
but has also become more fluid.[16] Bob Coles states that the "complex, messy, risky, and above all, long" routes into stable employment for youth "[call] into question the very conceptualisation of
'youth.'"[17] Though this book foregrounds the category of youth in
its study of cultural production and cultural policies, it also recognizes that this reconceptualization of the very category of youth suggests a broadening of both the key characteristics and the demographic
traditionally associated with youth. In its investigation of youth practices, this book will also turn to small-scale cultural organizations,
such as L'APLAS in Chapter 6 and Indyish in Chapter 7, that may not
have youth as their specific mandate but have particular relevance for
small-scale youth cultural production as they share commonalties in
their emerging, exploratory, and transitional qualities.

Beyond the economic and labour market forces that have led to
the prolongation of youth, Stéphanie Gaudet provides an overview
of how the cultural forces of "detraditionalization," or the relaxing
of social norms, have led to the "destandardization of life courses,"
which can result in the deferral of adulthood, as youth now have
greater life choices.[18] Gaudet foregrounds various new terms that
have been coined to capture this extended period of youth, including
Tony Anatrella's "adolescence," James Côté's "youthhood," Olivier
Galland's "post-adolescence," and Jeffrey Arnett's "emerging adulthood." Arnett has pushed to have this "emerging adulthood" phase
of life recognized as a distinct developmental stage. He notes the
extension of youth into the late twenties and argues that this is suggestive of a particular phase of brain development that is characterized by self-exploration, self-discovery, self-focus, and "a sense of
possibilities." Whether this extension of youth is caused by economic, cultural, or psychological forces, the symptoms are the same:

youth living a lifestyle that was once thought of as transitional but may now have longevity as a stage of life that is not necessarily a precursor to an older and more settled phase.

OUT OF THE BASEMENT: NAVIGATION AND NEGOTIATION OF BEDROOM ECONOMIES

While a decline in available full-time work might mean a prolongation of youth, there is also a lack of desire for permanent full-time work amongst many of the youth profiled in this book. Marc Molgat and Katharine Larose-Hébert note that research about youth values concerning employment shows a shift away from the idea that work is a societal duty; instead, youth think work should be interesting, expressive, and fulfilling.[19] Many of these qualities of employment have been associated with the creative industries, which are increasingly seen by youth as an alternative to the drudgery that is sometimes linked with more traditional and more stable forms of employment. Mark Banks and David Hesmondhalgh provide an overview of how the "utopian presentation of creative work" as a "freely chosen vocation" that is exempt from "much of the boredom and disaffection characteristic of enforced or materially necessary labour" serves to obscure the problems and difficulties of creative labour.[20] As they explain, creative labour is

> project-based and irregular, contracts tend to be short-term, and there is little job protection; that there is a predominance of self-employed or freelance workers; that career prospects are uncertain and often foreshortened; that earnings are usually slim and unequally distributed, and that insurance, health protection and pension benefits are limited; that creatives are younger than other workers, and tend to hold second or multiple jobs; and that women, ethnic and other minorities are under-represented and disadvantaged in creative employment. All in all, there is an oversupply of labour to the creative industries with much of it working for free or on subsistence wages.[21]

In this book, I seek to map out some of these difficulties of creative labour and do so by making use of the life stories of individual youth creative workers, starting in Chapter 1. Rising stars like Soulja Boy, Bieber, or Gevinson may contribute to this "utopian" conceptualization of creative work, but in this book, life stories of young cultural producers chronicle the process of navigating and negotiating the challenges of establishing oneself in the creative industries, and serve to mitigate this utopian thread. Though Banks and Hesmondhalgh examine the trend and implications of creative firms moving towards contract-based and freelance work rather than offering permanent full-time employment, *Out of the Basement* examines a different set of challenges than the oversupply of creative labour. It tracks the process of youth attempting to pursue their own small-scale creative ventures that are both entrepreneurial and community-oriented rather than attempting to find work in a creative firm.

Whether it is a result of a lack of available permanent employment or an active choice to turn away from it, the move towards ad hoc creative industries employment means an extension of a lifestyle associated with youth. For Angela McRobbie, work in the creative industries is "permanently transitional"[22] because it is unstable – the lack of stability in creative industries employment means a lack of life stability, which is a significant marker of adulthood as it has been traditionally defined. Despite this instability, public policies are still based in the norms of permanent full-time work. The Canadian Conference of the Arts (CCA) notes a discrepancy between current policy structures and the reality of work in the creative industries: "the public policy framework still remains firmly rooted in the industrial/agrarian paradigm dominated by the employer/employee relationship and lifelong careers with a single employer. Unfortunately, these realities are largely inconsistent with the concept of the creative economy. In the creative economy, an individual is likely to elect self-employment as the preferred mode of operation, seeking and obtaining income from a variety of sources and activities related to the creative process."[23] Due to this permanently transitional quality, we might also characterize the creative industries as intrinsically youthful. Indeed, the CCA notes that work in the creative industries means a "lifelong continuing reeducation or professional training circuit."[24] Making a living in the creative industries requires constant adaptation to new markets, new ways of doing business, new materials, and new audiences. The prolongation of youth through the continuing reeducation circuit that is required to deal with these changing logistics of the creative industries raises questions about our current systems of education and their ability to accommodate back-and-forth movement between work and school.

This book profiles youth ranging in age from eighteen to thirty-five who are attempting to make careers in the creative industries in small-scale and self-generated ways, and this age range suggests the extended period of youth that is seen in creative industries employment. Younger youth pursuing creative industries employment at ages where they are typically tied up with braces, homework, and soccer practices raises implications for systems of education, and older youth pursuing transient creative industries employment at ages where they are typically tied up with kids, mortgages, and staff meetings raises implications for retirement and pensions, parental leaves, extended medical coverage, and unemployment benefits. Sandra Franke notes these types of policy concerns that arise from the prolongation of youth and foregrounds the implications of youth having to build their own safety nets in the absence of a public policy system that is able to address this extension of youth.[25] Rather than suggest a neoliberal championing of the economic potentials of the creative industries and governmental encouragement of more workers to enter this field, *Out of the Basement* looks at ways in which cultural policies could be more responsive to the often low-income and challenging realities of small-scale self-generated creative work and forwards a creative ecology model based in sustainable community development.

Support and investment are needed across the cultural sector, but recognizing the differing needs and trajectories of youth who are entering this field could allow for policies to better match unfolding economic and creative directions. In this work, I do not seek to suggest that youth need more support than other creative workers. Instead, I advocate for developing more awareness of these emerging youth practices. The Centre for Expertise on Culture and Communities' (CECC) *Under Construction: The State of Cultural Infrastructure in Canada* report maps the need for investment in cultural infrastructure[26] across Canada, but also highlights that, in this regard, youth may have differing needs than other segments of the population: "We are also experiencing the coming-of-age of the baby boom echo generation, accompanied by new multidisciplinary cultural practices, preferences, needs, and expectations. On the basis of research for the CECC's *Building Blocks* project, it appears this generation is less interested in large, formal, single-use facilities and more interested in multidisciplinary facilities and smaller arts spaces (e.g., for music, art shows). It is also a generation interested in merging technology and art – which requires large open spaces that are flexible."[27] The danger of continuing to ignore these differences between emerging and established practices is that investments – in this case, in cultural infrastructure – will become outdated if they do not meet the needs of the young: youth participants in the CECC study "perceived a disconnect between emerging artistic practices and the facilities being championed, funded, and built today."[28] Due to this disconnect, policy can also become increasingly irrelevant over time, and this irrelevance can create harm, even sometimes criminalizing youth creative practices.

If generating one's own work in the creative industries makes use of logistical skills that are not taught in schools, youth must learn to navigate and negotiate their way out of basements and bedrooms as they attempt to make livings from creative works. This navigation and negotiation process forms one of the central investigations of this book. It's a grassroots stop-and-start process that requires full commitment, often without any direct link to financial rewards. This process has yet to be mapped out: youth activities often do not register in discussions of the creative industries, so there is a lack of knowledge about the experiences of youth as they face these industries. Colin Mercer discusses the need to "know more" about culture and argues for the need to improve quantitative and qualitative baselines through cultural mapping.[29] Importantly, Mercer highlights "the need for constant refreshing" of cultural indicators,[30] and this is particularly true when discussing youth creative practices that are in flux, evolving, or, as discussed above, are reconfiguring and broadening definitions of the cultural.

Across the book, common themes emerge from youths' discussions of their processes of attempting to make livings from creative industries work, such as the bleeding together of work and leisure time, the need for adequate spaces to carry out and house creative work, the fact that this work is often interdisciplinary and touches on for-profit and not-for-profit streams, and a confusion or lack of awareness of the policies and mechanisms of government as they concern cultural work. While the life stories of the youth profiled in this book foreground challenges and mitigate the often utopian conceptualization of creative work, there are stories of success, too – though the nature of these successes may also mitigate a rags-to-riches version of what success in the creative industries means. A central premise of this book is that these smaller stories and smaller successes, and their accompanying challenges, are stories that are not currently being registered, even if youth are increasingly seeking out creative work. *Out of the Basement* profiles individual youth experiences to allow youth to tell their own stories, so these voices can be heard. From these specific individual experiences, I move into broader examinations of the themes raised by youth while describing their experiences engaging in creative employment. Below, I begin the process of mapping youth entry and involvement with the creative industries with a discussion of cultural statistics revealed from 2006 Canadian census data that offer a snapshot of some of the current parameters of youth creative work in Canada.

MAPPING YOUTH ENGAGEMENT WITH THE CREATIVE INDUSTRIES

Scholars are beginning to notice what Michael Hoechsmann and Bronwen Low have characterized as a "wildfire of youth cultural production,"[31] but further work needs to be done to map the implications that this wildfire has for employment trends in the creative industries and for education policies. In the twenty-first century, the creative industries and cultural policy have become growing areas of academic research, as seen in the work of David Hesmondhalgh, Angela McRobbie, Kate Oakley, Stuart Cunningham, Richard Caves, Richard Florida, and John Hartley, among others. Coupling this interest is a growing awareness in the field of education that schooling needs to better engage, grapple with, and build young people's creative talents and interests.[32] Nonetheless, there currently remains a gap in empirical research between youth experiences in schools and their experiences of successfully working in the creative industries. This gap means that there is a lack of concrete data about youth involvement with the creative industries, but a trend towards small-scale and self-generated work in the creative industries can be pieced together from available research.

In his research, Richard Florida chronicles the rise of "the creative class," or the class of workers who use creative skills in their careers.[33] In order to make the claim that this "class" is growing, Florida foregrounds the increase in artistic work over the last century in the United States, commenting that "the numbers of people making a living from artistic and cultural creativity also expanded dramatically over the course of the past century and particularly since 1950. Professional artists, writers, and performers – so-called 'bohemians' increased from some 200,000 in 1900 to 525,000 in 1950 and to 2.5 million in 1999, an increase of more than 375 per cent since 1950. There were roughly 250 bohemians for every 100,000 Americans in 1900, a figure that increased to roughly 350 by 1950. That number crossed 500 in 1980, before reaching 900 for every 100,000 Americans in 1999."[34] Florida notes that his data comes from the US Bureau of Labor Statistics, but does not note which census category of employment he is investigating. In the Canadian context, the 2006 census showed that 346,315 Canadians were employed in the arts, entertainment, and recreation sector of the workforce. A more accurate picture of the "bohemians" that Florida describes, however, is perhaps found in a subsection of the arts, entertainment, and recreation sector, with the 51,860 Canadians who declared their employment status as "independent artists, writers, and performers" in 2006, which is roughly a 12 per cent increase from the 46,215 people employed in this sector of the workforce in 2001.[35] These numbers are small compared to Florida's US figures. Even adjusting for a much smaller population, these figures suggests that Canada has 166 "bohemians" for every 100,000 people, which is a lower number than Florida's 1900 figure. Florida's argument about the magnetic draw of "creative" cities may help explain this discrepancy, as Canadian cities have a shorter history as cosmopolitan / bohemian centers.

Current youth engagement with the creative industries may also be difficult to capture through examining census categories as many youth activities may fall outside of the category of "independent artists, writers, and performers," even if they are carving out careers with creative projects in "independent" ways. As we have seen, McRobbie suggests that youth cultural production includes a diverse array of activities that traditionally have not been considered cultural; these pursuits often become "gainful activities."[36] If these activities are shaping the future of creative work, then the category of "artist" that the census offers is too narrow to adequately capture trends in youth activities. Many census responders who would fit in Florida's "bohemian" category may no longer classify themselves as artists, writers, or performers, and many of these "bohemians" may not fill out their census forms at all.

The category of "independent artists, writers, and performers" may also not capture youth who are involved with the creative industries while also pursuing other kinds of work. Risa Dickens, who runs an artist network and online boutique called Indyish, comments that the artists on her website are not aiming to "make millions." They would just "like to meet their subsistence level [through earning a living from creative practices] – that's what we want. Just to make a living off of [art], that would be the ideal. And they work crazier hours trying to make that happen, working other jobs, trying to make it happen. Especially some of the younger people, working at McDonald's and shit, for like eight bucks an hour, and then going home and making complex beautiful Celtic traditional wedding rings to try to sell on Indyish because they make jewellery in their spare time – that's all they want to do."[37] Risa's suggestion that young artists are grappling with paid employment to try to support their creative projects until they are able to make a living from these projects is an accurate diagnosis of the conditions facing contemporary youth cultural producers. In 2007, the Canada Council for the Arts initiated a nation-wide series of forums about issues facing young artists and arts audiences that culminated in a report called *Next Generation of Artistic Leaders and Arts Audiences Dialogue*. This report found that "arts practitioners are not solely invested in singular aspects of creative practice or sectoral employment. Many participants have multi-disciplinary orientations, and work many different types of jobs to support their creative work."[38] In terms of earning a living, "very few participants said they survived from creative activities. Some artists said they felt fortunate to have found paying freelance work in jobs that are related to their field, such as arts instruction, arts administration or providing technical and logistical support to other artists or productions ... A small number of participants said they worked in fields completely unrelated to the arts sector as a means of supporting themselves."[39]

The reliance on other sources of income outside of revenue from creative work varies province to province in Canada, but, overall, a general picture of pursuing creative work while working other jobs is consistent. Albertans profiled in the *Next Generation* report commented that they were not able to support themselves from their creative work and had other unrelated jobs. Additionally, the increasingly high cost of living, including costs for housing and rehearsal and exhibition spaces, made many young Albertans feel compelled to leave the province. Similarly, in BC, "some noted that because of the high cost of housing in British Columbia, particularly in Vancouver and Victoria, artists and arts practitioners are forced to work long hours, often over several jobs to find the means to support basic living costs."[40] Young artists in Newfoundland and Labrador were faced with different problems due to the small size of the arts scene in this region, which necessitated finding jobs unrelated to their fields and resulted in frustration that creative work was relegated a hobby rather than genuine employment.

Those working in the arts are more likely than other types of workers to only have part-time work in their field, and the work that artists do in other fields may also influence how people choose to designate their occupations in the census and contribute to the relatively low number of "independent artists, writers, and performers." Hill Strategies Research's analysis of the 2006 Canadian census data shows that 42 per cent of artists declared that they worked part-time, which is significantly higher than the 22 per cent of workers in the population as a whole who indicated that they worked part-time. Similarly, artists could find employment from their artistic work for less of the year than workers in the population as a whole, as "68% of artists worked most of the year (40 to 52 weeks) compared with 77% of the overall labour force."[41] These figures, and those that follow, represent those people who designated "artist" as their status on their census form; others, especially the young, may not designate their status as such. If they did, these figures would likely be even lower.

2006 census data shows that 42 per cent of artists were self-employed, and this rate of self-employment was dramatically higher than the 7 per cent of self-employment in the overall labour force.[42] The incomes of self-employed artists were much lower than those of self-employed workers in the population as a whole: the average income for self-employed artists was $15,200 compared to an average income of $31,000 for all self-employed workers in Canada. On the whole, artists earned dramatically less than the average Canadian worker. The average earnings for artists were $22,700, whereas they were $36,300 for the Canadian population as a whole. When comparing median earnings, these discrepancies are heightened: median earnings for artists were $12,900, whereas they were $26,900 for the Canadian population as whole.[43]

In addition to low income and self-employment, artistic work is also characterized by the heavy presence of young labourers. The arts, entertainment, and recreation sector of the Canadian workforce (of which the independent artist category is a subsector) had one of the lowest median ages (36.3) of employees in all sectors of the workforce in 2006; only retail trade and accommodation and food services had lower median ages at 36 and 28.8, respectively,[44] and these types of work are sometimes temporary positions for youth while they are students pursuing training in other fields. The low median age of the arts, entertainment, and recreation field suggests that the increase in employment in this field in Canada between 2001 and 2006 is an increase of youth entering into this field rather than more mature workers taking up this line of work later in life. Overall, this census data gives us a picture of young self-employed artists who are not working full-time with their artistic pursuits and who are earning dramatically less than the population as a whole.

Part One of this book is structured around developing more knowledge about contemporary youth creative practices and employment. Chapter 1 uses individual life stories to map out some of the challenges of the navigation and negotiation process experienced by youth attempting to make a living through creative work. Chapter 2 continues this mapping project by giving an overview of the theoretical underpinnings of academic research in youth culture and youth practices. This chapter examines the possibilities and shortcomings of current conceptualizations of youth to direct academic research that speaks to youth realities at work and in the education system.

Part Two moves from mapping youth experiences and academic frameworks that theorize them to mapping the policy terrain that is directed – or not directed – towards youth creative work. This section of the book moves from federal to provincial to municipal policies and asks what the role of these policies is with regards to youth cultural production. Rather than provide an exhaustive overview of the overlapping nets of the three policy levels in Canada, I work towards reading policy through the lens of youth and interrogate particular pieces of policy to think through how they envision or ignore youth practices. In Chapter 3, I begin with the Canadian federal policy landscape and examine Canadian cultural policies in relation to their ability to foster youth experiences in the creative industries, and this leads into a discussion of how youth might be positioned when making the case for culture in Chapter 4. In Chapter 5, I move from the federal level to international comparisons and consider the possibilities and limitations of recent British cultural policies and the implications of these British cultural policies for education systems. For this investigation, I turn back to the Canadian context, and as education is provincially administered in Canada, I look at the framework for arts education in the Quebec Education Program. In Chapter 6, I turn to municipal policies and explore municipal policy issues in Montreal. In this chapter, I investigate municipal polices that have constrained small-scale youth creative practices, despite Montreal's branding of itself as a "cultural metropolis." In order to investigate the role of policy in relation to youth practices, I review not only cultural and employment policies, but also broader areas such as copyright, cleanliness, and noise bylaws in Part Two. As such, I theorize the ways in which policy works across and between fields, and shapes how youth activities are defined.

After this investigation of the relationship between policy structures and youth experiences, Part Three examines how community and youth initiatives help facilitate the process of youth navigation of the creative industries. In Chapter 7, I place emphasis on the concept of networks as they relate to youth cultural production and profile the Montreal-based artist network Indyish. In Chapter 8, I look at the international youth-led initiative Ignite the Americas and consider the possibilities and challenges of youth partnering with governments to work towards a more youth-centered agenda for cultural policies. I also investigate the ways in which Ignite the Americas makes connections between community cohesion, the creative industries, and youth employment. I continue this investigation with an examination of The Remix Project in Toronto, which also makes these connections and offers programs to youth to help foster their immersion in the creative industries. In the Conclusion, I return to life stories of youth and close out the book with profiles of two Montreal-based music promoters that highlight themes that have emerged from youth experiences across the book. Ultimately, I conclude that a more comprehensive youth policy framework and a more responsive education system are needed to better support youth involved in the creative industries.

1

Youth Voices

Life Stories of Navigation and Negotiation

To begin the project of mapping the new parameters of youth involvement in the creative industries, this chapter profiles the experiences of youth cultural producers through their life stories. These life stories continue to emerge throughout the book and serve to illuminate the interplay between the structures that youth encounter and the initiatives that they create as they attempt to determine what it means to make a living in the creative industries. Methodologically, the use of these life stories comes out of the turn to narrative and oral history research in the social sciences. Dan Goodley, Rebecca Lawthom, Peter Clough, and Michele Moore cite a growth in these types of research and comment that "our belief is that life stories – our chosen form of narrative – tell us much about individual and collective, private and public, structural and agentic and real and fictional worlds ... Stories fundamentally capture the diverse and changing nature of individual and social lives at the start of the twenty-first century."[1] Similarly, discussing phenomenological research, Max Van Manen underscores "the importance of interpretive models that place human situatedness central and are based on the belief that we can best understand human beings from the experiential reality of the lifeworlds."[2] In this book, I operate from this assumption that the lifeworld, or the world of lived experience, can teach us about the realities, in this case, of contemporary youth cultural production. Investigating what it is like to experience creative industries employment as a contemporary youth, I ask what these individual experiences can teach us about the challenges, as well as the successes, that youth experience in small-scale and self-generated creative industries endeavours. I analyze common themes that emerge out of the life stories of youth and highlight these themes as areas that need further study such that they can receive greater attention at the policy level.

Many of the life stories in this book started from my own experiences of being situated amongst a community of small-scale cultural producers, and I began drawing my initial sample from the vast pool of local cultural producers who are connected to my own informal social network in Montreal. As my partner attempts to build a career as a musician, I've witnessed some of the changing realities of the creative industries firsthand. Chapter 6 will discuss the particularities of Montreal and examine the conditions in the city that allow it to incubate creative work. Though these particularities may suggest the uniqueness of Montreal and the youth cultural producers who call it home, the central navigation and negotiation process of attempting to make a living is a common experience of youth as they face the creative industries, regardless of where they reside.

Case studies and interviews on their own are partial and limited representations of youth experiences, but they offer valuable insights into the contemporary dynamics of youth work in the creative industries. Discussing interviewing creative workers in order to generate knowledge about creative work, Angela McRobbie argues, "despite all the problems of dealing with personal accounts as evidence, testimony, or simply data, it still seems worthwhile to me to ask how these cultural workers experience this form of economic activity."[3] In this book, I also ask how small-scale creative workers experience this form of employment and focus on the Canadian context, in which research about this subject has been slim. The Introduction began to establish the trend towards youth small-scale self-generated creative employment through mapping statistical trends in Canadian census data. The life stories profiled here add to this picture by illustrating experiences and lending immediacy and personal details to a broader trend. Marcia Langton comments that "subjective experiences, varied social values, and multiple readings and interpretations can be accommodated in cultural maps, as can more utilitarian 'cultural inventories.'"[4] In this work, I seek to accommodate these "subjective experiences" and foreground what they have to offer to a cultural inventory of contemporary youth creative practices. While current policy structures often make no mention of youth, and may implicitly understand youth practices to be the same as other types of practices, these interviews contradict these assumptions through identifying the particular and unique features of youth creative work.

While life stories may offer interviewees' biases and limited experiences, they are a valid form of knowledge, especially with regards to learning what the process of navigating and negotiating the creative industries is like. This book endeavours to forge new discussions about youth creative work by drawing on and piecing together both academic and local community expertise. In addition to academic sources and policy documents, I draw on community reports from youth arts and other organizations, as this community knowledge offers expertise in profiling youth experiences.

Witnessing some of my peers' struggles has shaped my view that policy could and should be more responsive to youth creative work, and that more knowledge about this form of labour is needed, and these assumptions inform the work as a whole. Researching activities that I've witnessed firsthand in my community has the advantage of imparting unique expertise but has the drawbacks of partial and limited knowledge. The growth of oral history and narrative research emanates from a broader postmodern turn in the social sciences, and this postmodern framework informs my understanding of my position towards my research. Discussing the nature of postmodern research, Donna Haraway argues that the production of knowledge must be seen as situated, contextual, partial, and contingent. She states, "I am arguing for a politics of epistemologies of location, positioning and situating, where partiality and not universality is the condition of being heard to make rational knowledge claims ... we do not seek partiality for its own sake, but for the sake of the connections and unexpected openings situated knowledges make possible. The only way to find a larger vision is to be somewhere in particular."[5] As such, the researcher's own situated positionality can be seen as a suitable location from which postmodern research, claims, and conclusions can emerge.

This work makes use of non-probability purposeful sampling, in that "particular settings, persons, or events are deliberately selected for the important information that they can provide that cannot be gotten as well from other choices."[6] For this project, particular interviewees and case studies were selected on the basis of involvement with small-scale youth cultural production, either as practitioners or organizers. Youth who were employed in cultural firms as workers or interns, rather than creating their own small-scale activities, were not selected. To this end, intensity sampling was used: I selected "experiential experts" based in their public and extended involvement as small-scale cultural practitioners and organizers. I sought out interviewees who were both male and female, spanning the age range of eighteen to thirty-five, and who had at least two years of experience working in the field of cultural production. I aimed to profile a range of experiences from different creative fields. This initial sample was expanded and enriched through "snowball" methodology. Rather than setting out with a determined number of interviewees or case studies, the research proceeded organically, in that insider information from the initial group of informants added several useful case studies to the sample, which allowed me to reach a point of adequate data saturation. My interviews also extended to profiling programs, organizations, and policies that make specific mention of youth cultural production. Due to the use of non-probability purposeful sampling, my interviewees may not be representative of all youth creative workers; nonetheless, I aim to provide a useful and insightful portrait of my particular sample, which may offer some starting points for further study of a more representative sample.

This book foregrounds a lack of awareness and attention to youth cultural production at the policy level and forwards the life stories of youth as a mechanism to register their experiences. Rather than focus on the end products of cultural production, these life stories develop an understanding of the often challenging experience of attempting to make a living as a cultural producer, and interviews were structured around allowing the participants to tell their stories in these regards. Many youth were keen to tell their stories and have their stories heard. The lack of awareness of youth creative practices at the policy level means that some youth activities are illegal or criminalized, but these youth were still keen to have their names and stories forwarded in order to have their challenging experiences recorded. Due to the sensitive and personal nature of these stories, the informed consent process for this book meant not only having my interviewees sign consent forms that informed them of their rights but also continuing to check in with interviewees and have them review how they were profiled in the work as it evolved over several drafts. In some cases, as my work changed, so did my interviewees' situations, which resulted in follow-up interviews and edits that my interviewees recommended based on their changing situations and levels of comfort with disclosing personal information. In this chapter, these interviews begin to establish some of the characteristics of contemporary youth practices, and the work unfolds from this point by attempting to piece together policies, programs, and literature that are directed to the types of experiences profiled here.

SEAN SWAPS SUMMER JOBS: THE REDEFINITION OF WORK FOR YOUTH CULTURAL PRODUCERS

Sean Michaels's experiences demonstrate the diversity of pursuits that creative industries work may now mean for youth cultural producers. Employed as a music journalist, Sean writes fiction, performs improv comedy, runs a hobby music label, organizes a film festival, is a renowned blogger, and has pursued a number of Internet-based ventures. Not all of the activities that Sean is involved with are profitable or even intended for economic gain, but all of these pursuits, considered together, give a picture of Sean's involvement in the creative industries and are suggestive of the broadening boundaries of creative industries work for youth.

Tracking the origin of Sean's creative industries pursuits takes us to the spring of 2004. Gmail accounts were starting to pick up steam, but, at this time, the availability of these accounts was still limited to "invite only" from existing members. Due to the high demand for these email accounts, people starting selling their invites on eBay. In 2004, Sean was twenty-two and was studying at McGill University. He moved back home to Ottawa for a summer job working for Canadian Culture Online in the Department of Canadian Heritage, but, after moving back, he found out that his job had fallen through. Stuck at his parents' house in Ottawa, and noting the furor over the Gmail situation, on 17 May 2004, Sean started www.gmailswap.com, a message board where people could post what they would give for a Gmail invite. The rules were simple: no money could be exchanged, and no illicit activities could be offered (no sex, no drugs, etc.). The site took off as Sean wanted it to; for example, participants offered to courier homemade brownies across the continent, to tour visitors around Istanbul, or to act as a personal bodyguard in Chicago. In one interview about his site, Sean commented, "the best part has really been the extraordinary wealth of creativity, character, and human diversity that's been on show." He added, "my favorite's probably the flight-crew member who has offered to send postcards once a month from all over the world."[7] At its peak, there were a thousand new posts on the site a day. Soon, many major news outlets, including the *Washington Post* and the *New York Times*, had contacted Sean at his parents' house for interviews, where he was still sitting, unemployed. In July, he realized that he could sell banner ad space on the site, and this became his new summer job. As Gmail accounts became open to the general public, interest in www.gmailswap.com evidently waned, and Sean sold the domain name for six hundred dollars in March 2005. This Internet foray is suggestive of the contemporary explosion of creative practices as employment pursuits, as seen with McRobbie's argument that "internetting" might be one area of the "future of work."[8]

The Gmail site wasn't Sean's first Internet venture; in 2003, Sean launched the influential music blog www.saidthegramophone.com with two friends. The blog was the first of its kind to post free mp3s of new music. It is renowned in the music industry as a tastemaker and was voted one of the best twenty-five blogs by *Time* in 2009.[9] This site does not produce any direct financial benefits, as it does not sell any advertising space, but through this venture, Sean has created a career for himself as a music journalist while also having adequate time to work on writing fiction. In 2008, he quit his job as a legal secretary to write a daily music column for the *Guardian*'s website. He says,

> For the past ten years, I wanted as a career to write fiction, so I always resisted slipping into other careers that would supersede that. Even coming out of university, and I could have tried to pursue [paid] writing work, I resisted that. I didn't even look into doing that because I don't really want to spend all of my time writing about music for magazines. I started to work as a legal secretary and then this opportunity came along with the *Guardian*, which kind of stumbled into my lap. It was an issue of being presented an opportunity that felt like something I could accommodate within my writing career rather than would take over my writing career. So one of the reasons it worked or happened for me was its low-impact accidental nature rather than being something I sought out.[10]

Sean relates initially trying to resist paid employment working for others in creative firms so that his creative work could be for himself. Though Sean found out about the job at the *Guardian* through his "personal network system," he also suggests that many of his work opportunities have emerged out of his success with creating a name for himself with his blog *Said the Gramophone*:

> *Said the Gramophone* is I think 99 per cent responsible for all of the paid work that I've done. Maybe my hardcore skills would have been enough to impress [the *Guardian*], but it was my CV, and at the head of my CV was *Said the Gramophone*, which my editor knew of. When I starting doing a little more freelancing around 2007, it was always like, "Hi, I write for *Said the Gramophone*, this is what I'd like to do for you. What do you say?" My work for *The Believer*, which was one of the higher profile gigs I got, came out of a comment left on *Said the Gramophone* by one of *The Believer*'s editors, just saying [*The Believer*] is into something that had been written. I then emailed him, saying, "Hey, you are cool," just to express my appreciation for his work. He wrote back saying he would be honoured if I ever wanted to do something for them. So that clearly, literally came out of *Said the Gramophone*.

Here, Sean evokes the importance of the Internet and digital technologies that are central to contemporary creative work. These tools can play subtle roles, as Sean describes his blog and comments on it leading to freelance writing work, as opposed to multimillion dollar record deals, like in Soulja Boy's case.

Rather than specifically seeking out lucrative employment, Sean describes pursuing creative projects that are personally fulfilling and allow him to work with other like-minded people: "for me, it's always been important to identify, take a mental note of kindred spirits I meet in my sphere and then I'm always rolling around in my head how to work with them. What's fun about that is that it gives you ideas for projects that are fun. Because 'kindred spirit' isn't just someone you meet; it's someone you click with. You meet these people and you agree to do projects together and those projects are exciting and fun. There's incentive to finish them because they're projects you're excited about." Many youth involved in the creative industries prioritize working with like-minded people while also having modest goals of, for example, being able to pay their rent through creative enterprises and see their creative projects come to fruition, rather than seeking out the ability to reap in millions. Amy

Spencer argues that "in a society where the publishing and music industries are shaped by profit margins, what is radical about the participants of [the DIY] scene is that they simply want to exchange information about the bands, gigs, zines, etc. they have found exciting. The primary aim is to build unique idealized networks in which anyone can participate. Michael Cupid, an independent promoter from Bristol, explains that the members of the DIY underground aren't 'fixated with the promise of money, they are people who want to do something just to see it happen.'"[11] Here, Spencer suggests that youths' desire to pursue forms of cultural production might not necessarily be tied to motivations for economic gain. However, this desire "just to see it happen" may not be "radical" in nature. The alignment of these terms relies on an oversimplified binary of "authenticity" (i.e., do-it-yourself [DIY] scene) and "incorporation" (i.e., profit margins), which is not very useful for thinking about how subcultures and grassroots organizations actually operate. Chapter 2 will chronicle the ways in which early academic work on subcultures forwarded these oppositional/incorporated binaries. In some ways, this rhetoric has continued in contemporary discourses about grassroots and youth activities. Conversely, McRobbie foregrounds logistical and economic aspects as integral parts of subcultures; in her case study of punk subculture, she highlights the processes of buying and selling second-hand clothing in London flea markets.[12] I continue from McRobbie's approach to studying the mechanisms of youth culture in this work by investigating the tensions between commerce and creativity, and the ways in which commerce, creativity, and community intersect as youth navigate and work across for-profit and not-for-profit streams as they attempt to make a living and get creative projects off the ground.

Nonetheless, Spencer's foregrounding that young people may be motivated by the desire "just to see it happen" remains a useful concept when discussing contemporary youth activities. Indeed, Sean has spearheaded several creative projects that have no direct financial rewards: with others, he started an art blog, www.insidethe frozenmammoth.com, and also runs M60: The Montreal 60 Second Film Festival. Sean explains his motivations for seeking out these kinds of projects as follows: "If you have the resources to do something, and in a lot of the creative industries those resources are time and expertise, if you have those resources, then you can do it. The reason why most of us want to have money is so that we can do cool stuff … One of the main motivating factors for a lot of the arts stuff is the result: I want to have this forum for my writing that is widely read, maybe. Or I want to have this cool film festival, and the costs are nil."[13] That the costs for this type of work – creating online forums for writing or producing short films – are nil speaks to the impact of the digitization of media and the subsequent proliferation of youth cultural production. Though the desire to realize creative projects may be assisted by digital media, and though economic gain may not be an organizing concern for some creative projects, the challenge of earning a living while pursuing creative work remains.

Like many youth, Sean's involvement in the creative industries is not only motivated by the desire to realize personally meaningful projects; he is also seeking out a career, in his case, as a successful fiction writer. When interviewed about his fiction writing, Sean described a realization that the writing he does on his music blog, *Said the Gramophone*, which is often lyrical and personal rather than objective music criticism, has led to his growth as a writer of fiction.

> A month or two ago I was sitting with Dan Beirne – the other writer on the [*Said the Gramophone*] site – and I was complaining that I was writing very little short fiction. I've been working on these novels, and I wanted to submit things to magazines and for awards, and I said, "But I just don't have material to submit to magazines. I don't have very many stories." And Dan said, [referring to Sean's posts on *Said the Gramophone*] "You write several a week and have done so for five, seven years." And I was like, "Oh. Those are stories!" I'm obviously perfectly conscious of them as short short stories, but they live in different places in my mind. I think the big difference is that the stuff on *Said the Gramophone* comes to me essentially spontaneously. I write it, and maybe do a little bit of editing, and then it goes online. While the work of writing the more serious fiction I do is obviously edited and revised and laboured over, *Said the Gramophone* is written more off the cuff. So it does feel – not like practice – but like *a* practice, and that's part of what has helped me improve substantially as a writer over the past decade.[14]

Said the Gramophone, then, has not only led to paid work that allows for adequate time to pursue fiction writing; it is also its own type of fiction writing. Paid writing work and unpaid writing projects are both part of an accurate picture of Sean's creative industries work, which might be defined as a diverse and intermingling array of activities that might not always entail financial remuneration.

When interviewed in 2004 about *Said the Gramophone*, Sean said, "my dream job is to be able to write things I want to and see them published. I've not yet had any horrible jobs, but I'm looking forward to that delight in the new year."[15] Sean has been able to negotiate a balance between working on personal projects and working for money, and he seems to have navigated himself away from "horrible jobs" for good, but for many youth, as seen in the *Next Generation of Artistic Leaders and Arts Audiences Dialogue* report, part-time work unrelated to creative fields is a reality. Sean credits his ability to navigate himself away from unrelated work to his understanding of the importance of the logistical aspects of creative work.

One of the major challenges to creative people in order to make something of themselves, to translate their creations and abilities, I guess, into money, but also just progress out of their basements, is the amount of logistical work that needs to be done. *Said the Gramophone* only works because there is a functioning website. It only works because initially we answered enough of our emails that we built a community. I have to pitch articles to magazines. I have to apply for grants. I have to actually do the work of the writing and meeting my deadlines and finding larger-scale projects to do. There is all of this kind of work that is distinct from the [creative] work itself and I think that's an essential part of why I've made things work for myself. You can do it without being a total pinhead self-managing ... I've meet some of these people who are so [obsequiously business-oriented]. That's not what I'm advocating. But I feel that is one of the places that a lot of artists struggle. They know how to paint but they don't know what else, how else, to do that. I've picked this stuff up by just applying lessons I've learnt in other fields to this, but I feel that that's something that in terms of the professionalization of the arts, that's really important. Even how to invoice people, how to figure out what your rate should be, and all of this kind of stuff. That stuff is hard to intuit, and it makes the difference of someone being able to support themselves or not.[16]

Sean makes a number of important remarks here about the necessity of learning how to transform a creative project into a professionalized practice, and this book will look at some of the mechanisms that youth create to collect and share resources related to professionalization in creative fields.

AMY'S ATELIER: THE INTERPENETRATIONS OF ART, COMMERCE, AND COMMUNITY

While a surface-level reading of Sean's experiences may suggest that youth are easily able to steer themselves into their own self-generated creative careers, it is also important to register the challenges of negotiating one's own entry into the creative industries. Some of this difficulty comes from a disconnect between the types of creative work that youth are pursuing and what current cultural policies recognize. Amy Johnson's experiences speak to the frustrating nature of this disconnect and illuminate the back-and-forth nature of navigating and negotiating the creative industries, as she has both worked for herself, for a large corporation, and contractually for smaller organizations while she pursues creative work. Amy's experiences also speak to the intentionally small-scale nature of many youths' creative enterprises, which are at odds with policy structures that suggest that growth and expansion are key markers of success.

At nineteen, Amy started selling homemade wares in the indie craft fair circuit in Vancouver. At these craft fairs, Amy networked with other craftspeople and opened an online store to sell handmade goods. Other stores in Vancouver sold handmade goods, but Amy hoped to carve out her own niche in this industry by also conducting workshops to teach the skills needed to make handmade items. Because of the high cost of renting retail space in Vancouver, Amy eventually decided to move to Montreal. There, in May 2006, when she was twenty-two years old, she opened a retail/workshop space called Atelier Wooden Apples and sold handmade items made by artists ranging from sixteen to thirty-five years old. She states that when selecting the items to sell in her store, she looked for a "certain level of quality because there are a lot of stores in Montreal, and around, and on the Internet, that sell handmade things. I wanted higher-end things, sort of to prove that things could be made by hand and still have that look of quality."[17] Wooden Apples sold goods from predominantly Canadian, and more specifically Montreal- and Quebec-based artists, including "clothing, jewellery, silkscreen and screen-printed books and notebooks and art, mostly gift things." Amy explains the importance of selling local and handmade goods: "The store was never chocked-full of stuff. I would do lots of limited runs of things. And they'd been gone. I liked doing that. You can go to Urban Outfitters now and buy things that look handmade, but it's not handmade, and they're ripping off these people who are printing designs and are unable to copyright them. I wanted to have a space for those people who actually came up with those ideas to sell their stuff. The idea was always to have a full-time craft fair." Amy voices not so much a disdain for large corporate models of business but the need to foster local artists who often do not have adequate resources to promote and protect themselves. The vision for Amy's store was to be one such resource. Amy's articulation of her vision for her store speaks to a small-scale business ethos and suggests that the store was meant to be more than just a money-making scheme.

For Amy, skill-sharing workshops were another important aspect of Atelier Wooden Apples and also suggests this small-scale, not strictly for-profit ethos. Wooden Apples ran workshops, including introduction to the sewing machine, making your own body care and cleaning products, screenprinting, blockprinting, embroidery, knitting, and crocheting. Amy states: "It was really important to me that whoever was teaching the workshop was really interested in sharing skills, not doing it to make a profit. All of the teachers basically volunteered. They got vouchers for the store and they got to take any other workshops they wanted for free ... [The workshops] were all based on sharing information. They were never really complicated techniques or patterns. The intro was: here's the technique, now let's practice and work on it, and take it wherever you want. People would come back to the store with projects they'd taken on." Through these workshops that relied on volunteerism and skill-sharing, Amy's vision of Atelier Wooden Apples was that it would be a community space as much as it would be a place of business.

Youth activities may be moving towards the interpenetration of art, commerce, and community that Amy's vision for Wooden Apples suggests, but government policies and structures have been slow to recognize and support these endeavours. The combination of retail and workshop space was integral to the niche that Amy sought to carve out for her business, but it was difficult to find support for a business with this dual focus.

> I applied for lots of grants, but if I had been only workshops, I would have been able to get grants, but because I had the retail aspect, I wasn't able to apply. It was always like they were saying, "why don't you change your business? We'll give you money." They tell you to become a business then go back and re-apply as a nonprofit. If I had gone back, applied as a nonprofit, then only done the workshops, and not done the retail, I could have been an artist-run centre, but I couldn't have focused too much on the crafty things. It would've had to have been more printmaking and things like that that they consider art. What they consider art is really tricky. And that wasn't what I was doing, so it wouldn't have made sense for me to adjust it that much.

In addition to the problems associated with the hybrid nature of her business, Amy experienced frustration with the complicated bureaucracy of starting up a business itself.

> The Quebec government makes it hard to open a business. In Vancouver, they hold your hand a lot. It was so expensive to rent, but to open a business, they're like, "Fill out this form, now Jody's going to help you with the next form, then this is the thing you do after that." It's the total opposite here. Let alone language: it was fine. I was able to do it; I was able to do it in French. But it's like pulling teeth. You call someone, and they claim that they don't know, then you have to call someone else, and they send you back to the first person, and it's all just to get a form. It took me going to the government about six times, and each time them telling me I'd now filled out all of the necessary forms, and then finding out I hadn't and getting an angry letter from the government even though they were the ones who had told me I had filled out all of the necessary forms. It was horrible. But once I had the space and everything, it was fine. It just took a lot longer than I had planned to do all the paper work. Even stuff like putting up your sign. It takes months and months of going back and measuring and taking fifty photographs from different angles.

Quebec's youth policy document, *Young People Fully Involved in Their Own Success*, notes that "Quebec is facing an entrepreneurial shortage. Since 2000, it has remained below the Canadian average in terms of business start-ups."[18] Amy situates the difficulties of opening her business in a comparison between Quebec and British Columbia, as she voices frustration with what she identifies as overly complicated entrepreneurial bureaucracy in Quebec. Youth working in the creative industries may not start out with a background in business or a desire for immense profits, but they are still attempting to figure out how to realize entrepreneurial projects. Further examination of this problem of navigating entrepreneurial bureaucracy, particularly where it concerns youth, could allow for greater access and equity in creative business development and for more stability for youth endeavours in this area.

Overall, Amy had a difficult time sustaining her business, and she suggests that her workshop/community space/business hybrid was ultimately out of synch with current support structures: "I went to YES [Youth Employment Services] when I was starting up and I took a really good free tax information seminar with them that was incredibly useful. They should have more available, but things were really limited. Everyone was like, 'yeah, you're going to have no problem, of course there's money out there for you. You're female, you're under 25, you're doing something that's supporting teaching and creative learning.' And there was nothing. I found that surprising. It felt like there should have been someone out there backing me, but I was totally on my own."[19] Amy was "on her own" in the sense of a lack of support, but she is not on her own in terms of current trends in youth creative work, which indicates that support structures may have some catching up to do. In the end, Amy did not have enough start-up capital to sustain her business, especially after a particularly hard time with the recession in fall 2008, and Atelier Wooden Apples closed in January 2009. She remarks, "it was all financial. I was going at a rate that was normal but I didn't start with enough money. It takes four years to make a profit and I was going … I wasn't plummeting or anything like that, but there wasn't enough money in the bank to sustain me for that long." Amy started another on-line business, www.paperandpine.com, with a partner and planned to go back to school in interior design in fall 2009.

Chapter 1 suggested that creative industries work might mean a "lifelong continuing reeducation circuit," but this lifelong circuit might not necessarily involve the formal education system. After having decided to return to school, Amy was recruited into a job as a merchandiser at Urban Outfitters. As such, Amy found an alternative route into design work that did not emerge from or necessitate the formal education system, as she states that one reason she was recruited into the Urban Outfitters merchandiser position was because of the reputation she built for herself at Atelier Wooden Apples.

Amy describes taking on employment at Urban Outfitters with hesitation due to the large nature of the company; her vision for Atelier Wooden Apples was to generate her own small-scale business model that was distinct from Urban Outfitters. For this reason, Amy decided when she took her job that it would only be for a limited amount of time: she said to herself, "I'm going to do this for a year, I'm going to learn as much as I can, then I'm going to move on."[20] Though Amy decided to pursue stable full-time work, she did not regard this full-time work as a permanent career choice. Rather, it was regarded as one stage in career that would ultimately end up elsewhere, or as one stage of a larger navigation and negotiation process that would not stop with the acquisition of full-time work. After a year, Amy left with the plan to pursue freelance, contract-based work in design and related fields. She describes continuing to learn through informal systems: she considered returning to school to pursue the interior design education she had originally applied for, but instead created an informal internship with an interior designer with whom she collaborated on projects and developed her own portfolio of work, and planned to audit a particular class in the interior design program rather than take the whole program.

SERAH-MARIE AND *WORN FASHION JOURNAL*: LEARNING THROUGH DOING IN THE CREATIVE INDUSTRIES

Serah-Marie McMahon's experiences running her own independent magazine further illuminate the navigation and negotiation process of youth creative work that Sean's and Amy's stories have raised. While pursuing an undergraduate degree in fibre arts at Concordia University, in 2006, Serah-Marie started *WORN Fashion Journal*, an alternative fashion magazine that sets out to "embody a place between pop culture magazine and academic journal that opens new avenues in art and fashion theory by hovering where these two ideas intersect, connecting with fashion scholars and artists."[21] Originally a Montreal-based publication, WORN was initially also distributed in "Toronto, Ottawa, New York, and a store in Vancouver and a store in Winnipeg" and housed in Serah-Marie's apartment, with "eighteen boxes of the magazine under the sewing machine."[22] Through the process of producing the magazine, Serah-Marie describes herself as "learning, and every issue getting better, and learning more skills," despite not having any training or background in magazine-related fields: "I didn't study publishing in school; I didn't study writing. I didn't study photography – I mean I have a fine arts background – it really has nothing to do with magazines. I'd never written for anyone else; I had no experience, basically."

WORN remains a small-scale independent production but has expanded its distribution across Canada, the United States, and abroad over its seven years of existence. Serah-Marie states that WORN first started as a hobby but now has become a full-time job. At one time, Serah-Marie was able to pay herself a salary: "Not a big one. It's like I get paid pretty much what I would if was working, if I had a regular job at Second Cup [a coffee chain]. I get paid about that. It's better than nothing. I'm fine with that."[23] As WORN grew and expanded, its headquarters moved out of Serah-Marie's apartment in Toronto into a rented office in 2011, and the salary that Serah-Marie once paid herself was redirected to cover these costs. In issue 13 of WORN, the editors chronicle this move as the coming-of-age of the magazine.

> WORN was born in a Montreal living room, its infant years
> wedged into the spaces between other ventures – school and
> work. We spent our adolescence in Toronto, still living "at
> home." The conversion of a living room into a workspace was a
> temporary solution, like taking over mom's basement. And it did
> feel great at first, but you know, it wasn't really fooling anyone.
> As our numbers grew (staff, readers) it was clear we were out-
> growing our digs. So we packed our bags and moved out. This
> is the year WORN got its own place. An office – for real. We'll
> admit it was surprising. According to a report by UBS Canada
> in 2010, Toronto ranked at the world's ninth most expensive city,
> ahead of Paris and Dubai.[24]

By choosing to divert her salary to allow WORN to get out of the basement – or the personal apartment – Serah-Marie has prioritized the growth of her creative project over her immediate personal gain. The ability to acquire an office space is cited above as a more significant marker of success than a salary, especially in the context of the cost of living in Toronto.

Because she started her magazine project with no prior experience or training in this field, Serah-Marie characterizes the initial learning process of figuring out how to run a publication as an exhausting one: "I learnt that putting together a zine, no matter how independent, is a lot of jobs. It's not just being an editor. It's being an editor; it's being an event planner, a publicist, a distributor, a publisher, an art director, an ad sales representative. There's just so many parts. It's so big, and I've learnt how to do all the different aspects, which has been really, really good. I know a lot, but I'm really, really tired, and really, really close to failing. I learnt it was probably a bad idea to do it and school at the same time."[25] Serah-Marie comments that one element of this learning process was marshaled in through one of her first grant applications, the Canada Council New Magazine grant. In the process of applying for this grant, Serah-Marie was forced to grapple with the business end of her cultural production.

> [Applying for the grant was a] huge positive thing in terms of getting the business aspect of it in order, and whipping it into shape, because it's so often with independent anything ... I mean I'm not trained in business; I'm not trained in accounting: accountants are expensive. Many people who operate in that system, and I'm sure many young people, don't know how to do that. It's sort of like on the backburner, but that forced it into the foreground, which is good, because it's going to help build the foundation of what WORN's going to be so that it can always be there. It's a business ... You can't ignore [that] it's something that I'm selling. And if I can sell more, then I can pay people, and then everyone's happy. That part can't be ignored [and] I think that part was being put on the backburner.

Applying for grants might have unintended positive results beyond obtaining funding, such as this professionalization and organization of creative practices.

For Serah-Marie, part of the ongoing professionalization of her cultural production included choosing to move to Toronto from Montreal so that she could immerse herself in the independent anglophone publication community that she found thriving in Toronto but that was negligible in Montreal. In Toronto, Serah-Marie was able to connect with like-minded people pursuing similar projects, including magazines like *Shameless*, *Broken Pencil*, *Spacing*, and *Carousel*. She notes a spirit of openness and cooperation, not competition, amongst the people who run these magazines.

> The girls at *Shameless* were super awesome. They explained how mainstream circulation works to me. I had no idea. They sat down and they were like, "Ok, so this is what happens." They were really free and open ... Marc Laliberte [of *Carousel*], he hooked me up with a new printer that was a much better deal than what I had before. "Who prints your magazine? You know who you should go with? Here, I'll give you the number." That's so nice![26]

In addition to being supported by others who are pursuing similar independent magazines, Serah-Marie also describes Toronto as offering a greater pool of people who are interested in working on WORN, as the magazine has students who intern from Ryerson University and Humber and Centennial Colleges. Learning from others in the field, and having interns help and learn themselves, has allowed WORN to grow.

Serah-Marie identifies her move to Toronto as a positive element in the professionalization of her cultural production, but she also chronicles the continued struggles that she faces with the production of WORN. First, she states that the subject matter of her magazine, fashion, is often deemed "flighty" and "a stupid girl thing." She remembers the immensely frustrating experience of having her Canada Council New Magazine grant application rejected because her subject matter was not deemed "art": "Canada Council won't even consider an application from us. They just sent it back. It didn't even go through the board. Nothing. They just rejected us out of hand and said don't bother applying again because we don't qualify." Though WORN offers "an alternative voice" and "cultural commentary" on fashion, Serah-Marie describes constantly "coming across people who are dismissive of fashion as a serious matter." Serah-Marie has now successfully received an Ontario Arts Council grant for capital funding, but she explains that she initially made a phone call to the relevant grants officer to initiate the application process and was told, "we don't fund fashion magazines." From this point, Serah-Marie had to work to prove that her publication was exactly what the grant funds: a "critical analysis of culture." WORN bridges fashion, art, and commentary, but this bridge is often overlooked or not understood. Many youth cultural projects are interdisciplinary or innovative beyond established funding categories, and greater understanding of contemporary youth cultural production could facilitating moving beyond the dismissive attitudes that Serah-Marie sometimes faces.

Another of WORN's ongoing challenges is the struggle of finances. Serah-Marie speaks to the importance of access to small-scale sums of money to sustain her project, but more importantly, to allow it to grow.

> You don't realize, that expression, it takes money to make money? It's totally true. If we don't have money to send out review copies to people ... We sent a review copy to one specific blogger, she writes about us, and all of a sudden we get two thousand dollars worth of sales in three days. That makes a huge difference. But if you don't have the six bucks to send her the review copy in the first place, if you don't have it, you just don't have it. It doesn't matter if you're going to get it paid back in two weeks. If you don't have it, you don't have it. I'm pretty maxed out. My credit card is shot, so that's bad.

Here, Serah-Marie talks about targeted marketing strategies that she carries out for her magazine. This strategy requires small expenditures, but these small expenditures are not possible if there is no money to spend. Serah-Marie also discusses larger ventures and the difficulty of taking on larger investments: "We got offered a distribution deal for all of Europe, to be in newsstands everywhere. Four thousand copies: it would have been a big deal. We couldn't afford it; we had to turn it down. I couldn't afford to buy the copies to send there. It would have cost us four thousand dollars, and we wouldn't have gotten paid for those copies for a year and a half. In the meantime we'd have to deliver another issue, another four thousand dollars ... Just to carry that."

This distribution deal was out of WORN's reach financially, but Serah-Marie highlights smaller investments that are now becoming possible because of her 2010 Ontario Arts Council capital funding grant, which allows for "getting your name out there in a legitimate way." She will be able to increase her print run to have a direct mail campaign to "send copies to wholesalers and to libraries to get them to order the magazine and reviewers as well to get them to write about it." With this new funding, Serah-Marie will apply to the National Magazine Awards, which costs eighty dollars a submission. She notes that she has applied for these awards and was nominated in the past but was only able to do so because her husband paid the submission fees as a birthday gift, and she could not afford to apply again in subsequent years, though she was informed that she had a good chance of being nominated again. Additionally, she describes "a big conference every year called Magnet, which is magazine networking I guess. You can go to these classes and really learn about intricacies about publishing and it's really cool but $150 a course and it's three days and there's courses all day long. I'd love to go, but we can't afford that, but now we'll be able to go, and send a couple of people on the staff to go, so it'll help us learn and get ahead." With these references to $80 and $150, Serah-Marie suggests the small-scale nature of support that can be beneficial to youth cultural production. In addition to extra money, Serah-Marie cites access to workshops and networking as other opportunities emerging from her grant, which suggests that non-monetary types of support are also important to sustain and foster the growth of youth creative projects.

Ultimately, Serah-Marie explains that her commitment to producing an independent small-scale magazine generates ongoing challenges. One challenge stems from the choice to "try to sell magazines ourselves. I'm reinventing the distribution model." Rather than rely on revenues from advertising, which is the traditional method that allows magazines to make money, Serah-Marie sells her magazine directly to her readers and relies on these revenues to support the magazine. She describes the challenge of attempting to innovate when support mechanisms do not acknowledge or address new ways of doing business or new modes of cultural production.

> I think that having only these traditional methods in place is really stifling to people breaking out of what the norms are. For example, when we talk about distribution of publications, when the economy crashed a couple of years ago, things were really bad for publications. They were one of the industries that got hit the hardest because they had always had a model of relying on advertising to fund themselves ... When economies go bad, people

don't stop buying magazines. They buy magazines more because
it's a small luxury. But what happens is companies stop advertising. That is where you get hit. So all these publications got really
hurt. But because that's not what we rely on to exist, we rely on
our readers, because we have a reader-oriented distribution model, that wasn't a problem for us. Major distribution companies
don't accommodate that kind of distribution model because what
they do is you only get paid for what you sell. They take a very
large percentage because they expect that you make all your
money on advertising anyways. If you want to be innovative,
and make changes, and try to change an industry that is dying –
it really needs an entire re-haul – but because government and
everything else is ingrained in the way it is, it's very hard to
break through and try to make inroads and try to be innovative
and come up with new interesting ways of doing things unless
you are incredibly successful right off the bat. There's no room
to try it out and see what happens. You just have to be a pro at
it right away or there's no other ways about it.

Though Serah-Marie is discussing working outside of the traditional distribution model for magazines, these types of challenges
are faced by many youth when they are confronted with the difference between their modes of cultural production and the infrastructure that has been set up around older modes – modes that in fact
may be dying out.

Despite the various struggles of producing WORN, Serah-Marie
also highlights its many successes, foremost amongst them that she
"really like[s] the magazine." Like many youth ventures, WORN is a
labour of love, and for Serah-Marie, love has been able to be translated into a successful and established creative project. Serah-Marie
explains that one very rewarding experience is to be able to reach
people who connect with the vision of the magazine and "feel like
[she's] making a bit of a difference ... That is the point." She also
describes with pride the community of people who have come
together to work on WORN and "help each other," even if they live
in different cities and have "never met each other." Indeed, youth
cultural production is sometimes about more than just being successful with producing a project; it is also about being part of and
developing a community of people working together. For WORN,
this community extends beyond Serah-Marie's immediate circle, as

she has also been contacted by curators of museums, such at the Metropolitan Museum of Art, who want to write articles about fashion for WORN. Beyond these personal successes, Serah-Marie comments on the official accolades of getting nominated "for a National Magazine Award for a cover that I designed. To be in the giant room and to have your cover [enlarged]. We didn't win but we got an honorable mention." WORN's successes have led to other ventures for Serah-Marie; like many youth, Serah-Marie's creative projects extend across many platforms. She has been contacted by a publisher to write a book about the intersection of art and fashion and has a concept for a television show about "vintage hunters" that she'd like to put into production: "it's been exciting that WORN has led me to those opportunities, too."

Sean, Amy, and Serah-Marie's experiences outline some of the parameters of current trends in youth creative work and point to the successes, frustrations, and disappointments that many youth experience in the creative industries as well as to areas in which youth could be better supported in their practices. Much of this support could come from a recognition of some of the characteristics of contemporary youth cultural production: the redefinition of work, the interpenetrations of art, commerce, and community, and the back-and-forth navigation and negotiation process of learning through doing. Chapter 2 moves to an examination of literature in the field and asks how academics could foster a better understanding of contemporary youth practices and begin the project of working towards better support systems for youth.

2

Registering Bedroom Economies

Theoretical Contexts
of Youth Cultural Production

With the rise of the creative industries and their increasing visibility in cultural policies, research in the social sciences, sociology, and cultural studies has increasingly mapped and studied the changing nature of these industries. While some research has noted that creative industries work seems to be an emerging avenue of self-employment for youth,[1] empirical study of the field of youth cultural production is lacking. Because no one field offers a complete picture of contemporary youth cultural production, this chapter examines existing research from the sometimes disparate fields of research in creative economies, cultural studies, media education, and subculture studies and discusses the possibilities and limitations of the ways that these fields address youth cultural production. Ultimately, connections need to be made between these fields to work towards an adequate theoretical framework that registers contemporary youth activities in the creative industries. In creative economies research, youth activities are often not discussed, but when youth is foregrounded in subculture studies, abstractions prevail over concrete mappings of youth realities and the ways in which subcultural involvement can lead into the realm of work. To take up the search for a theoretical framework, this chapter gives an overview of the work of some researchers who touch on the areas of cultural production and youth culture in order to piece together a picture of contemporary youth realities as they face the creative industries.

DEFINING THE CULTURAL / CREATIVE INDUSTRIES

To map youth creative employment, we can first turn to the discussions of the creative industries and cultural policy that mostly emerge out of the fields of sociology, economics, and cultural studies. In this literature, there is a slippage in the usage of the terms "cultural industries" and "creative industries." Susan Galloway and Stewart Dunlop note that "the terminology currently used in creative industries policy lacks rigour and is frequently inconsistent and confusing. The terms 'cultural industries' and 'creative industries' are often used interchangeably; there is little clarity about these terms and little appreciation or official explanation of the difference between the two."[2] This slippage is not just semantic, as it has larger implications for the nature of the activities that get discussed and encapsulated by the terminology. Galloway and Dunlop further state that how we define the creative industries "has important consequences for how we measure these industries, and the type of interventions we adopt."[3] A further addition to Galloway and Dunlop's comments here is that the way we define the cultural/creative industries also prescribes what type of participants will be registered.

According to Stuart Cunningham, "cultural industries" is a term "invented to embrace the commercial industry sectors (principally film, television, book publishing, and music) which also delivered fundamental popular culture to a national population."[4] Indeed, the term "cultural industries" generally refers to industrial-scale production. In his discussion of the cultural industries, David Hesmondhagh refers to this industrial-scale production and the "project team" that is necessary to carry it out: "The creative stage of bringing cultural goods to market is carried out by a project team … These include primary creative personnel such as musicians, screenwriters and directors; technical craft workers such as sound engineers, camera operators, copy editors, and so on; owners and executives; marketing and publicity personnel; and, crucially, creative managers, who act as brokers or mediators between, on the one hand, the interests of owners and executives, and those of creative personnel. Examples of such creative managers include A&R staff in the recording industry, commissioning editors in the book industry, magazine editors and film producers."[5] If "cultural industries" as a term is hinged on the "industrialized" nature of the industries, youth will not warrant attention as players in the field; Hesmondhalgh's description of the "project team" will not be able to recognize small-scale grassroots activities that youth are typically involved with. As these activities may not be industrialized in their production, we may need to widen the connotations of "industries" such that youth activities have any visibility in cultural industries research.

In *The Cultural Industries*, Hesmondhalgh defines core cultural industries as advertising and marketing, broadcasting, film industries, Internet industries, music industries, print and electronic publishing, and video and computer games. Hesmondhalgh compares the "top 48" cultural companies with Fortune 500 companies to demonstrate that, while cultural corporations are increasingly profit-rich, they are not necessarily the top money makers of all types of industry (Exxon Mobil holds this position). Nonetheless, some of the cultural industries activities he researches are heavily-monied corporate activities. Hesmondhalgh also makes reference to the creative industries, which he defines as differing from these industrialized corporate activities: "In Europe, the term 'creative industries' is increasingly popular in policy circles as a means of encompassing not only the heavily industrialised and commodified industries which I have called 'cultural industries' but also the more craft-based activities of jewellery making, fashion, furniture, design and household objects and so on."[6] In distinction to this European inclusion of craft-based industry under the rubric of "creative industries," Hesmondhalgh excises these smaller types of cultural production from his focus,[7] but this broader definition may be useful for registering youth creative activities that may be craft rather than industrially-based.

Other commentators have warned against enlarging the term "cultural industries" to "creative industries," as this foregrounds a definition of creativity that refers to innovation, which can also been found in science and business. Galloway and Dunlop suggest that "any activity that involves creativity would necessarily be 'creative.' Defining 'creative industries' against such a measure is, if nothing else, far too wide to be useful for any purpose. Any innovation – including scientific and technical innovations – of any sort in any industry is creative, and, in such terms, any industry is, therefore, potentially a 'creative industry.' Conflating cultural creativity with all other forms of creativity fails to take adequate account of important differences between cultural and creative industries."[8] This movement towards a definition that departs from the traditional bases of the cultural industries – symbolic, cultural, or expressive values – has raised alarm that the specific conditions of labour in the cultural industries will be forgotten. Mark Banks and Justin O'Connor ask, "if everything can be creative – a management model, a kidney dialysis machine, package holidays – when wherein lies the specific value of cultural/creative industries?"[9] My purpose here is not to dilute an emphasis on cultural production to an overly wide definition of creativity that is based in a generalized notion of innovation, but to use terminology that is able to capture small-scale craft-based activities and hence include youth activities in creative industries research.

This broadening of the definition of creativity towards the idea of innovation is seen in the work of Richard Florida, who is the most well-known commentator to link the creative industries with economic development. His definition of creativity in the workforce in *The Rise of the Creative Class* is so broad as to include anyone who engages in problem solving on the job, such as nurses, business people, educators, lawyers, scientists, and engineers. Cultural production is not part of Florida's definition of creativity, as he instead foregrounds the ability to synthesize.[10] On the one hand, this definition of creativity is quite inclusive as it moves creativity away from a Romantic vision of isolated genius that is only available to a select few. In opposition to this Romantic notion, Florida defines creativity as a social process that is based in a variety of skills: "Creativity is not the province of a few select geniuses who can get away with breaking the mold because they possess superhuman talents. According to Boden, who sums up a wealth of research: 'creativity draws crucially on our ordinary abilities. Noticing, remembering, seeing, speaking, hearing, understanding language, and recognizing analogies: all these talents of Everyman are important.'"[11] Navigating the logistical elements of labour and professionalization in the creative industries may, however, require a different skill set than these abilities, and the particular challenges of creative employment could be useful elements of a definition of the cultural/creative industries that underscores cultural production.

While Florida's definition of creativity may be more inclusive by seemingly targeting more average skills and people, and may recognize the collective nature of creative processes, in practice, he does not deploy this definition in ways that address persistent social problems. Florida's delineation of "new" social classes actually points to the persistence of "creativity" being more accessible to the privileged. He champions the creative class' creative ethos, which involves bridging the gap between work and play, as a driving economic force, but the statistics he compiles suggest that the creative class is not actually the fastest growing employment sector, as the service class, which now works all hours to cater to the flexible work schedules of the creative class, actually forms the biggest chunk of the workforce.[12] Florida avoids engaging with service-class labour issues and realities by suggesting that his cleaning lady and hairstylist are actually not members of the service class because they use creative skills in rearranging his furniture and cutting his hair. Noting that his hairstylist drives a BMW and his cleaning lady's husband drives a Porsche, Florida suggests that these service industry jobs transcend economic concerns. Florida does acknowledge that some people are "stuck for life in menial jobs as food-service help, janitors, nursing home orderlies, security guards and delivery drivers,"[13] but comments about luxury cars, or other remarks – that highly educated immigrants driving cabs will soon move into the creative class, that students working in service industry jobs will also soon move up, that some entrepreneurial people working in the service industry will open restaurants and lawn and garden service businesses – undermine the seriousness of his engagement with the harsh realities to which he alludes. In the end, Florida's concept of the creative class is not useful for charting youth involvement in the creative industries as it is much too broad in its inclusive aspects that move away from cultural production and much too sweeping in its ignorance of persistent social problems that underlie creative work.

Definitions of the cultural/creative industries also matter for the types of support that are enacted in policy structures. Though Florida's notion of the creative class as an economic engine has excited many policy makers, taking up his definition of creativity at the policy level may require further examination. In the Canadian context, Lon Dubinsky suggests that much of the talk of culture and creative cities amongst policy makers has been "metro-centric" and wonders "what bodes for small places?"[14] Florida's model subsumes the cultural sector under an economic agenda while targeting big cities, but preserving a space for the cultural and targeting a broad spectrum of communities may be more appropriate for fostering cultural production. When considering how definitions of culture are put into public policies, David Throsby argues that economic and cultural policies need to be kept separate: "It can be suggested that cultural policy is distinctive precisely because it is *not* just economic policy, but relates directly to the legitimate social and cultural objectives that democratic governments are elected to pursue. Too strong a concentration on the economic contribution of the cultural industries may shift the focus away from the achievement of desirable social and cultural goals. This problem can be cast as one of getting the balance right between the instrumental role of the arts and culture in producing economic and social outcomes, and their essential cultural purpose."[15] Under Florida's rubric, cultural development becomes an arm of economic policy, but this may obliterate traditional cultural policy concerns that are not tied to economic development, which Jim McGuigan outlines as "the preservation of heritage, wider social access to cultural resources, opportunities for cultural production."[16] Kate Oakley states that the creative industries in the UK have been increasingly linked with innovation theory and "big money" at the expense of traditional arts or cultural policy, such that "several, carefully constructed arguments for public cultural funding" have been collapsed into "essentially one: it's good for the economy."[17] The pitfall of this type of argument is not only losing the cultural purposes of the creative industries, but also not being able to register any youth activities. As the creative industries gain more attention amongst economists through the potentials of cultural-as-economic policy, highlighting other non-economic concerns could allow for a recognition of the role of cultural production in the lives and employment of youth and communities.

THEORETICAL MODELS OF SMALL-SCALE PRODUCTION

One of the difficulties of capturing youth activities in the creative industries emerges from a lack of theoretical models to discuss small-scale creative industries. Raymond Williams's discussion of the social relations of cultural production is sometimes evoked by contemporary analysts of the creative industries. Williams chronicles four phases of cultural production: artisanal (handmade arts and crafts), post-artisanal (artisanal production supported by patronage), market professional (nineteenth-century model of emerging ownership over one's cultural production, including copyright and royalties), and corporate professional (employee in a company that produces creative goods).[18] With this last phase of the corporate professional, Williams refers to the corporatization of the creative industries, which results in salaried professional work and industrialized production. At the same time as the rise of this phase, Williams notes the survival of older, artisanal methods in "non-market" areas of cultural production, such as those that are supported by public subsidy. If we want to theorize contemporary youth cultural production, this opposition between corporate and artisanal will not capture the small-scale entrepreneurial model of contemporary youth activities, as these activities no longer occur in an autonomous sphere of "art for art's sake" that Williams's post-artisanal model suggests. The corporate professional model is not appropriate to describe small-scale self-generated youth cultural activities, but neither is it appropriate to revert to the nineteenth-century market professional model of cultural production that Williams's rubric provides. The impact of the digitization of media means that contemporary youth are fully immersed in a twenty-first-century world of cultural production, so we need new theoretical models to grapple with these new modes of youth cultural production.

In his article "Bourdieu, the Media and Cultural Production," Hesmondhalgh discusses Williams's contributions to theorizing cultural production but looks for more useful theoretical models in Pierre Bourdieu's work on cultural production in *The Field of Cultural Production* and *The Rules of Art*. Bourdieu's theory of cultural production debunks the aura of the creative genius associated with creative work by examining differing levels of power and capital that inform various positions within the field of cultural production. While these concepts remain useful, Hesmondhalgh critiques Bourdieu's failure to address large-scale cultural production, as he prioritizes small-scale or restricted cultural production. He notes that Bourdieu's characterization of the small-scale field relies on an overly polarized opposition to large-scale production; for Bourdieu, the restricted field is one of autonomy from the forces of commerce: "Bourdieu often writes of small-scale production as oriented towards the production of 'pure' artistic products, and mass production as oriented towards the making of 'commercial' cultural goods. He is also inclined to talk of the field of small-scale production as 'production for producers': in rejecting the market, he implies with this phrase, cultural producers in the restricted sub-field are left pretty much to talk to each other."[19] In Bourdieu's analysis, small-scale cultural production is "pure" because it is non-commercial "art for art's sake" that emerges from the avant-garde bohemia. This binary between "authenticity" and "incorporation" in cultural production does not capture the logistical and economic mechanisms of grassroots cultural production: a conceptualization of contemporary small-scale cultural production as the realm of the avant-garde bohemia that is in opposition to the mass market would be overly narrow and simplified. Bourdieu suggests that small-scale production is non-commercial production that rejects the mass market, but Hesmondhalgh offers a corrective that highlights the increasing interpenetration of small-scale and industrialized production with the example of small-scale production being folded into mass production, such as large film studios taking over independent production companies. However, the interpenetration of small-scale and industrialized production also means the digitization of small-scale production and the development of entrepreneurial knowledge (marketing, distribution) in the field of restricted or small-scale production. There is a lack of available research to theorize small-scale production in ways other than the insular "production for producers" field that shuns economic capital as suggested by Bourdieu; Hesmondhalgh notes that "restricted production has been neglected by Anglo-American media and cultural studies."[20] This neglect not only means a neglect of a segment of the creative industries, but more markedly, an absence of attention to youth activities.

REGISTERING YOUTH: REDEFINING CULTURAL ACTIVITIES

Angela McRobbie is one researcher who makes connections between the creative industries and youth activities and characterizes the involvement of youth in self-generated small-scale creative employment as a growing and significant trend. She states her interest in "the future of work in the creative sector" as well as "the growth in self-employment," of which an increasing part is "cultural work."[21] Thus, her investigation is into "small-scale cultural economies and livelihoods upon which so many people now depend for a living."[22] Her research foregrounds an understanding of the ways that former leisure activities have become sources of income for youth, in that "cultural practice for profit" is now "taking over a space in people's lives which we once would have called hobbies or activities."[23] Calling for more discussion and research into these new avenues of creative work, McRobbie suggests that "what we should now be talking about … is a sprawling sector of micro-economies of culture which now traverses the boundaries of social class, ethnicity and gender. Many young working-class people now become self-employed in the cultural field (as stylists, make-up artists, or by setting up club nights, or making dance tracks at home in their bedrooms) as an escape from the inevitability of unemployment, or in preference to an unrewarding job in the service sector."[24] Whether turning to the cultural field is an active choice or due to a lack of other available work, taking these bedroom economies of small-scale youth cultural activities seriously means mapping out how young people go about becoming self-employed in the creative industries.

Recent accounts of youth creative enterprises may be journalistic rather than academic. In the *New York Times*, Hannah Seligson chronicles a trend towards young graduates creating their own jobs due to a lack of available full-time work. One youth comments, "it's not a pure dichotomy anymore that entrepreneurship is risky and other jobs are safe, so why not do what I love?" In this regard, "entrepreneurship can be a viable path, not a renegade choice."[25] This trend towards entrepreneurship is based in the low start-up costs that are associated with the Internet and technology, such as using open-source software, building one's own website, and learning by doing. Seligson cites examples of new media and technology-based start-up companies, which may fit with McRobbie's definition of contemporary youth creative practices. One youth that Seligson profiles, Scott Gerber, has set up a Young Entrepreneur Council, which has youth members aged seventeen to thirty-three who share resources and knowledge. Gerber has "never taken a business or economics class."[26] Nonetheless, he is developing and sharing his entrepreneurial knowledge, and this lack of business background is common amongst many youth creating their own creative industries careers.

While there is a lack of academic research into the mechanisms of small-scale youth cultural production, some research exists concerning the nature of artist activities. Not all youth cultural producers would classify themselves as artists, but this research may still illuminate some of the logistics of small-scale creative activities. Following Richard Florida, Richard Lloyd discusses the catalyzing effect that artists/bohemians have on economic development through their role in the gentrification of neighbourhoods. He remarks, "this means that artists matter a lot in today's economy but not as producers of art."[27] In order to map out youth experiences, we need to shift the focus of this discussion. We need to ask not how "bohemians" are able to lure "real business": we need to investigate the business of bohemia itself. How do these people earn an income? What types of training and education are necessary to be a successful "bohemian"? Is this really the future of work, as McRobbie suggests? Florida's concept of the "creative ethos" suggests that bohemian values have merged with business ones such that work and leisure are no longer separable as work becomes play. He discusses this in terms of changes in corporate attitudes, but a counterpoint to this discussion would be the merging of work and play in the "bohemian" world, as success in this field requires industriousness and logistical know-how rather than creative ability alone.

Lloyd takes up some of this examination of the nature of bohemian work by looking at the activities of artists in the Chicago neighbourhood of Wicker Park. He characterizes artists not as a "resistant subculture" but "as useful labor" and asks "how their efforts are harnessed on behalf of interests that they often sincerely profess to despise."[28] Though Lloyd suggests that artists may espouse an anti-corporate rhetoric, he investigates the interpenetrations of art and commerce and argues that bohemian labour is not inherently resistant. This labour is harnessed on behalf of others, and there is a fluidity in the boundaries of working for oneself and working for others, as the offbeat appearance of artists is useful for certain types of business, such as funky cafés, bars, and restaurants, and bohemians provide both the labour of many service positions and the business for these service industries, as they frequent the establishments where friends work in an elaborate system of networking and maintaining social position. Similar to McRobbie's analysis of the economic and logistical aspects of punk subculture seen in London flea markets,[29] bohemians do not stand apart from the world of commerce and shun economic capital in favour of symbolic capital in Lloyd's analysis, as is seen in Bourdieu's outline of small-scale cultural production. Rather, Lloyd suggests that bohemians are embedded in flows and exchanges of labour and economic capital. These findings offer a point of entry into understanding the business of bohemia and the importance of informal personal networks for sustaining creative work.

Like McRobbie, Lloyd suggests that youth involvement in small-scale creative industries may be due to a lack of other types of more stable work, but Richard Caves notes that "most persons who credibly aspire to artistic careers have skills and qualities that fit them for success in other occupations."[30] Caves argues that most artists postpone the "serious career" in another occupation until middle age, and this may help to explain the relatively young age of independent artists, writers, and performers in Canada's 2006 census.

It is also worth considering whether the "serious career" in another field has not only been postponed but been abandoned by contemporary youth, who work towards having their creative work become their "serious career" through middle age in an extended period of youth. In his discussion of how the micro-economies of art function, Caves forwards a rubric of "simple" creative goods, or goods that are produced by one person (e.g., art work, novel, musical recording). Following Williams's model of the corporate professional, Hesmondhalgh comments that the second half of the twentieth century saw a rise in the "complex cultural industries," in which creative projects involve multiple people working at different levels, as in the "project team" discussed above.[31] However, when discussing youth cultural production, one youth may serve all the roles that Hesmondhalgh includes in his "project team": primary creative personnel, technical craft worker, owner, marketing and publicity personnel, and manager. This suggests a return to work in the "simple" cultural industries in new ways and configurations; for example, youth might opt out of working in "film" to start up their own ventures instead. They are on their own in the sense that they are working away from large corporations, but often seek out other like-minded people as allies and co-creators: personal networks and collaborations are often imperative for the success of these small-scale projects. In terms of "simple" creative goods, Caves emphasizes that those working in the creative industries, especially the visual arts, are highly educated people, but there are less opportunities for income earning from art than there are qualified people. For this reason, Caves discusses the importance of agents and managers, who function as gatekeepers. Writing in 2000, Caves still relies on traditional categories of cultural production (visual arts, performing arts, writing, musical recordings). In fact, Caves's work on simple creative goods makes no reference to the implications that the digitization of media has had for cultural production. This problem is most apparent in terms of his discussions of musical recordings, as Caves overstates the importance of having a manager in order to secure a record deal. Soulja Boy's story shows that for many young musicians, managers are no longer essential due to online forums that can be used to create a fan base, such as YouTube and MySpace; major record deals themselves may become unnecessary with trends towards self-released albums.

DIGITAL MEDIA AND CULTURAL PRODUCTION:
IMPLICATIONS FOR EDUCATION

"Simple" creative goods may have lost some of the "simplicity" that Caves ascribes to them due to the impacts of digitization on cultural production and of the Internet on distribution and networking. Hesmondhalgh comments that digital technologies, including samplers, sequencers, and MIDI, have had a substantial impact on music making since the early 1980s. He asks, "has digitalisation allowed 'ordinary' consumers more easily to become producers?" and "have these various technologies opened up access to cultural production and circulation, and greater choice for consumers? Have the barriers between production and consumption been eroded? Has digitilisation produced greater creativity and innovation?"[32] Hesmondhalgh replies that the answers "vary across the very different applications. Digital music technologies have been the subject of unjustified fears regarding their implications for music-making; on the other hand, they have been seen as more subversive and transformative than they actually were."[33] Digital music technologies may not be "subversive," but may be democratizing in that they open up possibilities for a greater number of people to act as cultural producers. Hesmondhalgh implicitly answers yes to his question about whether digitization has allowed "ordinary" consumers to become producers more easily. The relationship between digital media and the democratization of cultural production needs to be more definitively stated, however, especially vis-à-vis youth cultural production. Hesmondhalgh draws on Paul Théberge's work on "'the hyphenated musician' – the singer-songwriter-producer-engineer-musician-sound designer" who works out of home studios in bedrooms, dens, or basement rec rooms and is able to do so because of the digitization of music recording technologies;[34] situations like these further suggest the combining of all of the roles in the "project team" into one. This consolidation of roles that digital technologies can offer may mean greater access to cultural production and distribution for youth, as it is possible to forge a creative career with fewer resources. The "hyphenated musician" archetype is not exclusive to the music industry, but is representative of many youths' involvement in other areas of the creative industries.

Rupa Huq comments that youth have more opportunities to become cultural producers rather than merely act as cultural consumers through the advent of democratizing technologies, such as Cubase.[35] This digital recording software, and others like it, such as Acid Pro and Pro Tools, are not technically free, but are easily (illegally) downloadable. This software is currently producing a more dramatic change in music making than the digital technologies of sampling and sequencing that Hesmondhalgh references because it allows "ordinary consumers" to write and record music in their bedrooms without spending any money. This creates new pathways into music making that extend to more people. For example, Soulja Boy made his first album at home with FruityLoops, a widely available and extremely easy-to-use digital beat-making software. Soulja Boy's contemporary, Lil B, is emblematic of the proliferation of cultural production ushered in by the digitization of recording technologies. Over several months, when he was twenty, Lil B created hundreds of MySpace pages and uploaded thousands of tracks that he self-recorded in his bedroom studio. He explains that he considers himself a "real-time rapper": "If something happened to me today, I'm gonna put that on the song. Anything that I feel. It's kinda like me blogging, but with music."[36] More than just greater access to the means of production and the proliferation of cultural production, digital technologies also may mean a change in orientation towards immediacy rather than reflection in creative works and a real shift away from Romantic ideas of the cultivation of creativity through isolation and contemplation. These digital technologies are not only the means through which Lil B creates and distributes music; he has been known to "[shout] out specific Twitter followers, by name, at shows,"[37] which suggests a shift in how artist and audience relate. In addition to his prolific output of songs, he films "sort-of-music videos" with zero budget that are uploaded to YouTube, and he has published a self-help book titled *Takin' Over by Imposing the Positive*.[38] For Lil B and many youth like him, all of these aspects are part of his career, which illuminates how cultural production has become not only more widespread through digital technologies but also more diverse.

In a more local and small-scale context, formerly Montreal-based musician Merrill Garbus, known as tUnE-yArDs, self-recorded her debut album, *BiRd-BrAiNs*, with a borrowed digital field recorder from Concordia University. She mixed and arranged the album with Audacity, a free open-source audio editing software. This album was later put out by 4AD, a large British independent label that has released seminal acts such as The Pixies. Reporting this record deal, *Pitchfork* commented, "Merrill Garbus ... makes lo-fi, home-recorded weirdo folk that sounds like it was recorded with a Talkboy because it practically was."[39] One of the songs from this album, "Fiya," later appeared in a BlackBerry television commercial. That Garbus's lo-fi recording later became the soundtrack for a major corporation's television commercial suggests a fluidity or openness between art and commerce in ways that may have been more openly disdained by small-scale cultural producers around notions of "selling out" in the past.

Toronto-based musician Josh O'Regan, known by the moniker Diamond Rings, also has developed his music career around low-fi and digitized recording methods. Interviewed about his "favorite piece of musical equipment," he remarks, "my computer [is my favorite piece of musical equipment]. I can't imagine *not* using it. I started doing stuff with GarageBand – just trying to figure out how to make beats. But I didn't even have a laptop. I had to steal my roommate's laptop when he was away at work, so I could work on this album only at specific times."[40] The low-stakes investment that O'Regan describes led to his zero-budget album, *Special Affections*, which has captured international attention, and this process is suggestive of new points of entry into cultural production. However, the advent of digital technologies may also mean greater difficulty in making a living as cultural production becomes more widespread. As such, pertinent policies could still allow for better support of youth endeavours.

The digitization of media has not only democratized access to the music industry, as it has affected aspects of production, promotion, and distribution in the creative industries in general. For example, the M60 film festival, one of Sean Michaels's creative projects, operates under the assumption that anyone is able to make a film, and this assumption is only possible due to the digitization of film. One of the festival's organizers, Toby Harper, says, "the idea is if someone like me can make a movie, just about anyone else can, too. Trust me!"[41] Because this festival assumes anyone is able to make a film, it is open to all: filmmakers register to make a film on a first-come, first-served basis. There are no fees to register and no prizes or judges. All films are screened at the final event, and the purpose of the festival is the creation of the films themselves by "ordinary" people. Bill Brownstein calls M60 "the most democratic of film fests."[42] The

M60 example may not refer to a lucrative scheme or an employment opportunity, but does paint a picture of low-stakes cultural production within which many youth are immersed, and this environment may have implications for the employment pathways that they choose to follow. Youth are often involved in these low-stakes types of cultural production not only at home; they are also increasingly immersed in digital forms of cultural production through the rise of media education and arts education courses in schools.

Given the interest in the academic field of education in the life pathways of youth, one would assume that education would respond to these changing parameters of youth cultural production and employment. The impact of digital media on youth cultural production has been most taken up by those working in media education, and media education research investigates why and how creative work should be taught and evaluated. Julian Sefton-Green chronicles the changing reasons why creative work is valued in school curricula and notes that psychological perspectives emphasize children's personal development; cultural perspectives emphasize the ability of the arts to teach empathy and insight; cultural transmission perspectives emphasize how creative work teaches "appreciation of a society's literary and artistic heritage"; and vocational perspectives emphasize how creative work teaches skills that are desired in the workforce, such as "team building and negotiation skills."[43] Current rhetoric around creative work in media education emphasizes the cultural perspective of producing citizens who are equipped to participate in modern society though the instruction of digital arts in schools. Cultural production has long been taught in a variety of fields (e.g., creative writing in English, art class, music class, etc.), but media educators now suggest that "multimedia 'digital creations'" should be taught across the curriculum rather than in one isolated subject,[44] and that this form of cultural production is increasingly important in schools to mend the "digital divide" – not between those who merely possess computers and other technologies and those who do not, but between those who are developing relevant skills and aptitudes through their exposure to these digital technologies, and those who are lagging behind in this regard. Much of the discussion in media education research involves defining twenty-first-century citizenry as the ability to fully engage in modern culture, and abilities to critically read and produce media are being marked as skills that define academic and future professional success. Media education is not seen as a means to train future camera operators and magazine editors, but is seen as a means to develop an engaged and active civic body. Though providing basic vocational training is not the intent of media education, students still need to be given opportunities to practice and develop skills. To this end, perhaps an amalgamation of the vocational and cultural engagement perspectives could better grapple with contemporary youth cultural production.

This conceptualization of media production as preparation for civic life suggests a re-evaluation of creativity along lines that are reminiscent of what we have previously seen from Florida. David Buckingham comments that this re-evaluation of creativity necessitates moving away from a Romantic notion of artistic genius and towards a version of creativity that recognizes "the social, collaborative dimensions of creative production" and "the complex relationships between 'creative expression' and 'technical skills.'"[45] Unlike Florida, Buckingham retains a vision of cultural production as an integral part of his definition of creativity. To work away from notions of isolated individual creative genius, which is based in "inspiration," not teachable skills, Sefton-Green similarly conceptualizes cultural production as a collective activity that involves dialogue: creativity becomes defined as a social process rather than an individual act.[46] Henry Jenkins also defines creativity as emerging out of social processes, and earmarks appropriation, or remaking and extending previous media content (as in fan fiction or sampling), but notes that "this is not how we generally talk about creativity in schools," where the notion of individual effort and success is still retained, and "the tendency is to discuss artists as individuals who rise upon or stand outside any aesthetic tradition."[47] While the academic field of media education may be thinking through the rationales and execution of digital arts education, Jenkins's comments suggest a disjuncture between this conversation and models of arts education that remain in some school systems and also suggest the need for continued work so that schools can meet youths' needs and realities with regards to cultural production.

Research in media education also recognizes the extent to which youth are already engaged in cultural production on an informal, everyday level outside of their school lives. Julian Sefton-Green and Vivian Reiss assert that the home (and not the school) is the key site of cultural production, and educators need "to find ways of developing the knowledge about culture and digital production brought from the home to school."[48] Jenkins similarly suggests that Internet-based affinity spaces, rather than schools, foster and nurture digital cultural production skills. He reports that the Pew Internet & American Life Project study conducted in 2005 found that "more than one-half of all teens have created media content, and roughly one-third of teens who use the Internet have shared content that they produced. In many cases, these teens are actively involved in what we are calling participatory cultures. A participatory culture is a culture with relatively low barriers to artistic expression and civic engagement, strong support for creating and sharing one's creations, and some type of informal mentorship whereby what is known by the most experienced is passed along to novices."[49] For Jenkins, forms of participatory culture include "expressions," which involve "producing new creative forms, such as digital sampling, skinning and modding, fan videomaking, fan fiction writing, zines, mash-ups," and "circulations," which involve shaping the flow of media, such as podcasting and blogging.[50] These examples of "expressions" and "circulations" are not found in Hesmondhalgh's definition of the cultural industries but they are important activities to recognize if they are indeed to become the basis, as McRobbie suggests, of the "future of work."

THE QUESTIONS OF AUDIENCE AND ACCESS

While the digital cultural production activities discussed above may seem to be open to all, the questions of access and audience remain pertinent ones when discussing the parameters of youth cultural production. Jenkins champions the skill of networking, as he argues that networks not only foster cultural production but also provide an audience for its end products.

Many youth are creating independent media productions, but only some learn how to be heard by large audiences. Increasingly, young artists are tapping networks of fans or gamers with the goal of reaching a broader readership for their work. They create within existing cultural communities not because they were inspired by a particular media property, but because they want to reach that property's audience of loyal consumers. Young people are learning to link their websites together in web-rings in part to increase the visibility of any given site and also to increase the profile of the group. Teachers are finding that students are often more motivated if they can share what they create with a larger community.[51]

Here, Jenkins explains that those youth who are able to find audiences for their cultural production are able to do so through collaborating and working with others. Similar to Jenkins, Peter Levine argues that media production can enhance the civic engagement of youth, but Levine also stresses the difficulty youth experience in finding pertinent audiences for their creative work "in a crowded media environment dominated by commercial products."[52] Indeed, Hesmondhalgh notes that the seemingly utopian democratizing potential of the Internet was lessened by the professionalization and commercialization of its content producers.[53] The Internet might suggest a level playing field for all to participate, but much web content is never viewed. Jenkins argues that youth find audiences for their cultural production amongst affinity groups that share the same interests, but Levine states, "many adolescents do not belong to tight affinity groups, differentiated from the mass youth population."[54] As such, increasing access to cultural production through digital media does not necessarily mean equal success in the reception of creative works.

If youth have to "learn how to be heard" as Jenkins suggests above, how might educators teach this skill? Levine advocates for creating "highly interactive, gamelike environments in which youth can express public views and do civic work," expanding audiences by "marketing youth products by organizing face-to-face events," and enabling students "to create digital media products with relatively low investments of time and expertise."[55] On this last note of low-stakes cultural production, Buckingham also argues for "frequent and recursive" small-scale activities that happen regularly rather than in one "Big Production number."[56] Both Buckingham and Levine's articulations of the appropriate scale of media production further suggest a reworking of idealized notions of creativity and a reintegration of creativity into everyday practice. Buckingham's small-scale projects are a way for him to close what he sees as a "dichotomy between 'skills' and 'creativity' ... that has tended to characterize debates about media production"[57] or "approaches that prioritize the mastery of technical skills ... and approaches that emphasize self-expression and open-ended exploration."[58] If students are to find cultural production satisfying, they need to practice skills and self-expression in small-scale ways that find audiences. This approach does not assume that all students will carry on with careers in the creative industries, but it could well equip those who do.

Many commentators have raised important concerns that home-based skills in digital media are not in fact open to all; however, Jenkins argues that these skills are spread across social categories. The Pew Internet & American Life Project study found that "urban youth (40 percent) are somewhat more likely than their suburban (28 percent) or rural (38 percent) counterparts to be media creators. Girls aged 15–17 (27 percent) are more likely than boys their age (17 percent) to be involved with blogging or other social activities online. The Pew researchers found no significant differences in participation by race-ethnicity."[59] A comparison of different groups (rural, suburban, urban, gendered, ethnic) is unable to show that there remain problems of access and involvement within these groups. Hesmondhalgh comments on the potentials of the Internet to change patterns of cultural consumption and production but also notes that these changes have happened "mainly within a very specific section of the world's population."[60] The digitization of media may enable greater access to small-scale cultural production for youth, but this access is still rooted in industrialized areas, and there still may be disparity in access amongst different social groups. Jenkins cites statistics that seem to show a lack of discrepancy in the creation of media content across different groups, but he also notes a "participation gap" in "unequal access to the opportunities, experiences, skills, and knowledge that will prepare youth for full participation in the world of tomorrow."[61] What to do about this gap remains an open-ended and unanswered question in his report, as he asks but does not answer, "how do we ensure that every child has access to the skills and experiences needed to become a full participant in the social, cultural, economic, and political future of our society?"[62] Surely, to be a full participant in society also means to be employed, and responding to youth realities might mean that researchers forge greater links between cultural production, employment, and community development in order to work towards greater access to the means of cultural production for all and greater equity in creative industries employment.

AT THE CROSSROADS OF EDUCATION
AND CULTURAL STUDIES: HENRY GIROUX'S
UPTAKE OF THE YOUTH QUESTION

The field of education also investigates youth life pathways through an examination of how questions of power shape youth realities, most notably in the work of Henry Giroux. Giroux's research takes on interdisciplinary dimensions and intersects with the field of cultural studies, and some of his conceptual underpinnings of the category of youth are reminiscent of subculture studies research that emerged from the Centre for Contemporary Cultural Studies (cccs) in the mid-1970s.

The landmark youth culture work of early cccs research is *Resistance through Rituals: Youth Subcultures in Post-War Britain*, published in 1976; this work examines working-class subcultures in England with the assumption that outward displays of subcultural affiliation (for example, dress) are symbolic of class-based politically resistant sentiments and possibilities. Discussing subcultures, John Clarke, Stuart Hall, Tony Jefferson, and Brian Roberts state that working-class lived experiences "provide the real material and historical basis – under the right conditions – for a more developed class strategies of open resistance, struggle, and for counter-hegemonic strategies of rupture and transformation. The convergence of these various strategies of negotiation by a subordinate class in a more sustained class politics requires, of course, mobilisation, politicisation, and organization."[63] Though the authors recognize the need for "the right conditions" to produce social change, working-class subcultures are seized as a first step towards developing a counter-hegemonic class consciousness. One of the main critiques of this work is that practical everyday realities of youth are ignored in favour of championing larger trajectories of class struggle. The legacy of this work is that youth gets mobilized as a prism through which to see social change and social problems, and empirical studies give way to theoretical abstractions. Even in research that is aware of the mobilization of youth as a trope, like Dick Hebdige's *Hiding in the Light*, there is an analysis of the ways youth gets used as a trope, resulting in a twice-removed metanarrative of youth.

Another problematic legacy of subculture studies is that "youth" was mobilized as an overly broad category, even if only certain types of youth were actually been discussed, which according to McRobbie, resulted in a "male connotation of youth,"[64] though a white and working-class connotation of youth should also be noted. As early CCCS work has been revisited by the researchers themselves and other commentators, this early work's conceptualization of youth has been critiqued because of its tendency towards conceiving of youth in overly dualistic ways. Some of these binaries include simplified divides between street culture and domestic culture, between authenticity and incorporation, and between the oppositional and the mainstream, and these binaries result in a privileging of working-class males' "resistance" to the point that these types of activities come to stand in for the category of "youth." Indeed, McRobbie comments that "youthfulness became virtually synonymous with subculture" due to subculture studies' inability to register the activities of non-subculturally affiliated youth.[65]

Early CCCS work sees subculture as a symbolic and "magical resolution" to problems of class inequality and power disparities experienced by working-class youth, but it also sees this "symbolic" resistance as largely ineffectual or "fated to fail"; as such, "there is no subcultural career for the working-class lad".[66] The emphasis on "fated to fail" activities does not mean that the tone of this work is necessarily fatalistic. Rather, the privileging of working-class "resistance" means that research on youth activities focused on the symbolic. "Space" and "signs" are key areas of analysis, as subcultures are thought to "win space for the young."[67] The legacy of symbolically "winning space" remains with youth research; twenty years later, a similar trope is evoked by Giroux in discussing a pedagogical mode that challenges youths' claims to "authenticity": "this pedagogical practice also suggests providing students with the opportunity to move beyond the search for an authentic identity. Instead, a pedagogy of representation establishes 'spaces' where meaning can be rewritten, produced, and constructed rather than merely asserted."[68] Giroux's invocation of "spaces" here operates on a theoretical rather than a practical field, and Giroux's research often produces theoretical rather than empirical studies of youth culture, as did many of the foundational CCCS texts.

Giroux demonstrates an awareness of this abstract use of youth as a category, but argues that this conceptual approach emerges in a range of disciplines. He notes that "as a concept, youth represents an inescapable intersection of the personal, social, political, and pedagogical. Beneath the abstract codifying of youth around the discourses of law, medicine, psychology, employment, education, and marketing studies, there is the lived experience of youth."[69] Giroux notes the absence of investigation into the lived experience of youth, but carries out a conceptual analysis that ultimately positions youth as metanarrative through which we can analyze constructions of youth. McRobbie comments that this conceptual approach to studying youth is not only found in academic research, as "youth remains a major point of symbolic investment for society as a whole."[70] This symbolic investment in youth as a category becomes problematic if academic research hopes to make interventions that serve lived youth realities.

Many have noted that when youth activities have been defined as resistant, such research becomes a manifestation of the left-leaning politics of theorists rather than a concrete mapping of youth realities that serves youth. Giroux further suggests that, recently, youth has also been mobilized as a scapegoat by the right: "youth has become a central focus in the attack waged by the New Right against subordinated public cultures, especially those occupied by single mothers on welfare, poor inner-city youth, black youth, gays and lesbians, and working-class students."[71] This line of thinking forms a central theme in Giroux's work: that "youth" today is under siege, and that the corporatization of America and its accompanying increasingly conservative political environment results in the evaporation of youth culture. While charting forces of power that shape youth realities is important, it is also important to chart the ways in which youth exercise power themselves; they are not only circumscribed by the structures of power, but also take up their own initiatives. Ultimately, Giroux is an astute commentator of the ways in which "youth" gets mobilized, but he does not break out of this mode himself. Nonetheless, there is a growing recognition in the field of youth culture studies of the need to reconfigure earlier approaches to youth, class, and power in contemporary examinations of youth, including the need to focus on more practical youth realities.

Some of these reconceptualizations occur in the field of post-subculture studies, but these reconceptualizations are at times also problematic as they completely abandon the questions of power and class that were so central to earlier subculture studies work. David Muggleton and Rupert Weinzierl argue that post-subcultural studies has erred in its conception of human experience as fluid and fragmented and largely outside of questions of class; in response, they advocate a move towards "a position that recognizes the differentiation and multiplicity of points of power in society … Such a model dispenses with the theorization of subcultures as either oppositional or incorporated."[72] Similarly, Huq argues that "class, like the existence of gender, has not simply ceased to exist. It is more accurate to recognize that class and gender will forever be mediated by geography/locality, work/education, interactions with families and other relationships, forming complex networks of social processes."[73] For Huq, understanding how class interlocks with other structural forces also provides a better lens to capture the activities of multi-ethnic and diasporic youth, who did not register as subjects in early CCCS work.

FROM SUBCULTURE TO CULTURAL PRODUCTION: THE FUSING OF WORK AND LEISURE

Beyond these reconceptualizations of the categories of youth, class, and power, subculture studies has also been revamped in order to focus on more practical everyday realities of youth rather than on loaded symbolic investments. In his later work, Paul Willis focuses on the everyday "grounded aesthetics" of ordinary youth creative activities, such as making collages and mix tapes, dancing, and decorating bedrooms. Willis moves away from the analysis of the spectacular that is associated with early CCCS work and forwards a definition of creativity that is "not only part of everyday human activity, but also a necessary part – that which has to be done every day, that which is not extra but essential to ensure the daily production and reproduction of human existence."[74] In early CCCS work, "oppositional" subcultural activities were associated with the field of leisure, as "resistance" was futile in the field of work. This binary continues for Willis, as work remains an area that is stifling and cannot be creative, so leisure takes on particular importance as a site to exercise "necessary" creative practices. Willis may overstate this work/leisure binary, but it is important to recognize that service industry employment may be a long-term mode of work rather than a temporary after-school job for youth, and creativity may indeed not be possible in this sector of work. However, it is also important to recognize the potential for the bleeding together of work and leisure as leisure becomes work in order to be able to map new sources and challenges of employment for youth.

McRobbie makes comments about the "aestheticisation of everyday life,"[75] which in part recall Willis's discussion of "grounded aesthetics," but for McRobbie, unlike Willis, young people are not symbolically exercising creativity in their everyday lives; they are attempting to make actual careers from cultural production. Willis's work considers cultural consumption and creativity in the broad areas of clothing, music, TV, and magazines, but his work is interested in the relationships of these activities to identity formation and seeks to validate these activities as meaningful hobbies. Though he does not consider the employment ramifications of these hobbies, Willis also indirectly calls for policy changes in order to more broadly support these activities, stating that "it is this widest symbolic creativity which should be recognized and promoted ... to create the supportive environmental, economic and social conditions which enable [youth] to do better and more creatively what they do already."[76] Willis does not state, specifically, how these conditions will be created, and more academic work needs to be done to research what supportive "environmental, economic and social conditions" could look like, and how local, provincial, and federal governments could foster them. To be able to offer guidance in this area, academic work in youth culture needs to be more empirically grounded. This does not mean the abandonment of theory; rather, policy can be a meeting ground for theory and practice. Academic studies can offer the longitudinal lenses needed to track patterns in youth activities and provide the theoretical models to analyze the complexities of power and powerlessness in youth experiences.

Indeed, new theoretical models are needed to be able to grasp the bleeding together of work and leisure in grassroots youth creative activities. Sarah Thornton's work on club cultures offers a model that moves away from thinking of subculture as a discrete and well-formed unit, as she proposes the concept of subcultural capital as an alternative concept.[77] Drawing on Bourdieu's notion of cultural capital, Thornton suggests that subcultural capital is based in privileged insider knowledge of underground cool. She argues that subcultures are not about symbolic resistance towards the dominant culture; they are about demonstrating distinction to the undifferentiated masses, a homogenized crowd from which youth distance themselves through assertions of hipness. Thornton states that subcultural capital may not convert into economic capital, but it may convert into employment such as working as a DJ, club organizer, clothes designer, or journalist. Though Thornton's research emerges out of club cultures, if we conceive of subcultures along her definition – as affinity groups that are ad hoc communities with fluid boundaries – we can imagine other types of employment that may emerge out of subcultural capital than those mentioned above. Similarly, in attempting to re-evaluate women's involvement in punk, Helen Reddington comments that ad hoc subcultural organizational activities of the late 1970s paved new employment pathways, as women's "strong entrepreneurial flair involved in setting up a band, writing songs, organizing gigs, publicity, and so on ... presaged (and perhaps informed?) the 1980s focus on small businesses initiatives as the way out of economic recession."[78] Thornton has more modest claims about subcultural capital converting into employment and casts the employment opportunities she mentions as not necessarily financially lucrative. She argues that youth may slum it and opt for "classlessness" to transcend the "adult" demands and responsibilities of economic capital. For the youth profiled in *Out of the Basement*, the demands and responsibilities of earning an income are not evaded, however, as many of them share their work and commitment to make a living in creative fields.

In one of her later conceptualizations of subculture, McRobbie casts subcultural affinity spaces as an "opportunity for learning and sharing skills, for praticising them, for making a small amount of money." Subcultures may impart "future lifeskills in the form of work or self employment."[79] As such, McRobbie foregrounds the cultural production of subcultures in a material rather than a symbolic way, such that cultural production is "the creation of a whole way of life, an alternative to higher education, a job creation scheme for the culture industries."[80] McRobbie's work focuses on everyday activities and she advocates that youth culture research pursue "the dignity of the specific" instead of questions of class and ideology.[81] This attention to the specific has two outcomes: it allows for a reconceptualization of the loaded category "resistance" at "the more mundane, micrological level of everyday practices and choices about how to live" such that "it becomes possible to see the sustaining, publicizing and extending of the subcultural enterprise as a way of attempting to earn a living within what has been described as the aestheticization of culture (against a backdrop of industrial decline)."[82] Next, this focus on everyday practices that emphasizes cultural production offers a wider lens to capture a "more active

picture of the involvement of girls and young women, particularly
in relation to fashion and styles [and] it also would encourage a
more longitudinal dimension which would connect being in a subculture with what happens next, especially in the world of education, training, or employment."[83] This type of investigation requires
approaching research with pragmatic questions, such as, "what
were the social relations which informed the production of the
subculture? What preexisting skills were called upon to produce
the graphics and the posters and even the music itself?"[84] These
questions characterize subculture not as an inherently oppositional
grouping but as a space of teaching and learning that also has connections to employment. McRobbie also argues that more attention needs to be given to the changing parameters of young people's
work in creative fields through empirical, ethnographic, and sociological studies that can influence policy making, such that contemporary youth realities and experiences can be better understood
and supported.[85]

FROM FULL PARTICIPATION TO FULL EMPLOYMENT

Jenkins sees cultural production as paving the pathway for "opportunities to participate and to develop the cultural competencies and
social skills needed for full involvement [in society]."[86] Though
Jenkins does not make connections between "expressions" or "circulations" and the challenges of creating gainful employment for oneself, the narrative of Sean Michaels's experiences with blogging
leading into a career as a writer is one example of the connection
between small-scale creative projects and employment. Geoff Mulgan
and Ken Worpole made the bold claim that youth cultural production would perform "the historic task of bringing Britain back to
some form of full employment. Youth culture, alongside its offshoots
in style, fashion, music, and design has been one of the few areas of
the economy successfully to make the transitions to the late '80s,
creating jobs and finding new international markets."[87] While this
claim is overblown, it is important to explore the bridge between
informal subcultural leisure activities and paid work.

Full employment through youth creative work remains to come to
fruition, and perhaps a mitigating factor in this lack of full employment stems from barriers to equal access to participation. Creative
industries employment is not distributed equitably across differing

racial, ethnic, and class backgrounds, and the often informal, network-based modes of entry into creative industries employment, sometimes involving unpaid internships, may offer some explanation of these disparities. Discussing Florida's findings of a dearth of non-white citizens employed in the creative class, Oakley notes that the situation does not improve in the creative industries (which, in her definition, does not include high-tech jobs, whose inclusion would worsen the portrait).

> Despite the celebrated "creativity" of the BME [black and minority ethnic] population and the influence of urban black culture on everything from fashion and popular music to everyday speech patterns, the picture in the UK is ... bleak. About 4.6 percent of the creative and cultural industry workforce in the UK is from an ethnic minority background (Leadbeater, 2005) compared with 7 percent of the UK labour force as a whole. This is even more disturbing when one considers the concentration of creative industry employment in London, where over a quarter of the labour force is from an ethnic minority background – up to 35 percent in inner London. And the younger age profile of the BME population means that it should make up a relatively higher proportion of the economically active population than a simple per capita comparison with the white population might suggest.[88]

Jenkins's vision of participatory culture and media education sees creativity for all rather than job training for a few, but Oakley's statistics suggest there is a problem in translating this creativity/participation/involvement of all into equal employment opportunities for all. This lack of equity is another site of potential academic intervention, including researching the mechanisms that youth use to navigate employment in the creative industries in order to better understand inequities in access to these mechanisms.

These types of discussions are not currently happening, as there is an absence of attention to youth activities in research in the creative industries, even if youth are increasingly entering into this field and expanding conceptions of what creative work means. The capacity to register these youth activities may require a broadening of traditional definitions of the cultural industries such that non-industrialized types of cultural production can gain visibility. There is a need, though, to strike a balance and widen the definition of the cultural industries without slipping into an innovation model, in which youth activities will register even less. Mapping and theorizing contemporary youth small-scale self-generated creative employment requires a widened lens and working across disciplines and fields to better understand and support these youth activities. Academia can be a place to start this work so that policies, as will be seen in Part Two, can reflect an understanding of contemporary youth practices.

PART TWO

Structures

3

Does Youth Matter?

Cultural Policy in Canada

In Part Two, I turn to an examination of the Canadian policy terrain in which youth cultural activities are enmeshed. Because this policy terrain has federal, provincial, and municipal layers, as well as international ones, I examine a series of policy moments targeting each of these layers in the chapters in this section. John Foote notes that "to date ... there has been relatively little research and evaluation examining how the three levels of government actually interact on cultural matters in specific communities."[1] It is beyond the scope of this book to map out all of the interactions of federal, provincial, and municipal governmental levels in cultural matters; instead, I foreground a selection of policy moments and examine how they can offer an illumination of the relationship between youth and policy. Cultural policy in Canada is not only found in federal arts funding, for example, but emerges from disparate places and jurisdictions, such as employment, copyright, and noise and cleanliness bylaws. In this section, I take note of some of the gaps in federal, provincial, and municipal policies and examine how greater clarity and support for youth might be achieved through fostering a more cohesive framework for youth cultural production. Joyce Zemans argues that "national strategies are required to complement local and provincial initiatives. What we lack is the vision to see holistically,"[2] and Part Two investigates the effects of this lack of holistic vision on youth realities as they face the creative industries. In this chapter, I establish my general approach to studying policy and then begin to put this approach into practice by studying some policy documents.

FEDERAL CULTURAL POLICY IN CANADA:
PAST, PRESENT, FUTURE

Canada's federal cultural policy has long been directed to the project of building and preserving national identity. Many scholars cite the importance and impact of the Report of the Royal Commission on National Development in the Arts, Letters and Sciences, commonly known as the Massey-Lévesque Commission, which was begun in 1949 and released in 1951, and heralded an era of government intervention in the cultural sector. Though the 1950s and Massey-Lévesque Commission are commonly thought to have guided federal emphasis on supporting cultural institutions, Foote traces federal support of culture to the late nineteenth and early twentieth century, in which the government began to preserve and build cultural infrastructure through the vehicle of national institutions, such the National Gallery of Canada, the National Archives of Canada, the National Film Board, and the CBC/Radio Canada.[3] However, D. Paul Schafer and André Fortier suggest that pre-World War II growth of the art and cultural sector predominantly stemmed from individual efforts and private institutions rather than from government initiatives.[4] Nonetheless, the Massey-Lévesque Commission's articulation of nation and culture in 1951 provided a clear rationale for federal intervention in the arts and gave rise to national institutions such as the National Library of Canada (1953), the Canada Council (1957), the Canadian Film Development Corporation (1968), the Department of Communications (1969), and the Canadian Radio and Television Commission (1969).[5] Schafer and Fortier identify the first formally iterated link between cultural policy and national unity in the 1968 Broadcasting Act, with its statement that "the national broadcasting service should contribute to the development of national unity and provide for a continuing expression of Canadian identity."[6] This connection between Canadian identity and national unity permeates prior federal interventions in the cultural sphere, even if it is not so clearly stated.

This project of nation building was also linked to a project of the democratization of culture, which Greg Baeker defines as "broadening access to the products of one culture."[7] The "one culture" in question here is high culture, which has raised criticisms about the elitist nature of this democratization project. According to Zemans, distributing and creating access to culture was a particularly important project due to the features of the Canadian landscape, as Canada is "a sparsely populated country with significant regional disparities and isolation."[8] Creating access to culture in this spread-out population folded back into the project of forging national unity. In his discussion of the formation of the Canada Council in 1957, Paul Litt highlights how both projects of nation building and democratization of culture were at play and suggests that the Canada Council was "the product of the intellectual climate of the times." He states: "for Massey and his ilk, the big story of modern Western history was the spread of democratic rights and privileges. Rising literacy rates opened the possibility of cultivating the kind of responsible, civic-minded, and judicious citizenry required to make mass democracy work. In the Canadian context, this process was intertwined with nation building as the country defined an independent destiny in the postwar world. Canada needed culture both to succeed as a liberal democracy and to claim its place among civilized nations."[9] While the 1950s and 1960s may have emphasized nation building through the democratization of culture, the 1970s saw the rise of a new framework for intervention in the cultural sphere, with Secretary of State Gérard Pelletier's emphasis on the decentralization of culture between 1969 and 1975.[10] Baeker states that this era's emphasis on cultural democracy "not only [sought] the broader dissemination of one culture, but acknowledge[ed] the value of legitimacy of many cultural traditions and forms of expression."[11] The shift from the democratization of culture to cultural democracy is a shift from a top-down dissemination of culture to a horizontal decentralization, "relying more on organic and community-based approaches."[12] The second half of the twentieth century also saw the growth of provincial arts councils across Canada. Saskatchewan founded the Saskatchewan Arts Board in 1948, "the first agency of its kind in North America."[13] Ontario and Manitoba developed provincial arts councils in the 1960s, Newfoundland in 1980, and the rest of the provinces through the 1990s.

The move to a cultural democracy model in the 1970s was accompanied by the growth of the cultural industries, which ushered in an era of economic rather than cultural or national justifications for cultural policy. Baeker characterizes a "restricted vision" in this era's "pragmatic and utilitarian approaches" to cultural policy and notes a shift in cultural policy discussions "from 'participatory' activity to 'managerial' strategies, from calls for the democratization of arts

audiences to studies of economic impact."[14] In light of a lack of clear
vision and consistency in cultural programs and policies, John Meisel
suggests that what we need now is "a new Massey Commission"
such that we can "see and understand the whole cultural situation in
Canada and that we can learn how the various parts can best interact."[15] Though Meisel is wary of developing "a single policy framework," he highlights the benefits of "consistency, computability, and
congruence" to support cultural programs.[16] Despite the lack of an
overarching vision of culture, Foote credits the continued importance of developing and preserving national identity for the growth
of culture in Canada in 1970s, 1980s, and 1990s and for "the creation of a wide range of national policies and support programmes
designed to further develop arts, heritage and broadcasting." This
era also saw the beginning of federal support for the cultural industries "including film, sound recording, publishing, new media" as
well as "enactment of legislative amendments governing such legislation as the *Broadcasting Act* (1991) and the *Copyright Act* (1988,
and 1997 and 2002)."[17] Changes were also seen in the ministerial
organization of culture: in 1980, the Department of Communications
"absorbed the arts and culture programmes then housed in the
Department of the Secretary of State," and in 1993, the Department
of Canadian Heritage took over these responsibilities as well as "culture, citizenship and identity, Sport Canada and until recently, Parks
Canada."[18] This era not only saw the broadening of the definition of
culture, visible in the enlarging of the Heritage portfolio, but also
the broadening of federal intervention in culture, such that "the
trend in cultural policy in Canada is towards a holistic approach
from creation through to consumption."[19] If youth are increasingly
exploring self-employment through cultural production, this raises
the question of what role the government will exert in the twenty-
first-century context and how the new and different practices of contemporary youth will fit within a cultural policy framework. Though
a variety of cultural funding exists at the federal, provincial, and
municipal levels in Canada, these structures are often organized
around various artistic silos, and, as such, may be out of touch with
many contemporary youth practices.[20]

A variety of federal jurisdictions may have provisions for youth,
but there is no one federal policy that targets youth creative employment. Human Resources and Skills Development Canada (HRSDC)
has Youth Employment Strategy (YES) programs, such as "career

focus" and "summer work experience," which provide work opportunities for youth; "skills link," which targets youth who experience barriers entering into the workforce; and "youth awareness," which aims to make unemployed youth more aware of skilled trade sectors. None of these programs contain any overt connections to the creative industries in their descriptions or to self-generated employment in any field for that matter; rather, these programs offer funding to employers and community organizations to hire young people. Also at the federal level, both the Department of Canadian Heritage and the Cultural Human Resources Council (CHRC) provide youth internship programs. The Department of Canadian Heritage's program, Young Canada Works (YCW), is not solely focused on arts organizations or cultural production. Youth may apply to work in "visual or performing arts companies, film and video production" as well as "museums … arts organizations … and multimedia companies," but some of the options, such as "language schools, educational institutions, translation firms" take a broader definition of culture that is not necessary rooted in cultural production. CHRC also offers internships in cultural organizations, but its website states, "you cannot apply to CHRC for an internship. Instead, you must find an organization willing to apply, and hire you as an intern."[21] Youth engagement with the creative industries often takes the form of self-employment that is not affiliated with major organizations; as such, youth energies might be better supported by assisting these self-directed pathways than by causing them to create their own internships with organizations. Internships alone do not necessarily lead to sustainable pathways for youth in the creative industries. Steven Greenhouse chronicles the growth of unpaid internships and suggests that not all youth are financially able to take on unpaid work, nor do they all have access to the informal contacts and connections that are often crucial for securing prestigious internships.[22] Finally, "children and youth" are also specifically addressed by the Department of Canadian Heritage, but the majority of the programs offered by Heritage for youth, such as the "Canada Day Poster Challenge," are not employment centered, nor do they relate to involvement in the creative industries.

POLICY MATTERS

As noted above, there currently is not a complete picture of how federal, provincial, and municipal policy layers interact in practical and local circumstances and of how these interactions affect youth practices. The absence of research in this area may be part of a larger absence within the realm of cultural studies, where the field of policy studies has been the neglected and unsexy wallflower to its semiotic, feminist, and Marxist cousins. Angela McRobbie states that many cultural studies researchers have disdained more practical and empirical policy recommendation types of work in favour of edgier work in semiotics, textual analysis, and subversive things people do with their cultural commodities.[23] But if cultural studies has the relationship of culture and power under its purview, policy is a material instantiation of this dialectic and merits serious consideration. This mode of analysis follows from Tony Bennett's work, which asserts that policy must be part of discussions of culture. He argues for including "policy considerations in the definition of culture in viewing it as a particular field of government," such that the field of cultural studies is able to make pragmatic interventions into cultural policy.[24]

Since the 1990s, cultural studies research has taken up more of this cultural policy advocacy,[25] but more empirical work to support this advocacy remains to be done, especially with regards to youth creative practices. Research in this critical policy studies field typically raises questions, forwards critiques, and suggests new routes or changes in policy directions. For example, Mark Banks and David Hesmondhalgh perform close readings of UK creative policy documents, which they characterize as "bleak,"[26] and lament the lack of attention to labour issues in these policies. They suggest the need for cultural policies to take working conditions in the creative industries seriously, such that governments can work towards "prevent[ing] greater harm befalling those people who work within the [creative] sector."[27] Similarly, McRobbie characterizes her aim in researching the lived experience of small-scale youth cultural employment as "reformist, in that there is an attempt to connect sociological and cultural analysis with a concern for policy."[28]

In this book, I make use of life stories and interviews to think through potential cultural policy changes, and these methodologies are not uncommon in cultural studies-based critical policy studies research. For example, Charles Leadbeater and Kate Oakley conducted "dozens of interviews" with young cultural workers in order to "[draw] conclusions about how national and local policy could be made more effective."[29] Similarly, in her study of the British fashion industry, McRobbie interviewed eighteen graduates of fashion design school who were attempting to make a living as fashion designers in order "to contribute to the improvement of fashion as a place of livelihoods" for the young people working in this field.[30] Elsewhere, McRobbie makes wide-ranging recommendations and critiques of UK cultural policy directions, ranging from revising and expanding the UK's Small Business Support scheme, to making better links between universities and cultural industries, to reforming welfare, social security, and pensions.[31] Advocating for the use of case studies to map the contemporary working conditions that youth face in the creative industries, and to work towards making policy changes, McRobbie argues, "the case study ... performs a knowledge-generating function. It allows us the opportunity to see how things actually work in practice and how more general social, and even global, trends like those described by social theorists ... are translated or modified when they become grounded."[32] *Out of the Basement* emerges from this vein of critical policy studies, and explores the gaps in current cultural policies with regards to youth, and suggests what more supportive conditions might look like. In this chapter and throughout the work, youth life stories serve to ground the somewhat abstract discussions of policy at the level of lived experience.

Drawing on Bennett's work and the field of critical policy studies, I understand policy as a site of diffuse points and flows of power. In his analysis of "scenes," Will Straw examines the ways in which multiple policy streams shape and organize cultural movements. Discussing Aihwa Ong's work on cultural citizenship, Straw forwards an understanding of culture as "an implicit negotiation with the context in which it seeks to emerge. That context includes other people, artefacts, and the structures of power or institution."[33] Rather than positioning these structures of power to be directly administered, Straw maps the ways in which culture can emerge from "contradictions and hesitations of public policy rather than any enabling function."[34] For example, Straw credits the emergence of Montreal's disco scene in the 1970s not to any "formal cultural policy"; he argues that this scene "was shaped by multiple forms of public regulation and incentive," such as "alcohol licensing laws, municipal zoning regulations, public performance regulations controlling the use of recorded music as entertainment, Canadian content regulations to encourage the airplay of Canadian music (or French-language music), tariff regulations governing the importing of foreign recordings, agreements between nightclubs and local musicians' unions and so on."[35]

Similarly, Clive Robertson also emphasizes the multiple flows and streams of policy and suggests a critical study of policy that relies on a Foucauldian understanding of power production. He states that "critical studies of policy are recognizable by their re-affirmations of the possible production, and not just the seeking, of power from the 'bottom up,' and for their insistences upon the presence of questions about the stakes of political representation in policy formulations and analysis."[36] Under this rubric, policy is not only created and implemented at the governmental level. Referencing Jim McGuigan, Roberston wants to "trouble the 'practical operations that are merely administered' by emphasizing 'the relationship of policy to politics as a field of contestation between rival discourses, ideologies, interests.'"[37] By forwarding this view of policy as an active site of contestation, Robertson puts forth two possible definitions of cultural policy. First, drawing on Toby Miller, Robertson suggests "cultural policy as a site at which the subject is produced."[38] Second, drawing on McGuigan, Robertson suggests "cultural policy as being principally about the conditions of culture, the material and also the discursive determinations in time and space of cultural production and consumption."[39] If we read Canadian cultural policy with youth as our subject, what mode of youth subjectivity is called into being through its discursive structures? How does policy discursively determine the material conditions of youth cultural production? In what ways does policy produce youth subjects and conditions of youth cultural production in Canada, and in what ways can we read policy documents as fields of contestation between rival discourses and ideologies as they concern youth interests?

THE INFRASTRUCTURE OF CANADIAN CULTURAL POLICY: A CLOSE READING OF THE STATUS OF THE ARTIST ACT

Canada has no unified federal policy in the arts, and Canadian cultural policy is not writ large in any single instantiation. Nonetheless, the Canadian Conference of the Arts (CCA), Canada's oldest arts advocacy organization, argues that a "scatter shot" approach to federal cultural policy can be found through bringing together the "infrastructure" of legislation that concerns the arts: the Income Tax

Act, the Copyright Act, the Broadcasting Act, and the Status of the Artist Act.[40] A close reading of some of this legislation can provide an image of what mode of subjectivity of the artist is called into being through Canadian cultural policy. One may expect that, of these four acts, the Status of the Artist Act would most specifically highlight how the role of the artist and the conditions of artistic labour are encoded in policy, and as such, I begin my examination of cultural policy in Canada with this policy moment, and ask how and if the encoded role of the artist speaks to contemporary youth cultural employment.

Artist as Cultural Civilizer

In Canada, the Status of the Artist Act passed in 1992 and set out to answer some of the 1980 UNESCO Status of the Artist recommendations regarding artists' socioeconomic concerns. This legislation makes some initial comments about the broad role that artists play in society and opens by stating "the importance of the contribution of artists to the cultural, social, economic and political enrichment of Canada."[41] This overture suggests a multifaceted role of the artist, but the reference to cultural "enrichment" evokes a liberal humanist definition of the artist as cultural civilizer who betters humanity, in this case the Canadian public, through cultural works. Ruben Gaztambide-Fernandez identifies the liberal humanist conception of the artist to suppose that "artists are individuals with special talents whose role is to provide great works of beauty that contribute to the civilizing project of modernity; this is the view of the artist as 'cultural civilizer.'"[42] Gaztambide-Fernandez traces this conception of the artist back to the Renaissance, when "a new rhetoric of the artist as an individual with special faculties and personality traits emerged,"[43] but comments that this conception of the artist crystallized most forcefully in the nineteenth century with the work of Matthew Arnold. In the first chapter of *Culture and Anarchy*, "Sweetness and Light," Arnold states that studying culture is "the pursuit of perfection," which "then, is the pursuit of sweetness and light."[44] For Arnold, this pursuit involves class-based distinctions about cultural worth. Arnold makes remarks about the "Philistinism" of the rising middle-class in the late nineteenth century and suggests that the project of culture is to ward off the "vulgarity" and "animality" that is associated with "great middle-class liberalism."[45] Though Canada's Status of the

Artist legislation does not make these class-based claims, the idea of multifaceted "enrichment" through culture has had these connotations in the past.

Gaztambide-Fernandez foregrounds the lasting influence of liberal humanism in conceptions of the arts and of the artist, but he also suggests alternative modes of subjectivity for the artist than that of "the civilizer," including that of "the border crosser" and that of "the representator." While the model of the artist as cultural civilizer relies on an "art for art's sake" notion that artists improve humanity because art is a "civilizing" force, the model of the artist as border crosser relies on a notion of "art for politics' sake" and suggests that the role of art is to provoke change as it "challenges boundaries, rules, and expectations and disturbs the social order to promote social transformation and 'reconstruction.'"[46] Finally, the artist as representator relies on an "art for identity's sake" model in which the artist engages in "issues of representation, meaning making, and struggles over public space";[47] this model suggests that "artists produce works that inscribe political struggles over meaning and identification."[48] The latter two of these models may be more relevant to describe the goals of many contemporary artists, but Gaztambide-Fernandez highlights that there is continued emphasis on the model of the artist as civilizer in many art schools, citing that "most contemporary institutions of artistic education are grounded on the views of liberal humanism."[49] Gaztambide-Fernandez suggests a reconceptualization of education for artists in order to better grapple with the current climate and challenges faced by young artists through encouraging them "to confront the range of social roles they may be expected to fulfill."[50] If current Canadian legislation that addresses the role of the artist in society, such as the Status of the Artist Act, does not take up these challenges, how could Canadian cultural policy better reflect the complexities of contemporary cultural production and call into being the range of social roles that young artists may desire and be expected to fulfill, beyond providing "enrichment"?

The Artist as Nation Builder

Canada's Status of the Artist legislation not only calls a vision of the artist as civilizer into being; the act also ties its definition of the artist to a nationalistic vision of Canadian belonging. This vision is outlined in the following two provisions in the legislation, which state "the importance to Canadian society of conferring on artists a status that reflects their primary role in developing and enhancing Canada's artistic and cultural life, and in sustaining Canada's quality of life" and "the role of the artist [is] in particular to express the diverse nature of the Canadian way of life and the individual and collective aspirations of Canadians."[51] This rhetoric around Canadianess and the links between culture and national identity recall the framework of the Massey-Lévesque Commission. Even if this Status of the Artist legislation does not stem from the definition of art as high culture that underpinned the democratization of culture model, the humanistic vision of protecting culture and fostering nationalism remains in the rhetoric of this legislation. The wording of the Status of the Artist legislation suggests the continued importance of iterating links between public support for the arts and Canadian national identity, even if this vision of the role of culture may no longer be as central in the cultural policy landscape as it once was.

The Artist as Worker

Beyond this rhetoric of Canadianess and enrichment, the Status of the Artist legislation primarily concerns itself with the economic status of artists and sets out to legislate the rights of artists as workers. While there are initial overtures about the role of the artist in Canadian society, the definition of the artist outlined in the Status of the Artist Act is not the broader definition of the artist as "cultural worker" who plays a role in society as civilizer, border crosser, or representator. Ultimately, the vision of the artist in the legislation is pragmatically oriented; cultural work in the Status of the Artist Act refers to the rights of artists in the workforce as "independent contractors determined to be professionals."[52] The initial provisions of the act, which state that artists provide "enrichment," might suggest a privileged or elevated position of the artist vis-à-vis society, but the heart of the legislation is that artists are workers like any other. This legislation aims to normalize artistic labour, but it does not fully take into account that work in the creative industries is often unlike other kinds of work, as it frequently is contract-based, ad hoc, independent, and unregulated by unions and organizations, even if artists are granted rights to form unions. Indeed, "for some artists' associations, 'status of the artist' has become virtually synonymous with providing a statutory regime to enable unions and associations of professional artists to bargain collectively with those who engage artists and to regulate the bargaining process in a manner analogous to labour laws."[53] If we read the Status of the Artist Act with youth as our central subject, and ask if the mode of subjectivity called into being is relevant to the experiences of contemporary youth cultural producers, this provision of artists' rights to form unions and engage in collective bargaining may not speak to the characteristics of independent small-scale and self-generated modes of youth cultural production. Rather than seeing artists as responding to "extra-social callings to provide great works of art,"[54] contemporary cultural policies might define artistic practice as being engrained in and responding to society and being characterized by labour conditions that are distinct from other professions.

Here, it is important to bear in mind the differences between policy and practice. To what extent do the policy provisions of the Status of the Artist Act affect and enable the material conditions of artists as workers? Recalling Robertson's claims about policy, in what ways are youth discursively produced as subjects by policy, and in what ways does policy reveal the material and the discursive determinations of youth cultural production? Leadbeater and Oakley represent the work conditions of young people involved in the creative industries much differently than the Status of the Artist Act, characterizing youth cultural producers as "the Independents" because they often actively choose to pursue work away from major organizations.

> A large and growing share of employment in [the creative] industries is accounted for by the self-employed, freelancers and micro-businesses. These new Independents are often producers, designers, retailers and promoters all at the same time. They do not fit into neat categories. The Independents thrive on informal networks through which they organise work, often employing friends and former classmates. Although some are ambitious entrepreneurs, many want their businesses to stay small because they want to retain their independence and their focus on their creativity. Yet that does not mean they see themselves as artists who deserve public subsidy. They want to make their own way in the market.[55]

Leadbeater and Oakley are speaking to the British context, but Canadian reports have similar findings. In the *Next Generation of*

Artistic Leaders and Arts Audiences Dialogues report, "many participants spoke of entrepreneurial models when discussing their long-
range career plans. The goal for many participants is to be entirely
reliant on economic income generated through their practices, and
reliance on support from arts funders is often seen as a 'first step' towards this goal."[56] That this entrepreneurial model of the arts is often
fulfilled through self-employment and freelance work that is not
affiliated with larger unions or organizations is not something that
the Status of the Artist legislation addresses. In the *Next Generation*
study, some participants voiced a disconnect from unions and professional organizations, stating that they "feel that the membership and
designation within these types of organizations serves to limit them,
not only in terms of how they self-identify, but also what contexts
they are allowed to work in."[57] McRobbie notes a "blend of the bohemian individualism of artists and the business ethos of the commercial art director" in young creative workers, such that "union
organization along traditional lines is either seen as irrelevant or simply by-passed."[58] This model of cultural employment that exists away
from unions and professional organizations carries with it a host of
challenges and implications, from employment insurance to extended
health care and pensions, that simply granting "professional" status
to artists does not begin to address. Mapping out these ad hoc labour
conditions is a needed first step to consider what structures might be
put into place to respond to fluctuating labour conditions if unions
are no longer seen as the appropriate mechanism to fill this role.

  The *Next Generation* report does not take up a discussion of these
types of implications of independent labour, but does discuss the
disjuncture between current models of youth creative employment
and current funding streams: "flexibility in eligible project costs,
allowances for capital investments, grants for business training, and
workshops on the 'business of art' were only some of the key needs
identified by participants. Recognizing this entrepreneurial desire
will be an important challenge for arts funders, many of whom currently focus their efforts and resources towards supporting artistic
creation and organizational infrastructure."[59] These comments suggest that forging a career as an artist is more than pursuing the act
of artistic creation, and the youth profiled in this report desired support for the dissemination of their work and for the development
of skills relating to professionalization. Perhaps more stability for
young artists could be created through mechanisms that allow for
more flexibility, rather than by granting more professional rights.

All in all, in the "perception of most artists and arts administrators, a perception which appears to be confirmed by the available data, the [Status of the Artist] Act has not improved the economic status of professional Canadian artists."[60] Additional government policies and programs that recognize the parameters of contemporary youth cultural production might better address the economic situation of these artists. Support does not necessarily mean an increase in grants and funding, as support mechanisms could possibly include: "deducting artistic expenses against income; preserving the freelance status of artists for purposes of income tax and copyright; responding to fluctuating income levels; providing tax exemption for all artistic income or for royalties; providing tax exempt status for artistic grants; access to employment insurance, if only for the social benefits; ensuring appropriate pensions for artists; bankruptcy protection; health and safety; appropriate and affordable living and work spaces; providing appropriate professional development and training opportunities."[61] Pursuing any or all of these recommendations may allow for greater equity and stability in a field that is characterized by instability, and any of these practical recommendations might do more to improve the social and economic status of artists than the Status of the Artist Act. In the next sections of this chapter, I turn to two further policy moments and two youth stories that illuminate the disjuncture between contemporary youth cultural practices and policies.

BANDS AND BORDER CROSSINGS: MATT SHANE AND THE P2 PROBLEM

For emerging independent musicians, touring is a necessity to develop a fan base, gain visibility, create contacts, and become known. For emerging Canadian independent musicians, this also means crossing the border and touring to the United States. Gaztambide-Fernandez forwards a conceptual model of the artist as "border crosser," but artists also need to literally cross borders for work purposes, and this process may be complicated, if not criminalized, for small-scale cultural producers. Foote states that "Canada is active internationally in the field of culture by virtue of bilateral and multilateral cultural agreements,"[62] and easing the process for Canadian small-scale cultural producers to cross the American border for work purposes is an area of potential federal intervention. Matt

Shane, who formerly played drums in the Montreal-based band Think About Life, seized an opportunity to tour to the United States with the band after they had been playing together for several months. He describes touring to the United States as "totally essential. There are so many more cities in the States; the music scene is much bigger across the country ... Touring across Canada is a really, really expensive thing to do, whereas touring down the Eastern Seaboard, there are a lot of big cities on the way, so it's actually cheaper as well, and you're going to reach a much wider audience, generally."[63] Here, Matt speaks to the vastness of the Canadian landscape in relation to its relatively small and spread-out population, which makes touring Canada a costly and sometimes unrewarding affair for emerging bands, and makes the shorter distances and larger audiences of the United States more attractive. Matt narrates, "I had just moved in with this guy Spencer Krug who plays in Wolf Parade. They needed a band to go on tour with them; they needed an opening band," so he asked to go with them and was told, "Yeah, sure, no problem."

From a legal perspective, touring to the United States is in fact problematic, as it means pursuing paid employment, which requires a P2 visa: a work visa for artists and entertainers that is issued by US Citizenship and Immigration Services. For small independent touring bands, paying the costly fees of this visa is not realistic. Matt explains, "we couldn't afford a work visa, a P2 visa, because it costs – I don't remember how much it costs. It was over a thousand dollars; it was really expensive. We were a brand new band. We didn't have a label; we didn't have anything. We weren't going to pay out of pocket. It was already going to cost us way too much to go on this tour." Matt's estimation of the high cost of the P2 work visa is accurate: the "legal fee" is $645 and the "filing fee" is $420. Paying $1,065 per band member to legally enter the United States is not possible for most emerging bands. As Matt describes, touring is often a money-losing venture for small bands, as costs outweigh revenues. These bands may sometimes be lucky to get paid $50 or $100 a night, which is often less than the expenses of gas, vehicle rental, food, and accommodation. Although touring might sometimes be a financially dubious venture, it remains an important part of the process of becoming established, so bands continue to seek out opportunities to tour to the United States without first obtaining the P2 visa. Matt comments that this first Think About Life tour wasn't ideal: "We were so new ... and we were so shy. We were playing in front of really big audiences, way bigger than anything that we had seen, so it was just kind of a bad experience on the whole, not something I'd like to repeat." Despite the negative experience of being a new and inexperienced band and touring larger venues with a more established band, Matt suggests, "it was still good for us; I think it helped us in a lot of ways." Here, Matt highlights the importance of the act of touring. Aside from the quality of the performed shows, touring in itself raises the visibility of a band and helps them to become more established and recognized.

For many young musicians, as well as other types of performers, the solution to the problem of the P2 visa is to enter the United States illegally by hiding that the purpose of the trip is to perform. Think About Life created a fake recording contract to explain why they would be crossing the border with musical equipment. Matt explains,

> We knew of a recording studio in the States and they were sort of friends of ours, so we emailed them and asked them if they could just write a fake letter that we were going to come down and record at their studio and that was the purpose of the trip and that was why we were bringing all of our equipment across the border and that way we could get across without them [the border guards] hassling us. So we got this letter, and then we went down for the tour, and on our way down, it was absolutely no problem. He didn't even want to look at the letter, the border guard. He was just like, "what are you guys doing? Going to record, okay, see you later."

The "fake letter" is one strategy that Canadian bands may use to deal with the P2 problem, and the success of this mechanism depends on how thoroughly a particular border guard chooses to investigate the band and their story.

Although Think About Life was not thoroughly investigated when entering the United States, an unusual sequence of events presented problems for securely returning to Canada after the tour. The first event that later posed problems was an unusual form of payment.

> The last show that we played, I think it was at Syracuse University in New York. Because it was a university show and it was

sanctioned by the school, they had to write us a cheque. They couldn't just pay us cash because they need to file it for income tax or whatever. Every other venue pays you cash; that's the standard. So they made the cheque out, and before they made it out, they needed to sign it to an American citizen. It was just part of their legal stuff. I don't really understand it. So what we did, I was like, oh, okay, my friend Jim Holyoak is an American citizen. He has a US bank account. So we'll get them to put his name on the cheque. And that way he can cash it and he can give us the money afterwards.

Here, Matt discusses a cash economy that is the norm for small-scale performers and that typically eludes taxation. M. Sharon Jeannotte and Will Straw discuss forms of cultural creation that want "to be left alone" and not have "intrusive light [shone] upon willfully marginalized corners of cultural activity."[64] This evasion of taxation may be one such instance of desiring to be "left alone," but the broader picture of the consequences of a lack of governmental awareness about youth cultural production suggests that attention and intervention in these practices may be worthwhile. In Matt's story, he encountered a "random spot check" when returning to Canada with his band.

Apparently they sometimes do this, where there are just a couple of American border guards outside the Canadian border. We were unprepared this time. On the way down, we were thinking we got it covered, we're all set [with the fake letter]. But then on the way back, we were like, we're just going to go in Canada; it's not a big deal. [The American border guards] were just stopping everybody to ask really quick questions. Most of the people, it was RVs and stuff, and they were just passing them through. But for us, they stopped us, and they were like, "what are you boys doing?" "Oh, we're a band, we were just recording at this studio in New York." And they were like, "oh yeah, what's the name of the band?"[65]

After the driver gave a fake name to answer the question, the rest of the band "were just kind of like chuckling." At this point, the border guards "knew something was up, right away." The band was told to pull over for further questioning.

The driver initially started pulling the tour vehicle over to the wrong area, so the border guards "were really pissed off, because they thought that we were trying to get away, or something like that, so they flagged us down, and stuff like that. It was a big deal." During this process, Matt describes feeling calm, initially.

> We're thinking like, well, we don't actually have any evidence that we played any shows in the States. We have this letter from the recording studio; we're kind of okay right now. We're heading back to Canada; we've already done the tour, so it's not a big deal, right? And I had that cheque filed away in my diary in the bottom of my backpack, hidden, and I forgot all about it. So they were like, "stand over here, and we're going to go through the car." So they took out all the gear; they were taking apart all my drum hardware, and looking in, and there was absolutely nothing, and we were feeling pretty confident at this point that it was going to be fine, and then they came back out, and they said, "who is Jim Holyoak"?

After Jim Holyoak was identified as Matt's friend, Matt was taken aside for one-on-one questioning. Matt was informed that the border guards knew that the band was "up to something" and was told "we're not quite sure what it is, but we figure that you guys played a show, and this is your payment. And we can get to the bottom of it, or you can just tell us everything right now." Matt remembers being detained for "probably about two hours," during which time the band members were interviewed independently without being "allowed to go to the bathroom." (Matt states, "I think I had to pee really badly.") Matt characterizes an atmosphere of fear amongst the band members during this time, as they thought, "we might never be able to go back into the States and that would be terrible. That would be the end of our careers as musicians." Eventually, "one of the guys came out and he took us each in one by one without telling us what was happening," and each band member was fingerprinted and had mug shots taken, "side to side and the front." Matt describes a continuing feeling of fear: "I felt like we might get booked. We were really scared." Accompanying this fear, though, were also feelings of frustration about being treated like criminals when they were only low-income independent musicians. Touring to the United States without a work visa is illegal, but there was no "work" happening in the sense of income being earned through labour: "Needless to say, we lost far more money than we made on that tour. This was not a profitable thing; we spent a lot of money." Matt's phrasing suggests that it is taken for granted that small bands will lose money on tours. Indeed, work for many small-scale cultural producers may not necessarily always mean earning income.

At the end of their saga, Think About Life were "voluntarily deported" back to Canada. Matt explains that this "meant that we were free to go, and we were free to come back to the States, but it shows on our record at the border. But every time I go across the border now it shows up on the screen when they scan my passport that I have done something wrong." Matt comments that this constant flagging is "a real hassle," and, although he no longer is a member of Think About Life, he continues to experience difficulty while travelling to the United States. Matt states that Think About Life went on several other American tours after this first difficult experience, still without having the proper visas, and "they were nerve-wracking experiences getting across the border." For these subsequent tours, Think About Life developed a new strategy for border crossing: "What we ended up doing, both those times, is we split up completely. One of us would take the train, one of us would take the bus, at different times, and we would meet up. Our friend Brendan, an American citizen, would drive the gear [across the border]." Eventually, Think About Life became more established, acquiring "a label and manager and stuff like that," and after this point, "we ended up getting P2 visas." Though financially it does not make sense to get a P2 visa before a band achieves a certain level of stature, achieving this stature most likely requires doing some American tours, and as such poses a particular problem for the developmental phase of small-scale youth cultural production.

TOWARDS YOUTH-SPECIFIC CULTURAL POLICY

In order to recognize small-scale entrepreneurial models of youth artistic practice, greater awareness that the labour conditions facing young cultural producers are different than those facing more established practitioners is an important step. As seen in Matt's border saga, young emerging cultural producers have a specific set of needs. A better awareness of these needs could allow policy structures to be less of a hindrance to youth creative work. Discussing the characteristics of creative employment in Britain, Leadbeater and Oakley report that

> according to the [British] government's Cultural Trends survey, about 34 per cent of people working in the cultural sector are self-employed, compared with an average of 15 per cent for the economy as a whole ... The workforce in these industries is disproportionately young: a third of people working in the cultural sector are aged between twenty and thirty-four, compared with 26 per cent for the economy as a whole. The rate of self-employment is much higher in younger, newer sectors of the cultural industries and is lower in the subsidized and public cultural sectors, such as museums and galleries, which tend to have an older workforce. For example, about 30 per cent of the workforce in performing and visual arts, museums and libraries is over fifty years old, whereas a fifth of the workforce in the film industry is under twenty-five.[66]

The Cultural Trends survey that Leadbeater and Oakley are drawing on was compiled from 1991 census data, but more recent statistics suggest a continuation of the same trends. A British Creative Skillset report, drawing on census data from 2007–09, found that "many in the Creative Industries' workforce are young; two fifths (42%) in Creative Media is under 35 years and half (52%) in the Creative and Cultural sector is under 40 years."[67] 2006 data reveals that "while the rate of self-employment for creative occupations in the UK is roughly twice that of the general workforce it still represents only 28 per cent of the employment of those in creative occupations."[68] However, the rate of self-employment greatly varies across different creative industries sectors, with a 4 per cent self-employment rate in museums and a 64 per cent self-employment rate in music and performing arts.[69] Canada has no comparable cultural statistics to Britain's, but 2006 Canadian census data similarly reveals a low median age of creative industries workers and also reveals a rise in self-employment in the arts.

Addressing the "gestation" period of young artists, Leadbeater and Oakley state that "Independents often spend a lot of time (perhaps several years) early in their careers sorting out what they want to do, what their distinctive skill is and how they might make money from it. This period of exploration can be chaotic and unfocused but it is vital because often it is only the sense of vocation formed at this early stage that carries them through the uncertainties they will face later on. In this period cultural entrepreneurs often do not need business skills or large investments. They need quite small sums to keep going. At this stage they need access to micro-credit."[70] These concerns about the long period of youth creative career development are also evident in the *Next Generation* report, as participants "vocalized anxiety about the early years of their careers, particularly as they leave school and attempt to build their resumes, but also as they seek financial, professional and mentorship support through arts funders or arts audiences."[71] This early career period of becoming established may be more difficult and elongated in the creative industries due to the shifting and ad hoc conditions of labour in these industries, and these shifting conditions may need new types of support.

Leadbeater and Oakley argue that youth careers in the creative industries set out a specific set of policy challenges for governments due to the specific features of youth activities, such as the "preponderance of self-employment, sole traders and micro-businesses." While "government sponsored business support programmes and arts funding is tailored toward fewer larger organisations," Leadbeater and Oakley recommend "developing an ecology of hundreds of micro-businesses," which "requires a set of policy tools that most economic development agencies lack."[72] Canada is no better equipped than Britain to take on this task. Canada's cultural policy does not presently take up this challenge, nor does it seem to be moving in this direction. If Canada is to better support its young cultural producers, it might first recognize that these youth experience distinct situations and needs. Here, I turn to another policy moment and another youth story to again illustrate the disconnect between new forms of youth cultural practice and policies that run counter to their aims.

#MUSICBLOGOCIDE2K10

The events that came to be known as Musicblogocide demonstrate the crystallization of differing stakes around copyright policy. On 9 February 2010, Google removed several music blogs hosted on Google's Blogger that the company felt violated Blogger's Terms of Service, which includes adherence to the United States' Digital Millennium Copyright Act (DMCA). The music blogs that were removed all post free mp3s of music that readers can download, which is a criminal offence under the DMCA. Eliot Van Buskirk notes that, though the attention around this issue was directed towards Google's actions, "the biggest problem here is that the laws and organizations affecting music copyright don't make any sense when applied to music blogs,"[73] highlighting the disjuncture between emerging creative practices and existing laws. In his capacity as a music journalist, Sean Michaels chronicles the disconnect between the officially criminal act of posting and circulating copyrighted music for free and common practices in the music industry, citing the "de facto alliance between [record] labels and blogs." He states, "although such sites once operated on the internet's fringes, almost exclusively posting songs without permission, many blogs are now wined, dined and even paid (via advertising) by record labels. After the success of blog-buzzy acts such as Arcade Fire, Lily Allen and Vampire Weekend, entire PR firms are dedicated to courting armchair DJs and amateur critics."[74] Rather than being seen as disreputable or criminal, having free music posted on blogs to be downloaded has become a sought-out music industry practice.

Though music blogs may be an in-demand avenue of promotion, they are also much more than a simple mouthpiece for the music industry, as they represent a creative practice that requires curatorial and writing skills to be successful. For many bloggers, blogging is a labour of love rather than a direct income stream. Van Buskirk differentiates between music bloggers and "those who leak unreleased tracks or post entire albums," and references the "infectious enthusiasm" often found in the writing style of music blogs that "create[s] an audience for the music [bloggers are] excited about – an extremely valuable service for both fans and those on the copyright side of the equation."[75] Patrick Duffy, who ran one of the affected blogs, *Pop Tarts Suck Toasted* (and who has since retired this blog, for unrelated reasons), reflects on his blogging practice and references this labour of love for "almost every minute" of posting music and writing the words that went along with them": "I love writing my website. I loved covering music people weren't listening to. I loved introducing you to bands like The Antlers, Screaming Females, and Dinosaur Feathers."[76] Duffy's expression of love of music and of the practice of blogging is common in the blogging community. Michaels explains that some music blogs "are the most banal sort of pirates – offering links to download entire new releases" but that "these sites are ostracised by the blogging mainstream."[77] For those who are pursuing blogging as a creative practice, having one's music blog deleted means losing years of work. For *Masala*, one of the deleted blogs, this meant the deletion of "more than four years of archives."[78]

As supporters of the deleted music blogs voiced their discontent about Google's actions, the hashtag #Musicblogocide2k10 rose up the Twitter trending charts on 9 and 10 February 2010. Google product manager Rick Klau posted an official response to address the issue: "when we receive multiple DMCA complaints about the same blog, and have no indication that the offending content is being used in an authorised manner, we will remove the blog ... [If] this is the result of miscommunication by staff at the record label, or confusion over which mp3s are 'official' ... it is imperative that you file a DMCA counter-claim so we know you have the right to the music in question."[79] Michaels cites several difficulties in proceeding in the manner that Klau recommends. First, "many of Blogger's DMCA notices allegedly omit the name of the offending song. Bloggers aren't even sure what they are denying." Beyond this, Michaels notes, "the trouble with filing a formal, legal DMCA counter-claim is, that most bloggers don't know how."[80] Indeed, youth often navigate and negotiate their way through the legal ends of their creative output without any training or experience in this area.

With the #Musicblogocide2k10 hashtag continuing to top the Twitter trending charts in the days after the deletion of the music blogs, Google reversed its decision and reinstated the offending blogs, and the affected bloggers received apologetic emails from Klau. One of the affected blogs, *Masala*, posted this email from Klau: "what happened this week when we removed your blog was a mistake. As you no doubt know by now, we removed your blog citing repeat offences of the DMCA. The problem was that due to a processing error, you had not received notice of the DMCA complaints we'd received for your blog – which means you couldn't take corrective action or file a counter-notification. In addition to restoring your blog, we have fixed the error so that blog shut-downs will only happen when we can verify that prior notifications were sent."[81] After posting the apology email, the *Masala* bloggers explained their view of the circulation of music that (illegal) downloading provides, and this view differs from the vision found in current copyright laws.

At *Masala* we believe that music, like culture and art at large, is
a mix of influences and is largely derivative. No artist is creating
anything from scratch. We also believe that if the copyright laws
(DMCA) prevent culture and music from circulating and being re-
interpreted and mix, we're moving towards a monolithic culture
(to the economic benefit of a few). The music we're promoting
here is the incarnation of this idea. It's often music made by
young people wired to the world through internet or 1st, 2nd
or 3rd generation immigrants. People who are inventing themselves through and with the world they're living in, trying to
connect their local tradition and history with what they receive
from the outside.[82]

In this discussion of the disconnect between copyright laws and current cultural practices, the *Masala* blog highlights youth practices.
The blog emphasizes that young people are making music developed
from a reinterpretation of musical styles, enabled by exposure to
diverse music online. Young people are also posting and circulating
this music online in ways that differ from how music was circulated
in the past. Furthermore, they are voicing dissent and protesting in
new ways, as seen in the Twitter hashtag that quickly affected change.
Though the illegal digital downloading of music has often been
cited as a key factor in the downturn in the profitability of the music
industry, the *Masala* blog puts forwards a different view of the current state of making money in the music business: "Don't believe the
hype, every download is not a theft or one less sale. Music lovers have
a pretty limited bank account. But do support art when you can!
Recording music industry is shifting and doesn't make as much money as they used to and, on the other hand, the music industry at large
is doing ok (publishing, shows, merchandising, sponsorship etc.)."[83]
These changes in revenue streams – publishing, touring, and merchandising, rather than the sale of the primary cultural product alone
– are suggestive of the new economic realities of the creative industries that many young cultural producers face, and music blogging fits
into this larger picture of the restructuring of the creative industries.
Both Matt Shane's border saga and the Musicblogocide events
reveal moments that highlight how instruments of cultural policy
that are meant to support how money is being made in the creative
industries are out of touch with current revenue flows. In his
response to the deletion of his blog, Patrick Duffy of *Pop Tarts*

Suck Toasted earmarks music bloggers as the biggest supporters of the music industry.

> The people that create and write and update these sites with fervent passion are your biggest customers! We are the ones that buy the $100 box set of material released 10-years ago. We are the ones that collect the 7"s, attend the music festivals, and buy the t-shirts. We LOVE MUSIC and we LOVE Bands and no matter how you think you're helping your industry by sending the Web Sheriff or DMCA notices you are most certainly not helping. Instead you are looking like the dinosaur of an industry that you are, unable to adapt to the changing business model and falling apart at the seams as you try and fight little people that love what you do! It's time for you guys to look internally at your own policies and see what you can do better, rather than attack your biggest customers who are just trying to spread the word of the music they love![84]

Duffy again professes his love and passion for music, but also cites the need for youth-specific cultural policy, contrasting new and youth-oriented business models with "dinosaur" practices that remain in cultural policies.

ADDRESSING YOUTH: CANADIAN CULTURAL POLICY AND EDUCATION

As we have seen, the lack of awareness of youth creative practices at the policy level can collide with youth activities in undesirable ways. In the final section of this chapter, I turn to another policy document, *A Sense of Place, A Sense of Being*, and examine how it encodes youth roles and the extent of the awareness of youth creative practices and employment it demonstrates. Mirjam Gollmitzer and Catherine Murray highlight the lack of comprehensive policy framework for the creative economy in Canada and suggest that existing policy instruments can be found in four key areas: "education and training," "awards and contests," "business support," and "tax and social security policies."[85] Amongst these areas, one might assume that "education and training" would have a clear focus on youth, but even in this area, contemporary youth needs and practices are often not referenced.

A Sense of Place, A Sense of Being was produced in 1999 after public consultation by the Standing Committee on Canadian Heritage. The report outlines the role for the federal government to play in supporting culture in Canada. The document is organized around different phases of cultural production and consumption by addressing creators, training, production and distribution, preservation, and consumers and citizens. The only place where youth are specifically addressed in this report is in the subheading of "children and youth" in the "consumers and citizens" section; youth are not mentioned in the "creators" section. Grouping children and youth together defines youth in an infantile and dependent way. This grouping does not take into account the growing independence and autonomy of youth as they seek out their own pathways of cultural production; nor does it take into account the growing extension of the period of youth.

By placing youth in the "consumers and citizens" section, youth are addressed as arts audiences but not as cultural producers. The recommendations concerning youth and children in this section are most specifically targeted to children. The report recommends, for example, that the federal government create "access to cultural materials and activities for children" through programs and services and that the "Canada Council for the Arts review its policies and programs to ensure that they recognize, support and encourage cultural activity in the lives of children."[86] This vision promotes early exposure to the arts and culture, including Canadian "children's books, magazines, television and new media materials" so that children will become future supporters of the arts. The mode of subjectivity that is called into being here does not envision the multiple and fluid ways that youth encounter culture, including as producers. There is one reference in the "children and youth" subheading of the "consumers and citizens" section in A Sense of Place that suggests that artist visits to schools can "inspire the artists of tomorrow," but there is no reference to the youth involvement in the creative industries that is happening today.

It might seem likely that youth would be implicated in the "training" section of A Sense of Place, but youth is not specifically mentioned in this section. Some youth are not "students," yet are still in a learning phase of navigating and negotiating how to make a career in the creative industries. The document's recommendations around training that are most suggestive of youth are those recommendations that emphasize support for national training schools (the National Theatre School, the National Ballet School, the Canadian Film Centre, etc.). The discussion of these national training schools promotes a liberal humanist vision of education for artists.

> National training schools offer conservatory-type training that focuses on the needs of individuals intent on pursuing a career in the arts. These schools serve students who have determination and talent. The Committee supports the principle that Canadian students should be able to choose between a professional training program and a general arts program at a university or college. Accordingly, the Committee endorses the continued federal support of Canada's national schools, and recognizes the need to support new national training schools as the needs are identified.[87]

Discussing art education institutions, Gaztambide-Fernandez identifies that "few arts education organizations make explicit statements about the social role of the work they do. By and large, these institutions are explicitly dedicated to identifying and developing the skills of young artists with what are assumed to be inherent or inborn inclinations and abilities."[88] This vision of developing inherent inclinations seems to be the positioning of national training schools in *A Sense of Place*, with its statement that "training and talent are lifelong companions, and the greater the talent the more inspired and exacting the training needs to be."

Gaztambide-Fernandez outlines other possible models of training for artists, stating that the "curriculum of artistic education must challenge young artists to confront the contradictions of a postmodern, postindustrial, and electronically mediated society by affirming the role of the artist in the public sphere of a democratic society."[89] The mechanisms that training for artists could use to fulfill these goals might involve shifting "from imparting information and knowledge" and moving towards "becoming a space where information is exchanged and knowledge constructed on the basis of public interaction and not private study."[90] Gaztambide-Fernandez's vision of the structure of artistic education is one that is rooted in

> open public space where students connect with each other, share ideas about their work, exchange materials, and develop new techniques. Institutions of artistic education should provide

resources and offer instruction on those technical skills that become relevant to students in the process of creative consumption/
production. Young artists would take a lead in establishing their
own creative networks and identifying those practices that are
most relevant or salient to the specificities of their cultural practice. In this sense, institutions of artistic education would be
peripheral to cultural activity, while at the same time becoming
hubs where critique and technological support are readily
available.[91]

This vision is dramatically different than the vision of conservatory
schools that *A Sense of Place* sets out, as it suggests that youth need
to be active in producing the mechanisms to facilitate their own cultural production rather than be trained in a preset technique.

While the training section of *A Sense of Place* may promote the
conservatory school model, this is only one type of pathway in the
creative industries, and one that may be becoming outdated; cultural
policy might also explore other possible models to be relevant to the
needs of contemporary youth. Leadbeater and Oakley foreground
a disconnect between formal training and youth engagement in
the creative industries: "higher education does not matter because
degree courses provide people with formal training or skills in artistic production: only a tenth of people working in the cultural sector
have formal creative arts qualifications. Higher education is important to the new Independents because a period at university allows
them to experiment; university towns deliver large audiences for
experimental, cheaply produced culture and cultural entrepreneurs
often meet their future partners and collaborators at college.
Universities are incubators for cultural entrepreneurs."[92] These
remarks coincide with Gaztambide-Fernandez's suggestion above
that youth need to be supported in the creation of their own artist
networks and that artistic education institutions may be peripheral
to cultural activity. Leadbeater and Oakley recommend that post-
secondary education be more widely supported by federal governments, but not because it in itself leads to creative careers: "our
research underlined how vital access to higher education is for future
cultural entrepreneurs ... Expanding the reach of university education from the current 35 per cent of the eighteen year olds to more
than 50 per cent will be vital to expand opportunity. This is more
important than investing more in specialist institutions of artistic

training."[93] Like Gaztambide-Fernandez, Leadbeater and Oakley advocate for a different model for supporting youth creative endeavours than the model of artistic training found in *A Sense of Place*, and Leadbeater and Oakley's remarks are suggestive of the ways that support for youth activities could be broader than direct arts funding or cultural policies.

For Canada to be able to develop different and new mechanisms to support youth activities, quantitative and qualitative research into the nature of Canadian youth involvement with the creative industries is needed such that researchers can make policy-oriented recommendations that accurately reflect the parameters of youth creative practices. Currently, this awareness is lacking, and policies may inadvertently criminalize youth activities rather than support them. Part of this process of working towards supporting youth creative employment is making a broader case for the support of culture as a whole. In the next chapter, I examine how youth can fit into making this case.

Making the Case for Culture

Youth and Cultural Participation

The cultural sector in Canada faces a number of pressing concerns, and gaining and maintaining public support for the investment in art and culture is an ongoing project. Allan Gregg ties the difficulties of gaining public support for cultural investment to a broader picture of Canadians' disengagement with political life. In this discussion, Gregg cites youth as particularly disconnected with political processes. Making use of voter turnout as an indicator of political participation, he notes that in the 2000 federal election, "voters under twenty-five were only half as likely as those over forty-eight years of age to report a belief that voting was essential."[1] Chronicling the rise of activism but the disengagement with governmental processes amongst youth, Gregg turns to Naomi Klein, who states "that in her entire adult life, she could not recall one government initiative that she admired and was proud of. Voters under thirty-five who share her passion for societal improvement feel that the State not only fails to share that passion, but actively aids and abets those who oppose them."[2] Klein's comments do not paint a picture of lazy or apathetic youth, but suggest that youth energies and passions for societal improvement are not matching up with governmental processes.

Whether or not youth voter turnout can be improved through re-engaging youth with governmental processes, there may be more troubling indicators of youth disengagement from public life, and events such as the summer 2011 riots in London demonstrate the ways in which this disengagement can have explosive consequences. Referring to the Canadian context, Elizabeth Fix and Nadine Sivak note that "the engagement of Canadian youth, particularly the most marginalized youth, has become a pressing public policy issue in Canada in recent years. Incidents such as the rise in gun and gang violence in Toronto's 'Summer of the Gun' in 2005, the June 2006 arrests of seventeen Toronto area youth on terrorism-related charges, and the spike in Aboriginal youth suicides in Kascechewan [*sic*] in early 2007 have drawn media and public attention to the deep disengagement experienced by some segments of the Ontario youth population."[3] Fix and Sivak suggest that youth engagement has become a policy issue as a result of youth violence; Dick Hebidge critiques the absence of attention to ordinary youth realities and argues that, "in our society, youth is present only when its presence is a problem, or is regarded as a problem."[4] This raises questions of how we might increase the visibility of youth practices other than those than are, or are seen as, problematic as well as how government and public policies can better engage youth. Gregg suggests that making the case for culture should highlight culture's "galvanizing effect on citizenship" because culture has "the properties required to be the glue that brings citizens together, and bonds them into a sense of community."[5] This chapter looks at the role of youth in making the case for culture and the role of culture in fostering social cohesion. If youth creative practices are often unseen at the level of policy, can youth be reintegrated into the way the case for culture gets made, such that social cohesion and youth engagement with public life are fostered? This chapter opens by forwarding a creative ecology framework to make the case for culture in a way that targets the participation of youth. This framework guides the chapter as it examines moments of disconnection between government, youth, and culture, and suggests mechanisms to foster cohesion.

THINKING ECOLOGICALLY ABOUT CULTURE

When public investment in culture comes under attack, one argument that arts advocates sometimes turn to is the economic impact and earning potential of the arts. For example, Americans for the Arts, the United States' "leading nonprofit organization for advancing the arts and arts education,"[6] has initiated a series of impact studies about art and culture as an economic engine, entitled *Arts & Economic Prosperity.* Thinking ecologically rather than economically about culture would involve not only looking at the economic impacts of culture and but also forwarding the multifaceted relationships between culture and social life by making bridges across sectors. In their discussion of pertinent directions for Canadian cultural policy, Mirjam Gollmitzer and Catherine Murray suggest that "the goal is a theoretically and practically elegant integration of culture and the economy in policy practice."[7] According to David Throsby, this elegant integration requires a broadening of policy focus. Culture could "have greatest scope to generate economic and social rewards" by turning "to employment policy, to regional and urban development policy, to industry policy and other fields like labour and the social economy."[8] Discussing the social effects of cultural engagement, Dick Stanley has a similarly diverse list of culture's potential impacts, including "enhancing understanding and capacity for action;" "creating and retaining identity;" "modifying values and preferences for collective choice"; "building social cohesion"; "contributing to community development; and fostering civic participation."[9] A policy framework that attempted to target these areas would need to work across policy sectors and could also involve integrating youth. Stanley argues that "citizens must have the right and capacity to shape culture and influence the interpretation and creation of meaning. In a democratic society, we must be not only citizens, but cultural citizens ... It is therefore the responsibility of the governments to promote domestic culture to ensure that socially optimal amount of it is produced."[10] The benefits of culture that Stanley delineates are not only economic ones, and if government intervention is required to produce these benefits, this intervention could also be directed to ensure equal participation of youth in not only cultural consumption but also in cultural production and to ensure equal recognition of their creative practices.

Though registering these social benefits may be an important part of making the case for culture, these benefit-driven approaches may have some pitfalls. Reflecting on a career of working in the cultural field, John Meisel foregrounds an "arts-centered" tradition of the intrinsic worth of the arts and cautions that when "arts are lumped together with numerous other fields" such as "standards of living, social adjustment, [and] citizenship," then the importance of the arts "is likely to be watered down. Their unique character, contribution, and needs may consequently be undervalued and short changed."[11] Conversely, Catherine Murray provides an overview of the increased interest in the social effects of the arts. She states that the concept of increasing citizens' cultural participation has gained traction in the

Department of Canadian Heritage since 1993 and that "social capital studies" promotes "a sociological view of culture as micro and macro tool kits in the development of individual identity, civic literacy, and collective community."[12] However, she asks, "is culture just a means?" and comments, "the conceptual danger in a social capital approach is that it buries the cultural: treating it either as a by-product or enabler" of targeted functions.[13] If we are to regard culture as more than just a tool, this may involve returning to intrinsic approaches that foreground the cultural qualities of the arts and perhaps melding intrinsic approaches with instrumental approaches that foreground economic and social benefits.

Instead of solely focusing on benefits – economic or social – a creative ecology framework might also investigate the relationships between and amongst sectors and between economically and non-economically driven forms of culture or perhaps move beyond examining the benefits of cultural participation to also examine the conditions of labour in the production of culture. Kate Oakley refers to the "complex symbiosis that informs the cultural ecology of any town or city – with its mix of funding models, cultural forms, and working practices – that links a performance of *The Tempest* with a TV cop show and voiceovers for advertisement (the staple working life of a successful actor, for example)."[14] A creative economy framework that celebrates innovation and economic activity would see this blend of activities as "too messy, too wasteful and simply too hard to understand,"[15] but a creative ecology model might attempt to register and map the relationships amongst these funding models, cultural forms, and working practices in local lived experiences.

A creative ecology framework may have the capacity to recognize the participation of youth in cultural life and may also have the capacity to recognize the significance of youth creative practices even if young artists may not individually be earning significant incomes from these practices. The attempt to make sense of the economic impact of the arts looks at the relationship between the creative industries and the whole economy, but a creative ecology framework would look more broadly at the relationship between the creative industries and communities. Beyond the economic impact of the arts, we might also register youth creative activities in order for education systems to match the reality of their experiences so that communities are able to support these activities and engage youth, such that they can be healthy and functional communities.

Throsby notes the possibility of discussing the "core activities" of the cultural industries in terms other than economic ones: "If the cultural industries are interpreted primarily in economic terms, the policy spotlight will clearly fall on those sectors producing the greatest growth rates in employment, value of output, exports, etc. If cultural policy is directed more strongly towards achieving a government's artistic or cultural objectives, a different configuration of the cultural industries will be preferred, and a different group of core activities will be identified."[16] A creative ecology model that has sustainable community development amongst its objectives could spotlight small-scale youth cultural production or community youth arts organizations in its "core activities." These activities are not significant if we look at the creative industries in purely economic terms, and this may explain the current lack of presence of youth in Canadian cultural policies.

Moving towards a community-based view of culture means thinking through what sustainable community development might entail in a creative ecology framework. Amareswar Galla suggests that sustainable community development has the aim of "more sustainable and vibrant communities, more cohesive community networks, greater community confidence and direction founded in a sense of self and place, and an increased community capacity for holistically addressing its own needs ... It requires an inclusive framework that recognizes the cultural aspirations of different sections of the community, including groups that may otherwise be marginalized culturally, socially, and economically."[17] Following from this, Galla identifies four areas to target to integrate culture within sustainable community development: "strengthen and protect the cultural resource base for creative expression and practice"; "engage the whole community in valuing and participating in cultural expression and appreciation"; "provide relevant community infrastructure for the support of cultural activities"; and "develop the economic framework for cultural production and promotion."[18] Targeting these areas to work towards sustainable cultural community development may necessitate thinking about culture across sectors, including infrastructure, employment, and social inclusion and participation. In this process, it is important to recognize that youth may be a culturally, socially, or economically marginalized group. A creative ecology framework rooted in sustainable community development may be able to recognize this marginalization and work towards engaging youth, and one mechanism of working towards greater youth engagement might be recognizing their forms of creative practice.

Thinking about cross-sector sustainable community cultural development involves developing new frameworks for the creation of relevant policy infrastructure that emerges from communities rather than solely being administered by governments. Discussing the need to refocus on a bottom-up mode of policy making, Betsy Donald and Douglas Morrow suggest a move from cultural policy to cultural planning.[19] Greg Baeker comments that "cultural planning" means moving away from discipline-based approaches to culture (e.g., visual arts, performing arts, heritage) to place-based approaches: "Discipline-based distinctions grew up in part as a result of granting programs established by senior levels of government. These programs tended to place more emphasis on developing specific artistic disciplines than on connecting these disciplines with community interest and needs, or with strengthening connections across disciplines at the community level. Cultural planning reverses this perspective. It begins by considering the circumstances and needs of a specific community. More specifically, its point of departure is how the cultural assets of resources of the community can contribute to reinforcing a unique sense of place."[20] The shift that Baeker describes prioritizes specific places and community needs rather than artistic sectors as the origin points for the creation of cultural infrastructure, and this shift necessitates a re-envisioned government role from a top-down one of "public management focus on financing, regulating, owning" to a bottom-up focus on "enabling, supporting ('steering not rowing') combined with development approaches."[21] For Colin Mercer, cultural planning "does not mean 'the planning of culture' but rather, ensuring that the cultural element, cultural considerations, culture *tout court*, are there at every stage of the planning and development process."[22] Again, this entails working across sectors and thinking of culture not just as arts funding, but as a broad-based community resource.

In his fall 2008 cross-Canada forum tour, Canadian Conference of the Arts (CCA) director Alain Pineau solicited the public's opinion about the direction that the CCA's arts advocacy should take. In his Montreal forum, he discussed the use of the economic impact of the arts as a way to make the case for culture. Pineau suggested that arts advocates need to reach out to other sectors to make the case for the arts, but instead of exclusively relying on the economic impact of the

arts and the business sector, other sectors, such as education and
health, could be targeted to advocate for the overall impact that the
arts have on quality of life and well-being. Similarly, Throsby discusses that accurately charting the economic impact of the arts may
"legitimize cultural policy in the eyes of economic policy makers,"[23]
but argues that the economic impact of the arts alone will not make
the case for culture because this does not provide "an argument for
special treatment of the cultural sector" and "will not provide a special case for culture if other lines of investment are likely to produce
economic payoffs of similar magnitude."[24]

In *Making a Single Case for the Arts: An International Perspective*,
Alexandra Slaby outlines that some arts advocacy groups have moved
away from making claims about the intrinsic worth of the arts and
have moved towards instrumental approaches, focusing on benefits
of the arts in areas including but going beyond economic impact,
such as social impact, neighbourhood renewal, cultural employment,
and academic performance. However, Slaby claims that we need to
"combine core values and instrumental values" behind arts advocacy,[25] as using either approach in isolation is ineffective because
the core or intrinsic value of the arts – the "art for art's sake" model
– is hard to define, and the instrumental claims around the tangible
social impacts of the arts currently have a lack of concrete supporting data and weak methodological frameworks. Slaby cites the
2003 International Federation of Arts Councils and Culture Agencies
World Summit, which "rejected abstract, one-size-fits-all arts advocacy in favor of 'embedding' the value of the arts within local contexts, which has the advantage of gathering grassroots advocacy."[26]
Through foregrounding local contexts, we may be able to discuss the
intrinsic value of the arts without resorting to art for art's sake rhetoric and highlight the role of the arts in individual as well as community growth while also considering economic growth and employment
that may be small-scale and grassroots.

The lack of data behind claims about the non-economic instrumental value of the arts does not mean that this direction needs to be
abandoned; rather, continued research is needed to integrate these
types of claims within a larger creative ecology framework. In the
Montreal CCA regional forum meeting, Pineau cautioned against
using instrumental approaches alone to make the case for the arts,
but also noted the difficulty of emphasizing the economic impact of
the arts due to the lack of solid data to chart economic activity in

creative fields, as well as actual government spending in the arts. Kate Oakley notes the paucity of long-term quantitative data collection by academics and the use of anecdote to support claims about the creative industries. Oakley argues that "*somebody* needs to be doing the long-term evidence gathering. Otherwise, we are left entirely at the mercy of governmental rhetoric."[27] Indeed, Tony Bennett also calls for "the need for intellectual work to be conducted in a manner such that, in both its substance and its style, it can be calculated to influence or service the conduct of identifiable agents within the region of culture concerned."[28] Simply put, if we are to work towards better supporting youth and influence policies in their service, we need better data to stand on. If youth are disconnected from governmental processes, a more solid picture and understanding of youth activities could also be a part of working towards reintegrating youth with public life. In what follows, I discuss a policy moment that illuminates a lack of attention to youth and community development. I then examine how and if different models could allow for greater youth and community visibility.

CANADIAN CULTURAL POLICY: CAMPAIGN TRAIL AND RECESSION

Chapter 3 examined some cultural policy documents, but also argued that cultural policy is not only found in the infrastructure of existing legislation; it is also continuously produced through the "contestation between rival discourses, ideologies, interests."[29] Art and culture became a site of contestation between rival discourses and an issue of public interest in the October 2008 Canadian federal election as the government's funding cuts to certain arts programs (announced in the summer of 2008) became contentious issues. Additionally, the economic crisis that began to be illuminated in November 2008 had implications for the creative industries, and the government's response to these issues is also suggestive of the ways in which cultural policy is continuously produced. This moment highlighted the ways support for art and culture can come under siege by political figures, and also highlighted the lack of visibility of youth practices. At a time when youth are increasingly turning to the creative industries as a source of employment, the visibility of these practices at the governmental level in the Canadian context has been lacking, even if issues around government support of the creative industries gained more attention at the end of 2008 and into 2009.

This lack of visibility of youth involvement with the creative industries signals the neglect of youth issues at the governmental level, but also signals a general image problem of the arts and creative industries as a whole. In times of economic uncertainty, youth may be in particularly vulnerable positions, and their career pathways in creative fields may need support. With the economic collapse in November 2008, the financial sector and the auto industry were not the only greatly affected industries. The CCA chronicled that the stock market collapse heavily affected arts organizations, as many of these organizations are run on endowment funds. For example, the National Ballet of Canada projected a $900,000 shortfall in budgeted revenues due to the downfall in the stock market.[30] These economic struggles have direct implications for cultural workers employed at organizations run on endowment funds. Ballet BC (British Columbia's professional ballet company) laid off all of its dancers and much of its office staff at the end of November 2008 due to economically difficult times.[31] Economic challenges continued to face the ballet world through 2008 and into 2009, and the New York City Ballet also laid off several dancers in their early twenties from its corps de ballet in July 2009. While the economic recession of 2008–09 affected many types of workers, the difficulty of experiencing a lay off is particularly strong for young creative industries workers. Daniel Wakin suggests that "the emotions [of the laid-off ballet dancers] are especially acute because, more than many other workers, ballet dancers define themselves and their self-worth by their profession. Losing a job is like losing one's identity."[32] This intermingling of identity and career is common not only in ballet but in creative industries work in general. Layoffs that affected young cultural workers were often unheard in a media environment that was dominated with discussions of banks and bail-outs, but ballet merits discussion, too, especially if we want to get a sense of the impact of economic crises on the young.

Amidst the emerging economic uncertainty of 2008, Canada's newly re-elected minority Conservative government set priorities for governing in the Speech from the Throne on 19 November 2008. This speech, entitled "Protecting Canada's Future," did not foreground youth or the creative industries, or the particular difficulties either might be facing. The role of the creative industries in the economy was briefly discussed in the "Expanding Investment and Trade" section: "Cultural creativity and innovation are vital not only to a lively Canadian cultural life, but also to Canada's economic future. Our Government will proceed with legislation to modernize Canada's copyright laws and ensure stronger protection for intellectual property."[33] This reference to copyright laws foregrounds the infrastructure that supports cultural work and makes a connection between the creative industries and the economy, but this one brief mention of the creative industries does not target the uncertain realities of those people – which, increasingly, are young people – who work in the creative industries. Elsewhere, in the "Securing Jobs for Families and Communities" section, the speech does discuss workers. The only reference to youth in the speech occurs in the context of a discussion of family, in a comment that the government "will strengthen Canada's workforce for the future by continuing to support student financial assistance and taking measures to encourage skilled trades and apprenticeships."[34] This positioning of youth as students does not address the range of youth experiences and assumes that youth will later enter the workforce but are not currently working. Gollmitzer and Murray note that "sharp differences in status, training, credentials and the degree of professional independence obtained by various categories of creative workers exist. Most at-risk are youth, aboriginal and visible minorities and those in rural areas."[35] The Speech from the Throne did make reference to the needs of Aboriginal people, citing the need to ensure that Aboriginal people "fully share in economic opportunities," and mentioned education as a tool to assist in this project. However, the notion that youth, Aboriginals, and visible minorities may be in more economically vulnerable positions than the population as a whole in times of economic crisis, especially with regards to employment in the creative industries, was not acknowledged.

Rather than support youth practices or new trends in economic growth, the Speech from the Throne underlined the government's support for manufacturing and resource extraction, farming, automotive and aerospace industries, and "traditional industries," such as fisheries, mining, and forestry. The government's commitment to these industries also extended to "marketing Canadian products abroad and helping businesses to innovate."[36] This support, earmarked for the international marketing of Canadian resource-based products, came on the heels of cuts to federal programs designed to market Canadian cultural products abroad. In August 2008, Prime Minister Stephen Harper announced the cancellation of the PromArt and Trade Routes programs, both funded by the federal government, and both designed to support touring for creative workers and promotion of Canadian cultural products. Under these grants, creative workers could apply for support to travel to do readings, perform concerts, or enter film festivals, for example. The move to cut these programs seemed to suggest a departure from previous trends in Canadian cultural policy. In 2007, Richard Sutherland and Will Straw stated that "the Canadian government's cultural policy is becoming increasingly trade-oriented. This does not mean that trade was not previously an issue in the cultural field. However, whereas cultural policy was, in the past, designed principally to ameliorate the effects of international trade on Canadian culture, policies are more and more oriented towards allowing Canadian producers to take advantage of international trade in cultural products."[37] These comments note government support of marketing cultural products abroad, but this era may have come to an end. Rachel Maxwell suggests that, since 2006, the Harper government has relinquished public diplomacy and the emphasis on cultural aspects of foreign policy. The 1995 document *Canada and the World*, produced by the Chrétien government, configured Canadian culture as the third "pillar" of Canadian foreign policy, after economic growth and international peace and security. This demarcation of the role of culture in Canadian foreign policy was absent in the Martin government's 2005 document *A Role of Pride and Influence in the World*, as "cultural relations make few appearances throughout the entirety of the document."[38] Maxwell notes that, since the election of the Harper government, this turn away from the role of culture in foreign policy has continued.

Harper's cuts to PromArt and Trade Routes suggest a relinquishment of the importance previously placed on the international trade of Canadian cultural products, and this relinquishment signals a lack of understanding of the economic impact of the arts but, more broadly, an underestimation of the importance of Canada's creative industries for its image abroad. When preparing a culture and foreign policy report, John Ralston Saul found that Canadian foreign policy, domestic events, and sports were not visible abroad, and that "Canada's profile abroad is, for the most part, its culture. That is our image. That is what Canada becomes in people's imaginations around the world."[39] An important addition to Saul's finding is that it is often youth cultural producers who are seen as innovative in the eyes of the world. From the annual "Le Guess Who Festival" in Utrecht, Holland, which exclusively features Canadian bands, to the heavy Canadian presence in international music showcases, like Iceland's Airwaves music festival, to being name-checked by Indiana-based indie record label Secretly Canadian, and Athens, Georgia-based indie band Of Montreal, "Canada" is sometimes seen as being avant-garde and edgy because of its youth cultural producers. In advertising, we've seen Feist in trendy iPod ads, and when an Austrian public utility company used one of Owen Pallett's Final Fantasy songs (from his award-winning album *He Poos Clouds*) without permission, he forced the company to fund an avant-garde music festival instead of suing them. Young actors like Ellen Page and Michael Cera have garnered international praise as Hollywood's hip new generation, but they still choose to call their native Canada home. While Céline Dion and Shania Twain may represent a presence as heavy hitters in the international music industry, younger artists, like Grimes, Arcade Fire, and Fucked Up represent innovation and hipness to the world.

But this international image of Canadian youth cultural producers seems to be unseen by Canada itself. When arts organizations grapple with how to improve the image of arts and culture in Canada, the role of youth may merit more discussion. Youth may be developing economic and cultural directions that the world is taking note of, but that are not garnering enough attention on the home front. Similarly, policies may not take note of the nature of youth practices, and youth may feel increasingly disengaged with political life. These types of divergences can be further seen in the disconnect between the representation and the reality of artists' economic situations in the discussions of art and culture in 2008. On the campaign trail in September 2008, Harper cast Canadian artists as overindulged, stating: "I think when ordinary working people come home, turn on the TV and see a gala of a bunch of people at, you know, a rich gala all subsidized by taxpayers claiming their subsidies aren't high enough, when they know those subsidies have actually gone up – I'm not sure that's something that resonates with ordinary people."[40] While opponents and political rivals were quick to point out the fallacy of casting artists as "rich" due to the low average incomes of artists, another fallacy that was not foregrounded but is potentially just as incendiary is the bifurcation of "ordinary working people" and "artists," as if artists are not workers who are facing particular conditions of labour.

Furthermore, Harper's comments obscure the realities of young people entering into the creative industries: the young are certainly not those attending "rich galas" – if this phrase is erroneous for the majority of artists, it is particularly erroneous for the young. Putting aside the notion that successful artists are wealthy, Harper's remarks ignore the labour required to achieve this level of success. In an editorial response to Harper's comments, Margaret Atwood wrote, "well, I can count the number of moderately rich writers who live in Canada on the fingers of one hand: I'm one of them, and I'm no Warren Buffett. I don't whine about my grants because I don't get any grants. I whine about other grants – grants for young people, that may help them to turn into me, and thus pay to the federal and provincial governments the kinds of taxes I pay, and cover off the salaries of such as Mr. Harper. In fact, less than 10 per cent of writers actually make a living by their writing, however modest that living may be. They have other jobs."[41] If less than 10 per cent of writers earn a modest living from writing and need other jobs to support themselves, grants alone will not provide the necessary infrastructural support to help young people "turn into" successful writers like Atwood. Chapter 3 discussed other types of mechanisms that youth desire in the professionalization of their creative practices, including support for the process of distributing and promoting creative works. Forging connections between artists, community life, and cultural participation could be a mode of making the case for culture, and also could serve to cut the rhetoric of overinvestment and subsidization of individual artists and their "rich galas."

This move to broadening the case for culture away from individual artists and artistic creation was in part seen in the CCA's response to the economic recession of 2008. In late November 2008, Canada's minister of finance, James Flaherty, asked for suggestions for paths to take towards revitalizing the Canadian economy in a time of looming global recession. One of the CCA's recommendations to Flaherty was a reinvestment in art and culture through supporting communities and cultural infrastructure: "As part of the Employment Strategy, the CCA recommends that the Department of Canadian Heritage be provided with an additional $100 million to invest in the Cultural Spaces program to allow more communities and organizations to proceed with their capital development plans. This investment should be an annual increase for the next four years."[42] This recommendation does not specifically target youth, but targeting sustainable community development is one mechanism to support youth activities. When targeted to whole communities, and the differing needs within communities, creating physical and social infrastructure to support creative work is a mechanism to support youth cultural production that moves beyond grants to individual artists.

When the government unveiled Budget 2009 – a budget designed to deal with the economic crisis – there was an emphasis on maintaining arts and culture spending that was not found in the Speech from the Throne in November 2008, nor in the Conservatives' campaigning leading up to the 14 October 2008 election. With regards to the arts, Budget 2009 underlines the importance of the arts to Canadian identity and the need to support the creative industries as they experience the shock of economic crisis.

> Culture reflects who we are as a nation, how we see ourselves within our country, and how we appear to the world. Day-to-day, Canadians experience the essence of this rich and diverse country through the imagery and words of its artists, through works which demonstrate the best of talent. While resilient in many ways, the cultural sector is plainly also vulnerable to economic shocks. The Government wants to help ensure as much stability as possible for the sector at a time when the sector is facing difficult challenges. Budget 2009 provides over $335 million in support for culture and arts – recognizing the importance of our artistic institutions and the role they play in Canadians' lives.[43]

This $335 million might sound like a healthy injection of funds into the creative industries, but the bulk of this funding represented not new funds but rather a continuation of funds that had already been committed to cultural programs, leaving the CCA to comment that Budget 2009 was "more status quo than economic stimulus" in terms of culture.[44] While the government did not adhere to the CCA's suggestion to invest $100 million in Cultural Spaces, Budget 2009 did allocate $30 million of new funding in cultural infrastructure over two years, for a total of $60 million of investment in this program. However, the CCA notes that "these funds are largely designated for projects in Toronto and Montreal and that none will be available for much needed cultural infrastructure projects in other communities across the country."[45] This large-scale nature of investment was also seen in the $100 million of funding in Budget 2009 designated for "marquee festivals and events such as jazz and other music festivals that draw a significant number of tourists."[46]

One area of new funding in Budget 2009 was the Canada Prizes for the Arts and Creativity, which were intended to "bring the world's best new artists from a vast array of art forms to Canada to compete for the title of most promising new artist and for significant cash awards. These artists will be publicly adjudicated by a distinguished panel of established artists in each discipline ... Budget 2009 will provide $25 million for an endowment to support the creation of international awards to recognize excellence in dance, music, art and dramatic arts."[47] In its response to Budget 2009, the CCA notes that it is "difficult to object to any money being dedicated to arts and culture," but raises objections to funding being targeted towards mostly foreign artists in this award and signals that the "main disappointment" with Budget 2009 is "the refusal of the government to consider investing more in touring" of Canadian artists abroad, noting that "*Trade Routes* and *PromArt* were programs which specialized in this area and were cut under the 39th Parliament."[48] As of 2012, these Canada Prizes had yet to move forward, but there is something bewildering about cutting funds to support marketing Canadian culture abroad and reinvesting these funds in a Canadian-based award given to foreign artists. These changes in funding directions represent a lack of clear vision in Canada's cultural policy, as well as a continued lack of specific attention to the needs of contemporary youth cultural producers.

MAKING THE CASE FOR CULTURE: YOUTH ENGAGEMENT

As discussed above, one method some arts organizations have used to make the case for culture is to appeal to its economic impact, but this method may be insufficiently narrow to register youth and community arts activities. The Creative City Network is a cross-Canada organization uniting municipal staff who work in "arts, cultural and heritage policy, planning, development and support,"[49] and one way this organization is making the case for culture is through an argument about the personal and social development of children and youth. In this argument, psychological and vocational perspectives are emphasized, and the arts are seen to "help in the successful transition to adulthood and the development of in-demand job skills."[50] These in-demand job skills are not necessarily skills of artistic production; rather, they are more generic work-related skills, such as the ability "to complete tasks" and "teamwork skills."[51] This combination of the psychological and vocational benefits of the arts can be found in a youth engagement model, which also looks at the potential of the arts to remediate the harmful behaviour of at-risk youth. Fix and Sivak note that the youth engagement model has a longer history of implementation in the United Kingdom and the United States than in Canada, but is also starting to gain momentum here. Art is seen as a tool to reduce youth crime in the youth engagement model, but is also seen to promote social cohesion in a more holistic manner, as "research shows the enormous benefits to the health and well-being of children and youth when they have access to arts and creative activities. The results show increased learning and community involvement, a reduction in crime and high school drop-out rates, reduced psycho-social behavior and improved health and social skills."[52] The reasoning behind the success of art and creative activities in improving social cohesion is that the arts are "asset-based programs" that "focus on what children and youth do well."[53] In a UK study of the benefits of youth arts programs, Jenny Hughes cites that the arts are an effective way to foster social cohesion with youth because they "offer a non-traditional, non-institutional, social and emotional environment; a non-judgmental and un-authoritarian model of engagement; and an opportunity to participate in a creative process that involves both structure and freedom. At the same time engagement in the participatory arts requires respect, responsibility, co-operation and collaboration."[54] This conceptualization of the benefits of culture and youth engagement moves past an economic model and could be part of a creative ecology framework.

While the youth engagement model is sometimes defined as an asset-based model to improve social cohesion, youth participation, and citizenship, it is often used as a deficit-based model to target so-called "at-risk" youth. Joyce Zemans and Amanda Coles note "the youth policies that exist in various departments and jurisdictions, including justice/crime prevention/correctional services, employment/job training, community revitalization/development, education, health, and culture adopt the language of youth *problems* and *problem* youth. Federal support for youth arts programs is as likely to be from the National Crime Prevention Centre, Justice Canada or Corrections Canada as it is to be from the Department of Canadian Heritage."[55] Indeed, as the arts as youth engagement model starts to pick up steam in Canada, the Department of Justice has begun to act as funder of youth arts programs. Coles discusses the Department of Justice's Youth Justice Renewal Initiative, which foregrounds how youth arts programs help in "establishing positive peer and mentor networks" and in encouraging youth "to make positive choices as autonomous individuals."[56] The Youth Justice Renewal Initiative also emphasizes the role of the arts and recreation in crime prevention, noting that youth arts involves "the opening of pathways for kids to make a contribution (they can teach, coach, make pocket money...)."[57] This reference to money makes some connection between youth engagement, involvement with the arts, and employment, but the wording of "pocket money" and "kids" suggests that the Department of Justice does not see youth arts as a viable pathway to long-term employment.

Although long-term creative industries employment might not be targeted by the Department of Justice in the youth programs it funds, Coles refers to the success of youth arts programs in incubating this creative industries involvement for youth. For example, Coles profiles the Fresh Arts program that ran in Toronto in the early 1990s under the rubric of youth engagement, but has also been credited with "significantly influenc[ing] the course of Toronto's urban-music industry. A short list of its alumni includes rapper Kardinal Offishall, singer Jully Black, dub poet d'bi.young.anitafrika, music video director Lil'X, hip hop producer Saukrates and Flow 93.5 radio hosts Mark Strong and J Wyze."[58] Kardinal Offishall credits the program with bolstering his career as a performing artist: "I learned how to make music in the Fresh Arts program ... all of the things artists might have to pay a lot of money to do, we learned to be self-sufficient and how to be independent and ... that is how my whole career got started at a major level."[59] Here, Offishall cites learning the logistical elements of how to make one's way as a musician, and though he discusses the Fresh Arts program in terms of career development rather than youth engagement, this connection between youth engagement through youth arts programming and creative industries employment is not foregrounded in the youth engagement model. This model may enable many programs that foster skills necessary for employment in the creative industries to exist, but this also creates problems for sustainable long-term funding for youth arts programs beyond the initial pilot project phase that the Department of Justice funds.

In general, the Department of Justice funds these types of projects because growing evidence suggests that funding youth crime prevention is a cost-effective strategy. For example, Robin Wright, Lindsay John, and Julia Sheel conducted a Department of Justice-funded feasibility study in 2005 to determine if an outcome-based study of "community-based arts programs as a strategy to improve the psychosocial functioning of youth in conflict with the law and prevent recidivism" would be worthwhile. This "feasibility study" prior to the "outcome study" was conducted because arts programming with at-risk youth is "cost-intensive."[60] Nevertheless, this cost-intensive strategy is also seen as a cost-reduction strategy, due to the high costs of maintaining the justice system. Citing Rolf Loeber and David Farrington, Wright, John, and Sheel note that "youth who engage in delinquent acts are two to three times more likely than other youth to become chronic offenders as adults. In 2002, the federal government of Canada estimated the actual cost of crime – including the cost of private security, insurance, and impact on victims – is about $46 billion a year."[61] While the actual costs of "cost-intensive" youth arts programming are not listed in this feasibility study, budgets for these programs are presumably dramatically less than this projected cost of crime. This study of the feasibility and cost-effectiveness of youth arts programming in reducing crime also suggests a limited vision of youth and creative pursuits. A more holistic vision of youth engagement, community development, and creative industries employment might be a more suitable framework to better support contemporary youth involvement with the creative industries.

Part of making the case for culture could be creating and highlighting social cohesion by engaging youth into public life through arts programs. However, we need to move past the deficit model that is used to discuss the engagement of at-risk youth and recognize the need to engage many diverse youth for the roles they can play in strengthening and developing their communities. This may mean extending and connecting a youth engagement model with a larger creative ecology framework to make the case that including and integrating youth – not only "problem" youth but also youth who may be increasingly disengaged with public life as their practices go unrecognized – is an important part of fostering social cohesion. Currently, youth do not have visibility in cultural policies, even if these policies have implications for their success as cultural producers. We need models that are aware of the current parameters of youth cultural production, and policies that register these parameters, such that we might also work towards improving youth participation in public life. Youth are increasingly producers, not just consumers of art, and this segment of the population could become an important part of the process of securing the legitimacy of the arts in Canada.

Creative Britain and the Canadian Context

Youth, Education, and Entrepreneurship

In the developmental phase of Canadian cultural policy, the Massey-Lévesque Commission and its call for the formation of the Canada Council for the Arts looked to the Arts Council of Great Britain as a model.[1] Unlike Canada, Britain has taken up the creative industries at the policy level, most notably with Prime Minister Tony Blair's championing of "Cool Britannia," starting in 1997. The British government's support for the creative industries continued under the helm of Prime Minister Gordon Brown, and this chapter will look at the *Creative Britain: New Talents for a New Economy* white paper, published in February 2008 by the Department of Culture, Media and Sport. Britain's cultural policy does not stand as a model to purely emulate, as the take up of the creative industries in *Creative Britain* is based in an overly facile celebration of the potentials of the creative industries to correct problems of economic downtown. To this end, I do not seek to suggest that British creative industries policy should be imported into the Canadian context wholesale. Instead, I examine whether this policy has any possible applications in Canada. If *Creative Britain* sets out a particular vision for youth involvement in the creative industries and for arts education, how do these models compare to Canada's? The first half of this chapter examines the potentials and limitations of *Creative Britain* as a youth-centered policy, and the second half turns to an examination of arts education and youth policy in Quebec and asks if Quebec can learn anything from the British context.

NEW POLICY DIRECTIONS FOR BRITAIN

In 1997, Britain reorganized its cultural infrastructure with the election of New Labour and the creation of the Department of Culture,

Media and Sport (DCMS). From its outset, the DCMS set up the
Creative Industries Task Force (CITF), which was mandated to define, map, and measure the creative industries. The CITF released a
first *Creative Industries Mapping Document* in 1998 and a second
one in 2001, and these documents have been key to the uptake of the
creative economy as a central facet of the British economy by policy
makers. Canada has not produced similar mapping documents, and
this kind of large-scale inventory of national cultural resources is an
important step in the process of working towards more relevant cultural policies.

   Kate Oakley argues that the British uptake of the creative economy has taken on excessive dimensions, and she suggests that any
policy document on regional development in the UK will mention the
creative industries: "No region of the country, whatever its industrial
base, human capital stock, scale or history, is safe from the need for
a 'creative hub' or 'cultural quarter.'"[2] Oakley states that the creative
industries have been regarded as quick fix to serious economic problems of industrial decline and diminishing manufacturing industries
in the UK, but there is a lack of concrete evidence about the role that
the creative industries play vis-à-vis "economic development, regen-
eration and social inclusion."[3] Oakley also identifies problems in the
conception of much creative industries policy. She notes that many
cultural projects receive short-term rather than long-term core funding, and this promotes competition rather than cooperation amongst
organizations applying for funds. Oakley suggests that curriculum
in schools is narrow and promotes "early specialization" in students,
which might not adequately prepare them for careers in the creative
industries, as employment in these industries may require a diverse
rather than a specialized skill set. As we have seen through the narratives of youth experiences in this book, many youth seek out work
in the creative industries in interdisciplinary ways, are involved in
several areas of creative industries work at once, or move between
jobs in various fields in the creative industries.

   Some of Oakley's criticisms have been in part implicitly answered
by the 2008 policy framework developed by the DCMS, *Creative
Britain: New Talents for a New Economy*. This policy may in fact
envision long-term funding and may rework the cultural training
that children and youth receive in schools. This document is the
DCMS's first comprehensive plan for governmental support of the
creative industries in the UK and opens by noting that the "creative

industries must move from the margins to the mainstream of economic and policy thinking."[4] In order to "make Britain the world's creative hub,"[5] the document targets support for arts education in schools, aims to clarify the transition between the education system and work in the creative industries, and highlights support for creative businesses and research. While Chapter 3 noted that youth creative practices are not visible at the policy level in Canada, youth form a key underpinning of *Creative Britain*. Creating economic growth through the creative industries requires people to enter the field, and the document focuses on preparing youth to work in the creative industries and is in part directed towards gearing school experiences to relate to careers in the creative industries.

Through the creation of the "Find Your Talent" program, *Creative Britain* seeks to improve arts education in schools. This program expands the "Creative Partnerships" program, which targeted disadvantaged children; "Find Your Talent" now targets all British children and young people. "Find Your Talent" calls for the British curriculum to devote "five hours of culture a week for children and young people"[6] both in school and out of school at cultural sites. This program is centered around both arts appreciation and cultural production and, as such, envisions the role of children and youth both as arts audiences and as cultural producers. Possible activities of the "Find Your Talent" program include having the chance to "produce creative writing, or listen to authors," "use library and archive services," "visit exhibitions, galleries, or museums," "learn about and make films, digital, or new media art," or "learn a musical instrument."[7] *Creative Britain* suggests that visiting sites means that curriculum becomes clearer to students and their skills are consistently improved.

Though there are links between school learning and interacting with the wider community in "Find Your Talent," the program is situated in an individually-based understanding of cultural production, and it does not suggest collaborative or community-based work as much as it suggests self-discovery through the arts. Mark Banks and David Hesmondhalgh characterize New Labour cultural policy as denying "the institutional and collective basis of cultural production."[8] Indeed, *Creative Britain* does not answer the call of media education academics such as David Buckingham, Julian Sefton-Green, and Henry Jenkins, who advocate for creativity to be understood as a social and collaborative process. Understanding these social and collaborative dimensions of cultural production are important for moving towards a creative ecology framework, but, as we will see below, *Creative Britain* stems out of an economically-based model of cultural policy.

CREATIVE BRITAIN: NEW TALENTS FOR A NEW ECONOMY: IMPLICATIONS FOR YOUTH AND CULTURAL EMPLOYMENT

A strength of the *Creative Britain* policy is that it works towards offering a comprehensive framework to address cultural employment. This policy document focuses on the transition between school and work, which is an important transition to consider, as there currently is a gap in research between youth experiences in schools and later experiences in the workforce. *Creative Britain* provides measures to "help untangle the complicated and fragmented paths into a creative career and provide new opportunities for training and work experience" to "ensure that young people have real opportunities to develop ... For too many at the moment, the chance to start a career in the creative industries means moving to London, working for free or knowing someone who can get you a foot in the door."[9] Success in the creative industries often requires adeptness in navigating informal networks, and the informality of these networks can also lead to social exclusion, as not everyone has access to these networks when they are so intangible. One measure that *Creative Britain* outlines to formalize these informal networks is to create "clear career paths,"[10] and one mechanism to foster this clarity is the creation of five thousand new internships a year by 2013; the document also includes a goal of having an internship available for any qualified high school graduate who desires it by the year 2013. The DCMS hopes that more transparent access and more available internships will result in a more diverse workforce, as it "not clear that opportunities for the recruitment of unpaid young people as interns, common in most creative industries, are distributed evenly across all socioeconomic groups. We expect an important spin-off from better routes into creative careers to be an improvement in the diversity of the industry."[11] Here, the assumption is that internships provide clarity in navigating the murky waters of creating careers in the creative industries, but internships can often cyclically repeat without leading into permanent employment.

Without more equitable hiring policies and more available jobs, internships themselves cannot create equity.

Furthermore, internships may not be the primary mechanism that youth elect to develop careers for themselves in the creative industries. British research characterizes youth cultural producers as "the Independents," as they are opting to pursue creative careers in self-generated ways rather than seeking out employment/internships in creative firms. *Creative Britain* does not address the unique needs that youth in this demographic have as they enter into the creative industries. The document proposes a Young Enterprise Quickstart Music Programme to assist young entrepreneurs who want to operate their own music businesses by providing them with support from business and industry mentors. This plan creates links to major record labels and names industry partners such as Sony BMG, which does not address the ad hoc and independent nature of much youth involvement in the music industry. *The Economist* chronicles the economic struggles of major record labels and gives an overview of how artists like Madonna, The Eagles, and Radiohead may be on the vanguard of the trend away from releasing albums with major labels and have instead chosen a concert promoter, self-releases, or Internet releases, respectively.[12] These trends may be even more pronounced for small-scale youth musicians, and the *New York Times* discusses the growth of independent record label sales while major record labels find themselves "hamstrung in their traditional ways of doing business."[13] *Creative Britain* underlines the government's role in giving "support for creativity from the grassroots to the global stage,"[14] but the assumption here is that grassroots involvement in creative fields will necessarily attempt to move into global arenas, which has the connotations of the industrialized cultural industries. It is difficult to imagine where youth pathways in the creative industries that are intentionally small-scale and community-oriented would fit in the DCMS policy framework. There are no provisions in this document for grassroots cultural production that desires to remain at the grassroots level, and there is no vision of grassroots community development through small-scale creative industries that include youth.

Beyond internships and business mentorship, *Creative Britain* sets out to find other mechanisms to correct a lack of diversity in the creative industries and seeks to proliferate more information about career pathways. The policy calls for the creation of the *Creative Choices* website, www.creative-choices.co.uk, which the DCMS touts as the "first industry and user-led online service to fully exploit the potential of social media and give individuals a pathway to shape their own destiny," noting that the "core of the new service will be the ability to find and compare all the courses, jobs, people and placements that are available across the sector." Similar to the creation of more internships and "effective advice literature,"[15] this website is charged with minimizing confusion about how one might go about creating a career in the creative industries: "Any young person contemplating a higher education course could find it difficult to make an informed choice from the extraordinary range on offer. For example, there are currently over a thousand courses that include 'film' in their title and over 350 with the word 'television.' There are nearly one hundred courses related to computer games listed in the Skillset/British Film Institute database, and the number of courses related to information technology runs into the thousands."[16] Again, these mechanisms assume that the solution to problems of equity is based in improving the quality and access to training; this assumption does not examine the nature of hiring, employment, and success in the creative industries themselves. Discussing a 2007 DCMS policy document, *Staying Ahead*, Banks and Hesmondhalgh argue that this document raises but does not deal with problems of inequity in creative industries employment: *Staying Ahead* does not "elaborate on the causes and consequences of these social disparities. Nor does it suggest how labour markets might be progressively reformed in order to overcome these problems."[17] This problem continues in *Creative Britain* as equity issues are raised but then subsumed under a meritocratic model of creating one's own success in the creative industries, as youth are expected to "shape their own destiny."

The rhetoric of *Creative Britain* is rooted at the level of the individual and relies on a development model of nurturing individual creativity and "discover[ing] talent where it might otherwise have lain hidden."[18] This individually driven model suggests that "talent" is innate in everyone and only needs to be "unlocked" or "found." The document states that "only an individual can decide to put in the huge effort required to reach the top of these professions ... but for those talented individuals willing to put in that effort, government should do everything it can to remove any barriers to achieving their ambition."[19] With these statements, *Creative Britain* does not address that there may be systemic barriers that preclude individuals from being "willing" to put in effort. Angela McRobbie notes that "New Labour appears to be inventing a new youth-driven meritocracy"[20] and that the individualization of the workforce means "freelance, casualized and project-linked persons, and ... a more fiercely neo-liberal model in place with the blessings of government for overseeing the further de-regulation and commercialization of the cultural and creative sector."[21] Though McRobbie is not specifically addressing the *Creative Britain* policy document, her claims also ring true when considering this new DCMS policy. Youth are foregrounded in this policy, but a neoliberal model of economic development is truly at its core.

Establishing networks that youth can access is another aspect of formalizing the informality of careers in the creative industries in *Creative Britain*. One part of this initiative is the creation of academic "hubs" that link schools with further and higher education. The goal here is to provide "end to end" development of creative skills for youth aged fourteen to twenty-five. *Creative Britain* aims to achieve this goal through the sharing of curricula, industry contacts, and facilities between schools and universities, and by providing mentoring for students and exchanges for staff. These collaborations between universities and community youth arts programs can be found in Canada as well; for example, the Beat of Boyle Street is a collaboration between the music program of the University of Alberta and the Boyle Street Education Centre. The Beat of Boyle Street uses hip hop as a tool for engaging primarily Aboriginal at-risk youth and targets individual development, youth voice, and crime deterrence. The program provides university credit courses in areas such as digital design and media and offers instruction to assist youth to make music, remixes, rap, spoken-word poetry, and hip hop dance tracks. Their website states, "creative expressions connect with a vital component of young people's lives, and are readily accessible for individuals who find written and oral communications difficult. In addition, creative expression can open doors for youth to establish positive habits related to self-image. The Beat of Boyle Street, therefore, creates an opportunity to move youth-at-risk from activities related to crime and self-destruction toward positive alternatives."[22] As such, the Beat of Boyle Street targets goals of youth identity, self-expression, and empowerment, but does not explicitly target youth involvement with communities or economic development. In that the stated mission of the Boyle Street project does not address youth as workers, it demonstrates a clear difference to *Creative Britain*. Although the Beat of Boyle Street focuses on capacity building, which could potentially relate to careers, this is articulated around personal development lines. Another key difference is that the Boyle Street project and others like it can often be found in major city centres (the Boyle Street project is located in Edmonton), and *Creative Britain* proposes giving access to these types of opportunities to youth in regions outside of major urban centres and aims to implement these programs for all youth.

We may be able to find comparable programs that deliver some of the same provisions of *Creative Britain* in Canada, but these projects are often the result of the initiative of hardworking people who are committed to working with youth and who are often youth themselves, and these programs often do not have long-term stability. *Creative Britain* may work towards providing long-term stability for youth arts programs by developing a comprehensive policy framework for the cultural sector. This desire for more sustainable funding is often voiced in surveys of youth organizations. The Arts Network of Children and Youth initiated a survey of Canadian youth organizations, called *Undervoiced Voices: Strategies for Participation*. The survey found that "short-term project-to-project funding, although useful in some situations, poses numerous problems, particularly for youth-led organizations and should be addressed through core funding involving a staggered multi-year, multi-funder approach."[23] Similarly, the Grassroots Youth Collaborative (GYC), an organization that is made up of representatives from six youth-led, nonprofit, community-based organizations in the Greater Toronto Area, has produced a report on best practices and challenges for youth-led organizations. The report, entitled *Youth on Youth: Grassroots Youth Collaborative on Youth Led Organizing in the City of Toronto*, notes that one of the struggles faced by these organizations is a lack of core and multi-year funding, as well as "organizational and program stability, sustainability, and capacity."[24] These challenges also result in high program/staff turnover, as staff often feel "overwhelmed ... and undersupported."[25]

Working towards better supporting youth organizations in the ways outlined in the *Youth on Youth* report would require a paradigm shift in policy making such that youth needs are highlighted and supported by a coherent vision. Responders in this report felt that, while there is a current climate of rhetoric in Canada that supports youth activities, actual policy and commitment in this area is lacking: "many of the focus group participants felt that the recent embrace of youth issues and youth-led organizing in the discourse of government and funding agencies and bodies was more rhetorical than actual, judging from the actual commitment of tangible resources to youth-led organizations by the latter in the experience of GYC member organizations."[26] This report highlights a desire for an integrated approach to youth policy that positions youth as community members with a "larger vision and strategy aimed at increasing the health, strength, and social infrastructure of communities."[27] The *Undervoiced Voices* report also calls for a more comprehensive vision behind youth policy, citing the need for a "holistic, long-term, community and human development approach" such that youth may also potentially be included in policy making and funding processes through "more cross-sectoral collaboration and communication not only amongst the funders themselves but also between funders and fundees."[28]

Creative Britain might explicitly yoke youth with employment and economic development, but it does not ground these links in any larger vision of community development or creative ecology. As such, it does not speak to the broader issues in the *Youth on Youth* and *Undervoiced Voices* reports. Values of culture other than economic ones are mentioned in *Creative Britain*, but the economic impact of the arts is consistently underlined. On the one hand, *Creative Britain* is unique in that it highlights the role that youth have to play in the creative economy. On the other hand, this policy is quite limited, as it primarily underscores the value of the arts as an economic engine. Given its emphasis on the economic impact of the arts, *Creative Britain* could cause a surplus of creative industry hopefuls. The document continually suggests the need to create a "wider pool of talent" of available workers and assumes this pool of talent will be able to find available employment in the creative industries.[29] Due to "global competition" in the creative fields, the "creative industries need the best possible business support structures in place and an abundant pool of talented people with the right skills to meet the needs of an expanding creative sector."[30] The creation of this abundant pool may lead to joblessness and only accentuate the contract-based and freelance nature of much creative industries employment. *Creative Britain* is undergirded by the notion that "working in the creative sector is the ambition of many young people,"[31] and the DCMS suggests there is a need to create more links between

"education [and] the world of work."[32] Links between education
and the world of work, especially in terms of the creative economy,
are important to forge, but the rhetoric of the document stems from
an instrumentalist view of the purposes of education and the role of
the arts in the lives of youth and in the well-being of communities.
Banks and Hesmondhalgh foreground the concern that cultural
policies that target systems of education result in "business-oriented
education" where systems of education are expected to develop
workforce skills to meet the needs of creative businesses.[33] How,
then, can connections between higher education and the creative
industries be framed not solely to meet the needs of business but to
meet the needs of youth?

Operating from an economic view of culture, *Creative Britain*
develops a vision of Britain where "local economies in our biggest
cities are driven by creativity,"[34] but this vision of "creativity" is hazy
and undefined. The document underlines "the Government's fundamental belief in the role of public funding to stimulate creativity"[35]
throughout, but the theoretical underpinnings of creativity are never
specified. At a debate about the future of the creative industries in
Britain, Terry Illiot, the director of the Film Business Academy at Cass
Business School, pointed out this lack of clear conceptualization of
creativity in *Creative Britain* and suggested that "without an underlying theory of creativity on which to ground itself ... the many ideas
and schemes in the paper would founder, and the industry would suf-
fer many unintended consequences as a result."[36] *Creative Britain*
risks falling into the definition of creativity as "innovation" and
"problem solving," which is so large and celebratory that it fails to
grapple with the limitations and challenges of creative employment
and the particular characteristics of labour in the creative industries.

While *Creative Britain* may be flawed and limited in many aspects
of its conception, it does demonstrate an understanding of the link
between the creative industries and economic growth that current
trends in cultural policy in Canada seem to overlook. At the debate
on the future of the creative industries in Britain, English Arts
Minister Estelle Morris stated that the reason behind New Labour's
championing of the creative industries as a major area of economic
investment is "quite simple. It is the expansion. It is the sheer numbers of people who now work in that sector: jobs, employment,
income for families. That is something that is unanswerable. The
amount of money that the creative industries now bring to the GDP,

£60bn a year – 7.3% of our total wealth – and the sector has been doubling in relationship to any other sector, growing at twice the rate of any other sector. Politicians understand that language."[37] This matter is perhaps not as simple as Morris states, as Canada has yet to develop a comprehensive policy framework for its cultural sector, even if figures produced by an independent think tank, the Conference Board of Canada, suggest that the cultural industries earned $84.6 billion or 7.4 per cent of the GDP in Canada in 2007.[38] *Creative Britain* might offer interesting avenues to explore in terms of cultural policy development for Canada, but this cultural policy development might be better joined with a more holistic vision of community development that is not solely driven by an economic engine and that highlights the role that small-scale youth cultural production has to play within the ecology of the creative economy.

ARTS EDUCATION AND CULTURAL AND YOUTH POLICY IN QUEBEC

As we have seen, in its targeting of youth involvement in the creative industries, *Creative Britain* outlines a particular vision of arts education. Of course, arts education is not unique to Britain; within Canada, education is administered provincially, and, amongst these provincial jurisdictions, Quebec is often touted as an arts-friendly haven. Given that Quebec is known within Canada as the province that most highly recognizes the significance of culture, I have chosen to study the province to see how extensive its cultural infrastructure is and to examine to what extent this infrastructure relates to youth practices. Quebec participants in the *Next Generation of Artists and Arts Audience Dialogues* study noted that "Quebec is considered an attractive place for artists from across the country, due to the size of the perceived audiences, and lower cost-of-living expenses in urban areas like Montreal."[39] Quebec may be known for broad audiences that support culture, but making a career in the arts in Quebec is not struggle-free. In the *Next Generation* study, "some participants [from Quebec] said that they are often forced to make sacrifices in time and money to support their involvement as artistic creators and professionals. Many participants said they believe they are making an investment or making sacrifices to gain the experience they expect they will need as professionals. Others, however, said they were beginning to question their involvement in the arts due to personal and financial struggles."[40] Moreover, long-term funding to support and sustain community arts organizations may be no more available in Quebec than in any other province: "Many have the misconception that art programs are readily available to all children and youth in Canada and are well funded, when in fact only a small percentage of families can afford to send their children to arts programs and in some communities they do not exist. Only 25–30% of children and youth in Canada ever have a 'creative arts experience' in their life outside of the school setting. As well ongoing, operational funding does not exist at the Federal, Provincial and Municipal levels to support and sustain community based programs."[41] Developing core funding for community arts programs remains a challenge across Canada, and more comprehensive policy structures might be able to work towards more stability.

Nonetheless, at the policy level, Quebec is noted for its existing cultural legislation, including a provincial Status of the Artist Act; in fact, Quebec was the first jurisdiction in Canada to implement such legislation in 1988, and the Quebec legislation informed Canada's federal legislation development in this area in 1992.[42] Other provinces have since implemented their own Status of the Artist legislation, such as Saskatchewan in 2002 and Ontario in 2007. Monica Gattinger and Diane Saint-Pierre identify that Quebec has always had a strong articulation of national identity and culture, and "up until the 1960s, government initiatives were based on one major objective: protecting, increasing and transmitting, for purposes of prestige and philanthropy, Québec's national heritage in all of its forms."[43] After the 1960s, Quebec cultural policies turned to "supporting creation, developing infrastructure for production and broadcasting, professionalizing cultural activities, and promoting widespread participation,"[44] as well as forging links with foreign countries within la Francophonie. According to Gattinger and Saint-Pierre, in the 1980s, culture in Quebec became aligned with the economy, and the industrialization of culture saw the development of Quebec's cultural policy, the *Politique Culturelle du Québec*, and the creation of the Conseil des Arts et Des Lettres du Québec in 2002.

Though it is not specifically cultural in nature, Quebec also has a comprehensive youth policy framework. The first version of this policy, introduced in 2001 and entitled *Bringing Youth into Québec's Mainstream*, sets out to ensure that youth achieve "full citizenship" by fostering solidarity between generations and to acknowledge the importance of youth with "consistent youth-oriented action by the government."[45] Above all, this youth policy framework is tied to a nationalist vision of Quebec's maintenance and renewal by its younger generation, who will "build the Québec of tomorrow."[46] In order to achieve the aims of full youth participation and belonging in society, the themes of youth health, education, and employment have been emphasized across its 2001, 2006, and 2009 incarnations.

Culture is not a main part of this vision of youth citizenship, but it does crop up in these policy documents. In *Bringing Youth into Québec's Mainstream*, "culture, creativity and innovation" are tied to the project of "engaging society in a culture of generational renewal." This commitment to culture begins with a nationalist vision of "a lasting artistic and cultural heritage," and the document outlines strategies for young people to become invested in Quebec's culture, such as to "involve young people in the development of resources and cultural property; make young people even more aware of the history of former generations and the characteristics of Québec culture which shape their very identity; make young people aware of the original, diverse and dynamic artistic and cultural practices in Québec by providing better access to facilities where all types of art forms are shown."[47] The majority of these provisions are mechanisms to ensure that Quebec youth will continue to act as consumers and preservers of culture, but there are also provisions that address youth as cultural producers.

> It is important therefore to continue to foster this vitality by encouraging the creative work of young artists and the upcoming generation. To allow young people to express themselves, develop their creativity and innovate, the strategies to be pursued must aim to: promote creativity among young people, and provide better access to places where they can express themselves creatively; welcome, recognize and support the artistic creations of young people, by showing the creations on a local, national and international scale; support the creativity and artistic expression of young people through school and extracurricular activities to develop their critical judgment and increase their contact with the artistic community.[48]

These strategies see youth as active producers of culture, but there are no specific links here between cultural production and employment/

entrepreneurship, which form major themes of the policy elsewhere. In the subsequent incarnations of Quebec's youth policy, there are even fewer provisions that relate to culture; the 2009 document *Investing in Youth: Empowering Québec's Future* mentions the need to "encourage artistic expression and introduce young people to arts and culture at school" and "encourage young people to pursue leisure and cultural activities" as "complementary" measures.[49] Quebec may have well-defined cultural infrastructure, as well as a well-defined youth policy, but these two policy areas are discrete and distinct, and a melding of these two policy areas might better support youth creative practices.

This lack of connection between youth, culture, and employment continues in Quebec's vision of arts education for children and youth in schools. Gattinger and Saint-Pierre identify the growth of an economic emphasis on culture through the 1980s in Quebec, but the Quebec Education Program (QEP), revamped in 2004, does not primarily envision arts education as a mechanism for career pathways or economic growth, as is seen in the British *Creative Britain: New Talents for a New Economy* policy. Rather, the QEP is oriented around liberal humanistic lines of self-development, which is also connected to a nationalist vision of a well-formed citizenry. The QEP sees this personal development as integral to society as a whole; in his foreword, Quebec Minister of Education Pierre Reid comments that the QEP is "preparing young people to become full-fledged citizens." In the QEP, arts education is presented as an important mechanism to ensure Quebec national identity, as it is said to "develop, affirm, and safeguard cultural identity" in the face of the "homogenization of cultures" produced by "commercial interests" that "have a stake in the arts."[50] This bifurcation of "real" art and "commercial" art does not recognize youth interests in working in "commercial" fields of the creative industries. Instead, a humanistic rhetoric of personal enrichment is seen in the discussion of "the creative dynamic," which the QEP defines as a "process and a procedure" that begins with "inspiration" followed by development of the work, and then distancing oneself from the work.[51] While the QEP proposes that learning "cultural references" is part of arts education, this rhetoric of "inspiration" seems to divorce art from socio-historical contexts and frames art in the language of individual expression and distanced reflection. In this way, the language of the QEP recalls the individualistic rhetoric of the "Find Your Talent" program, as neither sees art as a collaborative, social, or community project. Ultimately, neither the QEP nor the "Find Your Talent" program answers Henry Jenkins or Ruben Gaztambide-Fernandez's calls for an arts education or for training for artists that designates art as a social process based in public interaction, that emerges out of affinity spaces where students create their own creative networks, or that works towards affirming the role of the artist engaging in a democratic public sphere.

When the QEP does address careers in the arts, it is rooted in the rhetoric of personal development rather than in purely economic terms like in *Creative Britain*. The QEP states:

> The arts stimulate bodily awareness, nourish the imagination and contribute to the development of self-esteem. In practising an art, students draw on all aspects of the self – body, voice, imagination, culture – in order to convey their perception of reality and world-view. They make use of a symbolic language that opens up new perspectives on themselves, others and their environment. Arts education, in helping to empower students, contributes to the construction of their identity and the enrichment of their world-view. It also helps narrow the gap between academic learning and the working world. When pursued on a consistent basis throughout their secondary studies, it can pave the way for studies leading to a wide variety of professions and occupations related to the arts and culture.[52]

Of interest in this passage is the space given to a description of the enrichment of the student in comparison to the space given to the description of "professions and occupations" in the arts. Developing skills for the realm of work or future post-secondary study is part of the QEP, as this document suggests that schools' "threefold mission" is to "provide instruction in a knowledge-based world," "to socialize students in a pluralistic world," and "to provide qualifications in a changing world."[53] Careers related to creative fields are presented through the "cultural references" of the arts education section of the QEP and include "artist, media designer, designer, architect, photographer, filmmaker, television producer, videographer, graphic artist, computer graphics artist, art critic, art historian, illustrator, comic strip artist, artisan, art teacher, museum curator, conservation and restoration technician for art works and objects, museum educator, etc."[54] The careers named in this broad list demonstrate an awareness of the importance of the creative industries even if this is not a main focus of the arts education section of the QEP; these careers would also seem to belong to commercialized sectors of the arts that the overall mission of arts education in the QEP seeks to curtail. Beyond this mention of careers in the arts, though, the QEP does not include in its vision of arts education any discussion of the logistics that are required to make a career in any of the above areas. Students are invited to learn that these careers exist, but they are not invited to see themselves in these careers or move towards obtaining them.

While the QEP may not include an explicit vision of youth careers in the creative industries, its vision of arts education does value cultural production. Like the "Find Your Talent" program in *Creative Britain*, the QEP casts youth as both arts audiences and cultural producers. The QEP makes mention of the benefits of "visits to cultural sites" and "meetings with artists,"[55] but more focus is allocated to cultural production. Each of the subject areas in arts education (drama, visual arts, dance, music) is structured around developing subject-specific competencies, and these competencies are oriented around learning by doing. The wording of each competency varies according to the specific subject, but all of the competencies follow the model of creating a work, performing this work, and then learning to appreciate other works. This suggests that cultural production and arts appreciation are joined and artist and audience are articulated to emerge out of the same process. This focus on project-based learning in the QEP lends itself to youth later pursuing their own creative practices; however, a broader vision of creativity as a social process, and clearer links between the world of arts education and the world of work in the creative industries, could make arts education more relevant to the needs of contemporary youth.

JEUNES VOLONTAIRES: PROJECT-BASED
ENTREPRENEURSHIP FOR YOUTH IN QUEBEC

As discussed above, *Creative Britain: New Talents for a New Economy* makes provisions for youth-directed projects but may not be relevant for youth small-scale, self-generated practices because it envisions industrialized forms of creative work rather than assisting youth in developing their own local forms of cultural production. Quebec also has funding for youth-directed projects, and Jeunes volontaires is one grant that specifically targets youth and aims to help their entry into the workforce. As a structural mechanism to facilitate youth creative projects and employment, this program has possibilities and limitations. To examine this program, the end of this chapter returns to a life stories methodology and profiles three small-scale creative projects that Jeunes volontaires has funded: an experimental folk choir called the Coal Choir, a sitcom about a fictional band made with foam core called *The Mittenstrings*, and a web-based television series called *The Bitter End*. Through the creators' profiles of their projects in this final section, we hear how Jeunes volontaires fits into their larger trajectories of trying to get their creative projects off the ground and attempting to make a living.

Katherine Peacock and the Coal Choir

While Jeunes volontaires is not specifically an arts grant, Montreal-based musician Katherine Peacock identifies that it is known through "word of mouth of artists" as "fairly easy to get."[56] For this reason, the grant has a certain visibility amongst young cultural producers in Montreal. Indeed, when I attended a public information session about the Jeunes volontaires grant, all of the examples of potential projects given by the grants officers were arts-related (music, dance, photography, writing) even if the grant is not specifically earmarked for art projects. Jeunes volontaires runs monthly information sessions, and there were nearly fifty youth present at the one that I attended, which demonstrates the demand for support for small-scale youth projects. Funded through Emploi Québec, Jeunes volontaires offers project grants for youth aged sixteen to twenty-nine who live on the island of Montreal and "have trouble entering the labour market." The grant allows them "a chance to acquire skills while working on a project that [they] have designed. [They] can develop and implement projects in fields that interest [them], e.g., agriculture, arts, culture, communications, community services, environment, tourism."[57] Projects can run from nine to fifty-two weeks, and Jeunes volontaires is framed as an opportunity to "enhance your knowledge, improve your skills, creativity and self-reliance, work with professionals, make contacts and friends [and] gain an enriching experience."[58] Youth are paid to work on a personal project that they develop themselves, but the Jeunes volontaires grant is designed to increase employability rather than to facilitate careers in the project area. The grant program has built-in mechanisms to promote this job readiness, such as requiring youth to produce an operating budget and to find a mentor who has experience related to the project.

Despite this framework of job readiness, Katherine's experience with this grant program was that it "in no way helped [her] furthering [her] career."[59] This problem suggests a tension between the job readiness that is the official mandate of the grant program and the career development that many youth – who already have clear conceptions of the cultural production they want to pursue – desire. These youth may not necessarily have trouble entering the labour market per se and may not need to work on developing job-readiness types of skills. In fact, the demographic that Charles Leadbeater and Kate Oakley characterize as "the Independents" are highly qualified people. British data from 2008 and 2009 suggests that people employed in the creative industries have much higher rates of post-secondary degrees than the population as a whole (54 per cent vs. 35 per cent), and "freelancers in particular tend to have degrees."[60] The bureaucratic work that the Jeunes volontaires grant entails may amount to more busy work than support for professionalization of creative practices for these highly educated people.

Katherine was first introduced to the Jeunes volontaires grant when an ex-bandmate applied for it for their now defunct band, Dorian Hatchet. She explains that "he made it sound like it's all this bureaucratic stuff and then they give you a bit of money to do your music," but Katherine's own experience of working with this granting organization proved to be more difficult. A year after the completion of the Jeunes volontaires grant for Dorian Hatchet, Katherine decided to apply for her own project, the Coal Choir, for which she composes music and leads. She describes her application process as a difficult and frustrating experience.

> A year later, I was like maybe I'll try to do it myself for the choir and that's when I found out all the bureaucratic stuff. I right away realized what I wanted to do was no way in keeping with what they wanted. They want you to have a highly marketable product that will make you make more money in the future. Basically they want to see that you're geared towards making money. A choir is about community. The sort of music that is only possible through government support. The whole idea, they didn't like it, that we were going to perform three shows at the Mile End Mission, kind of benefit shows. That was a big no-no.

The whole idea of community benefits were not what they wanted. [My mentor] realized what they wanted so she was like "well, through this, Katherine could learn how to produce and orchestrate," all these kinds of marketable skills.[61]

The difficulty that Katherine raises here arises out of a disconnect between her desire to develop her artistic practice in community-oriented way – which is in fact her career objective – and the program's emphasis on the development of marketable skills.

Despite the lack of enthusiasm for Katherine's small-scale community-based project that was not seeking to make a profit, Katherine feels that the structure of the grant does not allow for projects that are larger in scale. She states, "they give so little money that all I wanted to do was all I could have done. There's no way you can record an album on $900," the project budget she was allocated. Here, Katherine refers to the small operating budget that the Jeunes volontaires grant provides. The grant also provides a small stipend of pay – $300 per month, unless the recipient has received employment insurance within the last four years, in which case the stipend is greater. The Jeunes volontaires grant does not allow the recipient to work at a job for more than twenty hours per week and assumes that the recipient will consecrate twenty hours per week to the project. At $300 per month, twenty hours of work per week on a project translates into $3.75 per hour. That nearly fifty young people attended an information session that runs monthly suggests both the demand for these small-scale funds and the willingness of young people to undertake the bureaucratic Jeunes volontaires application process to access this small amount of project money. Small-scale grassroots cultural production often relies on informal networks of favours and assistance from friends, and, despite her frustrations with the Jeunes volontaires granting system, Katherine comments, "it was nice to be able to pay my friends a little bit, like a kind of honorarium for recording and mixing," but the amount of money offered "was all kind of token stuff," and "there's no way that that small amount of money can help you establish yourself in the marketplace!"

Beyond these frustrations, Katherine credits her experience at Jeunes volontaires with giving her the confidence to seek out other grants: "It's kind of got me in the bureaucratic mindset, like, OK, I can jump through these hoops." However, Katherine felt an overall lack of support from this program and questions if she should have been given the grant at all. She explains:

> What would have been better would be seeing what I was actually trying to do and maybe making suggestions about what could have been better. They could have been like, "Jeunes volontaires is about trying to get young creative entrepreneurs set in the marketplace, so this is not for you but this is how we can help you get a different kind of grant." They kind of just dismissed [Katherine's project] and were like, "we'll wave you through" … So I think it would be good if they took a little more care. Even after you finish a project, maybe they could refer you to other grant organizations, and that would be really helpful. It was kind of like, "Boom, that's the end of this, no talk about any other options" … I've been trying to get different kinds of grants since, and have no idea.

While the Jeunes volontaires grant seeks to assist the transition into the workforce, what Katherine voices here is a desire for a larger framework behind granting organizations, such that the services she references, including referrals to other granting organizations, are possible. Jeunes volontaires might be specifically targeted towards youth, but the types of support that Katherine discusses suggest the need for more awareness of the contemporary parameters of youth creative practices and for connections across sectors and organizations.

Lily Lanken and The Mittenstrings

Lily Lanken cites a more positive relationship and identification with the Jeunes volontaires grant system; however, she also voices similar frustrations as Katherine. With her brother Sylvan, Lily pursued a Jeunes volontaires grant in order to produce a "sitcom-format video … about a fictional band, The Mittenstrings."[62] Lily recounts that she found out about the grant because a friend of hers had received one. She heard that "there's this money you can get" because it is a "grant for people starting out."[63] She explains that she applied to receive a grant to do a "video project with musical element. My brother and I had done a [music] video of these little cut-out drawings and stuff for a song of our aunt's … I got into these cut-out things ... I think it's a neat medium to work in, then I had this idea for a story. It was about a fictional band, and then we would write the songs for the fictional band and then they would do whatever. So it would be like a little miniseries." Lily describes that the origin of her project developed from an affinity for working with cardboard foam core. Though she has a background in studying visual arts at Concordia University, her vision for her project was interdisciplinary, as it would contain elements of art, video, and music. Describing the interdisciplinary nature of the project, The Mittenstrings website explains that "all elements were hand-drawn and painted. The videos are composed of live-action shots, a sort of moving tableaux; the authors have come up with the term 'inanimation' to describe the action. To give each character in the sitcom a unique voice, Lily and Sylvan enlisted the vocal talents of numerous friends. Finally, all songs in the sitcom were written and recorded by Lily and Sylvan."[64]

Lily credits her Jeunes volontaires mentor and her friend who already had a Jeunes volontaires grant with assisting and encouraging her navigation of the grant application process. She characterizes this process as "fairly efficient," but she also cites that the funds she received could not be considered enough to complete the project without financial assistance from other sources. Additionally, Lily spent much more time on the project than the grant outlines and compensates for, both at the weekly level (twenty hours of work per week are required, which Lily exceeded), and with the length of the granting period itself (which was twelve months, but Lily worked on completing the project for a year and a half in total). Lily also suggests that Jeunes volontaires' emphasis on vocational or trade apprenticeship is outdated and irrelevant. She states, "It only seems to be art related [in terms of who applies for this grant] but it obviously was from a time when people did apprenticeships ... It was supposed to be more like you were a carpenter." Lily was also frustrated with the Jeunes volontaires grant stipulation that grantees must rent rather than purchase equipment with their grant money. She explains, "We got the money, started the project, then realized we couldn't do it without a camera. If we rented it, we would have paid for it"; that is, they would have paid the price of purchasing a camera in the amount of rental fees that they paid. Despite these irritations, Lily comments, "JV was really important," and it was the birth of The Mittenstrings as a live musical project: "that's the thing that came out of it, that we became a band, so that's one good thing."[65] Nonetheless, Lily's frustrations speak to the lack of relevant and up-to-date models to support youth small-scale cultural production. Jeunes volontaires has been taken on as structural mechanism to support small-scale youth cultural production, and the program has become known as such by word of mouth from one cultural producer to another. But it is not in fact designed to support these projects, and this discrepancy sometimes produces frustrations that are additional elements to wade through in the navigation and negotiation of making one's way in the creative industries.

Etan Muskat, Dan Beirne, Brent Skagford, and The Bitter End

Like Katherine and Lily, the creators of the web series *The Bitter End* highlight the community-based and collaborative nature of how they marshaled their creative product into being. Youth are sometimes motivated by the desire to bring creative projects into realization "just to see it happen," often without the promise of immediate financial reward. Rather than perpetuating a binary of DIY "independence" and industry "incorporation," examining how youth navigate and negotiate their way through for-profit and not-for-profit streams, including grants like Jeunes volontaires, can provide a more useful framework to understand the mechanisms of contemporary youth cultural production. For the creators of *The Bitter End*, this granting body was one mechanism to bring their project into being and launch themselves into creative industries work, but was not the defining element of their ability to produce a creative project. Rather, this granting body was one amongst multiple pathways that came together to produce *The Bitter End*.

The Bitter End web television series began as an idea for a network television show. Etan Muskat states, "It started as a pitch for a network series and we just started guessing at what the show would be like in a pitch document kind of thing."[66] Though this pitch to Canadian networks was unsuccessful, co-creators Etan Muskat, Dan Beirne, and Brent Skagford still wanted to pursue the project and hoped to develop their skills and the marketability of their show by having a completed project to shop around. Dan comments, "So we turned it into an improv show, just to start doing something with these characters. We did that for eight or nine months ... We did about twenty improv shows and then decided that we would try and get a little money and turn it into a web show and went full force at it for basically all of 2009."[67] *The Bitter End* creators have a background in improv, or improvised live comedy, and used this background as an incubator to develop their television series. They are also situated within a community in the improv scene that has been important for the development of their work. Etan explains, "One of the things that has kept us here [in Montreal] is a certain community, in terms of specifically performing improv live. Marc Rowland, who we've been working with in our live shows for a long time and is part of the cast of *The Bitter End* when we do it live, just opened an improv theatre with some other partners, which has become our new performance home. A lot of our creative energy comes out of improv." Etan notes that the creative output of *The Bitter End* is not tied to one particular genre, as it is able to move between live comedy and web-based television show. Furthermore, Etan highlights another important aspect of youth cultural production: the importance of physical infrastructure, in this case, a theatre, to house and nurture cultural projects.

These community elements have been important for *The Bitter End* not only in terms of the creative inception of the project, but also in the creators' abilities to tap into a network of like-minded people who are willing to assist the development of the project through volunteering their labour and equipment. Etan accounts for a donated camera, lighting kit, and locations, and the donated time of the cinematographer, crew, and extras. He says, "If we were to budget out the actual professional costs of this series, it would be exponentially higher than what we actually spent, just because we got performances, crew, equipment, locations, all this stuff donated. It's kind of hard to calculate. People working for free, that's the secret."[68] *The Bitter End* creators also credit the importance of informal mentorship and having connections with other people working in the field. Brent states:

Pat Kiely and Darren Curtis from Kidnapper Films both appear in the series and kind of functioned as our test audience, giving us a lot of advice on editing the show to make it snappier, funnier, and clearer, as did Seth Owen from Automatic Vaudeville. And while most of the series was shot in my Mile End apartment or the apartments of other friends, the Kidnapper guys also let us turn their office space on Clark and St Viateur into a night school for one shoot. One of our friends even let us destroy a wall in his bathroom in an episode where Les works on a demolition crew. His bathroom wasn't scheduled to be renovated until later in the summer so he essentially had no wall in his bathroom for a month. Yeah, the community really pulled through for us on this.[69]

Brent invokes a model of cooperation, not competition, amongst people working within similar genres, and this element as well as the element of non-compensated labour is important to recognize when mapping the parameters of contemporary youth cultural production.

Working with a certain community in a particular city not only assisted the creators in being able to produce *The Bitter End*, as the particular conditions of small-scale cultural labour in Montreal are to a certain extent thematized within the show itself. When CBC radio host Jian Ghomeshi asked Etan about the specific conditions of producing a television program in Montreal, which Etan identified as "not exactly the centre of English language Canadian television," Etan responded that Montreal informs the "feel" of the show in terms of the subject matter because "a lot of people in their twenties in [Montreal] are doing creative work but are still sort of making the transition to adulthood and that's very much the subject matter of the show."[70] The creators of *The Bitter End* are part of this demographic of young people trying to make a living from creative work, and the show follows the story of Bernard, played by Dan, who is attempting to pursue a career as a fiction writer while working a day job in a photocopy shop and assisting his romantic interest in putting on a slam poetry series at a local café. This combination of doing unrelated paid work, pursuing a career in a creative field, and participating in community-based not-for-profit events is representative of many youths' involvement in the creative industries. Similarly, *The Mittenstrings* miniseries that Lily and Sylvan Lanken produced also thematizes small-scale cultural production in its content, as the series follows the story of a fictional band while they attempt to make a living from a career in music. Lily and Sylvan in a sense became this band and took on this story as they performed and toured with the music that was originally written for the series.

The Bitter End creators tapped into their community to get their show produced – a show that is in part about the struggles of getting things produced – and they also sought out financial support to create their project and to get a start in the creative industries. To "get a little money," *The Bitter End* creators turned to Jeunes volontaires. As the project leader on the grant, Dan says, "I was the closest with it. Basically, the way I would describe my experience is pretty positive but I didn't really know how to work the system. We could have gotten more money than we did."[71] *The Bitter End* grant project budget outlined that certain people would be involved during certain periods, but these people chose to work beyond their compensated periods. Additionally, the creators themselves worked well beyond the amount of hours that the grant requires. Etan explains that they were motivated to begin their project before the grant period began: "we actually did the writing – all the writing and preproduction happened before the [grant] period started because we just wanted to get going on it, and we knew we would have to wait a couple months."[72] In addition to this head start, *The Bitter End* creators worked much more than the allotted twenty hours a week of the grant; in fact, Etan says, "we probably worked more than a full-time job on it." *The Bitter End* creators received $3,000 to produce their project, but feel "we probably could have got twice that or three times that if we'd sort of done things a bit better" in terms of putting into the budget a more accurate forecast of the actual time that would be spent on the show. Etan comments, "The amount we got probably covered a little under half of our total budget. If we'd had a more definite conception of the amount of work – I think we knew more or less how much work there was going to be, but if we could have put that in more definite terms we probably could have covered more of our budget and had to invest less personally." Though the creators invested personal funds into the production of *The Bitter End*, that a professional product was able to be realized for $3,000 of grant money speaks to the importance of small-scale sums of money being available to incubate and support small-scale, self-generated youth cultural production.

In addition to Jeunes Volontaires, another support structure that *The Bitter End* creators drew on to foster their creative project was the Canadian performers' union – the Alliance of Canadian Cinema, Television and Radio Artists (ACTRA). *The Bitter End* was produced through "a model that didn't force [the creators] to pay the actors … [there was] a co-op agreement where [the actors] would donate their time for free in exchange for a percentage of ownership." Etan cites that these two structures that offer support for small-scale projects are at odds with one another: "JV saying you can't make money off this, and ACTRA saying we own the money you make off this to be distributed amongst the cast. So those two things kind of cancelled each other out." Even if many youth go into Jeunes Volontaires with projects that they ideally would like to make a living from, Jeunes Volontaires promotes the development of marketable skills rather than the creation of a lucrative project; any profit that is made from the project must be reinvested into the project rather than kept. The two support systems that *The Bitter End* creators made use of being at odds with one other highlights a lack of clear vision and broader support framework for youth small-scale cultural production.

While *The Bitter End* has not yet become a profitable product that requires the ACTRA provisions to be put into place, Ghomeshi, in his interview with Brent and Etan, comments that this lack of profits does not come from "a moral stance" or an opposition to commercial gain or mainstream broadcast forums, as they ideally would like to showcase their show on network television. Brent states that they "just really want to keep making it" and continue with a second season "by any means necessary."[73] *The Bitter End* hasn't found success with major television networks, but they are part of a growing body of Internet-based television work, and this avenue for distribution may be becoming a genre in its own right instead of a precursor to broadcast television distribution. Ghomeshi outlines that "do-it-yourself web TV is beginning to catch on. There are a number of web-based comedies and news programs out there."[74] Web TV may be poised for popularity, but the question of how to earn income from digitized forms of media that can be distributed on the Internet for free has yet to be answered. Brent explains that "there's a lot of really interesting things happening on the web right now. The industry is only just developing, nobody really knows where it's going, especially when it comes to generating revenue, so we figured we'd just put something out there."[75] Dan comments that he has witnessed the growing popularity of web-based television, but these ventures have yet to be monetized: "The whole time we were making this, people were coming up to us saying they were doing the same thing, making their own web show ... It really feels like the Gold Rush, everyone's doing this right now but there's no system in place to make any money."[76] Brent responds, "It's a rush, but there's no gold."[77] These questions of monetization and the growing popularity of web-based TV speak to the changing nature of the creative industries, and many youth are grappling with how to earn a sustainable living in these volatile times of restructuring in many creative fields.

The Jeunes volontaires grant, the QEP, Quebec's youth policy, and *Creative Britain: New Talents for A New Economy* all offer possibilities with regards to supporting youth cultural production; however, none of these policies or programs are adequately broad to fully address contemporary modes of youth engagement with the creative industries. Katherine, Lily, and Dan, Brent, and Etan's experiences with Jeunes volontaires suggests that they, like many youth, try to fit their creative practices within whatever possible structures exist to support these practices, but these structures may not be completely appropriate and lack a larger vision that supports youth creative work.

6

Montreal, City of Strife?

Agitation, Negotiation, and Visions of the Scene

With the international attention that has been focused on its independent music scene,[1] Montreal has become renowned for its cultural caché and its ability to foster cultural production. Studying scenes offers a point of entry for schematizing the post-subcultural milieu; Will Straw forwards a focus on scenes for investigating the organizing principles of "highly local clusters of activity" as well as "practices dispersed throughout the world."[2] Straw characterizes scenes as "elusive, ephemeral" in that they can constantly be in flux in space and time and can be defined in multiple ways.[3]

> Is a scene (a) the recurring congregation of people at a particular place, (b) the movement of these people between this place and other spaces of congregation, (c) the streets/strips along which this movement takes place (Allor 2000), (d) all the places and activities which surround and nourish a particular cultural preference, (e) the broader and more geographically dispersed phenomena of which this movement or these preferences are local examples, or (f) the webs of microeconomic activity which foster sociability and link this to the city's ongoing self-reproduction? All of these phenomena have been designated as scenes.[4]

While a scene can be variously defined as its people, its movement, its streets, its places and activities, its dispersal, or its microeconomic activity, Straw argues that scenes have a "productive, even functional, role within urban life" in that they are "one of the event structures through which cultural life acquires its solidity."[5] Thinking through how a scene is organized foregrounds the specific material conditions of cultural activity, and in this chapter I examine the localized scene of independent cultural production in Montreal and focus on some of the microeconomic conditions that enable and constrict youth cultural production. I investigate how meaning has accrued around Montreal as a scene and ask what is at stake in the various representations of this scene. With the renown that the Montreal independent music scene has received, what visions of this city and of this scene are proliferated, and to what end? Are these visions in service of and supportive of the milieu that they represent? What role do these visions play in raising the visibility of small-scale cultural production and in working towards more supportive cultural policies?

Amongst the representations of the independent scene in Montreal, a particular vision and origin story dominates discussions of how the city came to act as an incubator of independent cultural production. For example, Geoff Stahl traces the "social and aesthetic lineage" of the Montreal independent music scene from nineteenth-century Parisian salons, 1960s happenings in New York City, and Montreal's own Sin City days of "seedy glamour" of the 1930s, '40s, and '50s.[6] In addition to these bohemian, avant-garde, and hedonist roots, Stahl chronicles that an Anglo-bohemia flourished in Montreal in the 1990s and 2000s due to economic, cultural, and political forces such as the economic downtown of the 1980s and 1990s, the demetropolization of Montreal as an urban centre, and the anglophone flight from the city due to the threat of Quebec sovereignty. In this origin story, these factors coalesced to produce a milieu that was welcoming to artists and cultural producers. Stahl highlights the "continuing appeal" of Montreal for independent cultural producers due to these factors as well as others.

> A stagnant real estate market and rent control has meant cheap apartments throughout the city, especially on the cherished Plateau, which has the highest density of self-identified cultural producers in Montreal; Montreal's industrial districts in the Old Port and further north in Mile End were gutted as the city inched slowly towards a post-industrial economy, freeing up warehouses and lofts that many artists used for living, recording, and performance spaces; the city's four universities offer the lowest fees in North America, which has meant that a number of foreign and out-of-province students are drawn to the city, a fact which gives the city its youthful, energetic ambience; the cost of living

is reasonable even for those living on welfare or unemployment insurance, which means that those who wish to pursue an artistic lifestyle rarely have to worry so much about eking out a marginal existence with undue amounts of suffering (in fact, the difficulty of pursuing a creative life in another, more expensive city has driven a number of artists to Montreal); Montreal is close to bigger, cultural vibrant and diverse cities such as Boston or New York, each with their own distinct independent music scenes (anglophone independent labels, musicians and distributors have established affective and industrial ties to these cities, as a way of compensating for Montreal's weak support structures).[7]

Though the origin story of Montreal's independent scene can be continually expanded through the layering of additional contributing factors, the base story of economic privation remains, and the sum of these factors is considered as an indirect form of cultural policy that incubated favourable conditions for small-scale cultural production. In the case of Montreal's independent music scene of the 1990s and 2000s, the relationship between economic depression and creative flourishing has lead Stahl to characterize the mythology of Montreal that its musicians both inhabit and produce as a "subcultural utopia" and "a kind of middle-class escapist utopia."[8]

This identification of the Montreal scene as a utopian space is not based in an excess of opportunities and resources, but in a willful differentiation from them. This vision of the Montreal independent scene thriving out of conditions of economic scarcity is replicated across narratives about the emergence of this scene. It is a story that is told about Montreal and that Montreal tells about itself. *Spin* magazine's 2005 profile of Montreal as "the next big scene" includes interviews with Montreal musicians and scene makers who narrate the story of economic depression, struggle, and the effects of the threat of Quebec secession on the development of Montreal's independent music scene.[9] Similarly, the *New York Times*' overview of the emergence of the Montreal music scene prizes the "artistic regenesis" that flourished when "Anglophone-oriented money, people and resources pulled out – much of it for Toronto – leaving vacant buildings."[10] A 2010 travel profile in the *New York Times*, "36 Hours in Montreal," retraces much of the same origin story of the Montreal music scene with its reference to the "gritty stages" that gave successful Montreal bands like Arcade Fire their start.[11]

This chapter acknowledges the unique economic, cultural, and political forces that have allowed for the development of a milieu that is able to incubate independent cultural production in Montreal, but seeks to discuss other types of small-scale culture beyond the focus on music that has dominated much of the attention on the independent Montreal scene. The youth who were profiled in Chapter 5 are all Montreal-based, but neither Katherine's experimental folk choir, Lily's foam core sitcom, nor Dan, Etan, and Brent's web series would readily fit into the normative vision of Montreal's independent scene. A "scene" might be "one way of speaking of the theatricality of the city – of the city's capacity to generate images of people occupying public space in attractive ways,"[12] and music may be one of the most visible and spectacular forms of cultural production, such that "the production and consumption of music lend themselves more easily to a mobile urban sociability than does involvement in other cultural forms."[13] Nonetheless, the forces that impact the independent music scene also impact other forms of small-scale cultural production. Susan Semenak explains that "everyone knows about Montreal's happening indie music scene," but "there is another homegrown creative movement in Montreal gaining steam and garnering attention, and it too has emerged from oh-so-hip Mile End. Call it a handmade revolution, or the new DIY."[14] This "handmade" scene is made of artisans in their twenties and thirties who sell their wares at craft fairs like Montreal's Puces Pop, which "has gone from being a tiny, underground gathering to a thrice-yearly event that attracts more than 7,000 shoppers. It is now billed as one of the biggest indie craft fairs in North America."[15] In addition to local craft fairs, these artisans also make use of Etsy, an online marketplace that exclusively sells handmade wares, and "many Montreal artisans now manage to earn a living from their art or craft. They have become entrepreneurs, not hobbyists."[16] The conditions that have made Montreal attractive to musicians have also made the city attractive to handmade artisans, as well as writers, actors, performers, and other youth pursuing their own small-scale forms of cultural production. If the Montreal scene becomes synonymous with its independent music scene, this obscures the particular conditions of labour experienced by youth pursuing non-music-based forms of cultural production.

Beyond widening our definition of what the Montreal scene encompasses, this chapter also troubles the image of Montreal as a utopian escapist space through examining a series of moments that crystallize competing stakes and investments in the infrastructure that surrounds cultural production. The representation of the bohemian artist and cultural production thriving in times and places of economic scarcity valorizes conditions of deprivation and masks and romanticizes real struggles and challenges even as they are highlighted. This mythologization of deprivation as an integral part of artistic labour is at odds with working towards more supportive cultural policies for youth cultural production. If the Montreal scene is said to have successfully emerged out of implicit cultural policies, how can we map a course for explicit cultural policies that are supportive of youth cultural production? I offer a corrective vision of the independent scene in Montreal that suggests not an escapist utopia but a site of strife, negotiation, and continued investment and commitment from its young residents to maintaining the conditions that allow for the flourishing of cultural production. I return to the notion that scenes are "enmeshed within broader economic relations and regulatory regimes" and highlight how Montreal municipal cultural policy can directly affect and can be at odds with youth cultural production.[17] I then chronicle the initiatives taken up to safeguard favourable conditions for small-scale cultural production.

QUARTIER DES SPECTACLES, CASA DEL POPOLO, AND SUPPORT FOR SMALL-SCALE CULTURE

One strand in the narrative of the mythology of Montreal as a subcultural haven has been the availability of spaces that support cultural production, such as affordable rents that allow cultural producers to pursue a minimum of paid work, and empty warehouses that serve as affordable studios and rehearsal spaces. Beginning in the 2000s, the declining industrial area in Montreal's Mile End neighbourhood was re-appropriated and revitalized by artists and cultural workers, which made it an important magnet for all types of cultural production. In the late 2000s, this situation began to change as some of these industrial buildings – former textile factories that house artist studios – were resold with multimillion dollar price tags. Pied Carré was founded in January 2010 as a nonprofit organization to represent the more than eight hundred cultural producers working in the area (known for having one of the highest densities of creative workers in Canada) and to work towards protecting and maintaining these artist spaces. This organization stresses the urgency of intervening in the commercial real estate speculation in this area, as this speculation is driving artists out. For example, the building at 5455 De Gaspé was sold for $8 million in 2008 and resold in June 2011 for $37.8 million. The new owner of this industrial building, Allied Properties, has stated that it will renovate to attract high-end office clients, and current tenants anticipate that they will not be able to afford the increased rents.[18] Unlike residential leases, commercial rents are determined by the market and are especially vulnerable to real estate speculation. For these reasons, Pied Carré calls on municipal and provincial levels of government to take concrete actions to protect the conditions that have allowed cultural production to flourish in the area, such that Montreal has come to be nationally and internationally known for its independent scene.

In addition to this problem of real estate speculation, finding spaces to house small-scale cultural activities also presents a persistent challenge due to licensing, zoning, and other municipal policies. Montreal music venue Casa del Popolo, which showcases emerging artists and has "gained a big reputation for bringing in up-and-coming local and international acts over the past nine years"[19] had to stop having live music in 2008 after city licensers uncovered that the venue was having concerts without the required *salle-de-spectacle* permit. At a 2010 Pop Montreal symposium session about noise bylaws (profiled at the end of this chapter), director of L'APLAS (L'association des petits lieux d'art et de spectacles) Sebastien Croteau characterized the process of obtaining live music permits as nearly impossible for small concert venues due to a lack of available and accessible information about these permits.

> I challenge you to try to find information on the city's website about how to get that type of permit and the rules that govern that type of permit. It's really not obvious. We have a lot of small venues that opened and did just about all of the legwork to legally open a small venue. Then a city inspector came and said, "You don't have the proper permit. You have your restaurant permit, but you don't have your concert permit." And these small venue owners didn't have any idea at the beginning that they needed that type of permit.[20]

In contrast to Croteau's characterization of a lack of information about proper permits, Casa del Popolo owner Mauro Pezzente suggests, "certain laws are there, everyone knows about them, people are breaking them."[21] Nonetheless, these salle-de-spectacle permits are difficult to obtain. After the Casa was closed by a city inspector, Pezzente was able to obtain the required permit to legally have live music after a year of bureaucratic wrangling and has resumed live music at the Casa, but comments, "there are so many specific bylaws that are archaic and need to be updated – they could be less general and more specific to the location ... Everyone needs to lobby local government to open the city up to being more friendly towards music ... You look at other cities and they have so many live music venues. It's 100 per cent about the licensing here." In this comparison to other (unnamed) cities where music venues are abundant, Pezzente suggests a vision of Montreal that differs from the normative image of the city as an ideal incubator of musical production. Pezzente also highlights the direct role that municipal cultural policies play on a scene – in this case, the independent live music scene – and the need for continued work to create policies that are supportive of small-scale culture.

Emerging small-scale cultural activities also face the struggle of receiving funding and support in Montreal, as established, large-scale cultural activities tend to have easier access to cultural infrastructure funds. Pezzente characterizes the city as unfriendly towards live music, but this description might more aptly represent the city's attitude towards small-scale forms of cultural production. The city's attitude towards larger, industrialized forms of culture is markedly different from its attitude towards small-scale cultural production. In 2007, the City of Montreal developed a comprehensive ten-year action plan for itself as a creative city entitled *Plan D'Action 2007– 2017 – Montréal, Métropole Culturelle*. In theory, this plan targets both small-scale and large-scale culture, as it underscores support for "initiatives that encourage emerging artists and diversity" as well as for Montreal's well-known festivals and museums.[22] In practice, a primary area of attention and implementation in the inaugural years of the plan was the Quartier des Spectacles (QDS), a designated music festival zone in the downtown core that opened in 2009 and received $120 million in federal, provincial, and municipal funding as well as additional funding from private corporations. This heavily funded area contrasts with the support that small-scale spaces receive. Profiling the development of the QDS, Kelly Ebbels comments,

Small venues and festivals, which have played their own role in making Montreal an international culture destination, are struggling for attention. Compared to the QDS' hundreds of millions of dollars in investment, this year saw just a $90,000 grant given over three years to the city's Association of Small Art and Performance Spaces. Also this year, a new Industry Canada grant was announced for festivals – but only "marquee" festivals, with attendees of more than fifty thousand and an overnight touring plan, need apply. Just For Laughs and the Jazz Festival have already secured a significant chunk of this funding. Patricia Boushel, a producer at the celebrated Pop Montreal music festival, laments that the city's vision of promoting culture has amounted to supporting "hyper-funded areas of the arts – for artists who have gotten over their developmental phase," instead of for the smaller venues and creative forces at work on the edges. "As far as the city is concerned," she says, "the only festivals of value are Just For Laughs, Cirque du Soleil and the Jazz Fest."[23]

The mythology of Montreal's independent music scene suggests that independent culture thrives from being in the margins and out of the spotlight, but the example of the closure of the Casa del Popolo highlights the negative repercussions of the lack of attention and active support of the small-scale scene. The closure of the Casa for a year can affect hundreds of bands, who will not perform, as well as the surrounding infrastructure of bartenders, promoters, and poster artists and distributors whose employment revolves around live music. A lack of support for developing artists and for the spaces in which they create and showcase their work also means a lack of support for small-scale youth practices; continuing to fund these "hyper-funded areas of the arts" because they are seen as economically viable and profit-producing may mean a neglect of community development and sustainability and a lack of attention to the role of youth within communities.

These challenges faced by small-scale artists and the infrastructure that supports them point to shortcomings in municipal cultural policies and their implementation. Since the publication of Richard Florida's *The Rise of the Creative Class* in 2002, the city has gained attention as a key locus of economic development, and considerable investments have been made in developing the "creative city," both in the United States and in Canada, as well as internationally.[24] In 2004, Nancy Duxbury characterized Montreal as an "Innovative

Knowledge City" in that "cultural activities are not seen as part
of the knowledge and innovation milieu" of the city.[25] The 2007
Montréal, Metropole Culturelle action plan reflects a shift in the city's
vision of itself towards a creative city in Floridian terms, as it suggests
the "'Montréal brand' consists of a number of 'products.' A few examples of these are the overall success of our creative work; the quality,
quantity and diversity of festivals; development of the Quartier international (international district); and our built heritage, particularly in
Old Montréal."[26] In this action plan, maintaining and developing this
"brand" is tied to the national and internationally competitiveness of
Montreal as a city, suggesting a larger-scale understanding of culture.
Discussing the "principles of practice" of taking "innovative action"
in communities, Duxbury underscores the importance of "visionary
fit," as "the community's vision must resonate with its particular circumstances and possibilities, including assets and constraints."[27]
Due to the attention Montreal's independent scene has gained at
home and abroad, counting this scene and its small-scale cultural
producers amongst the city's cultural assets would provide a more
accurate vision of Montreal. Thinking through what defines culture
in Montreal returns us to Colin Mercer's question of what counts and
what is counted in inventories of culture.

The City of Montreal may not have yet taken measures to actively
support the development of grassroots culture, but local small-scale
cultural producers also create their own infrastructure to enable this
development. Ian Ilavsky, cofounder of Montreal-based independent
record label Constellation Records, offers an alternate vision to
Florida's about investment in cultural infrastructure and mechanisms to develop a scene in a city.

> We [Constellation Records] had one band, Godspeed You! Black
> Emperor, who became [successful] – certainly [not the level of
> success that] now seems to come to the top end of indie bands –
> but that group of people, besides being incredibly politically co-
> herent in the decisions they made faced with opportunities with
> success also, without even thinking twice, took everything they
> made, which wasn't even a lot of money, and pumped it back
> into the local scene. The Casa [del Popolo] and the Sala [Rossa]
> [two important music venues] exist because Mauro [Pezzente]
> from Godspeed You! Black Emperor put the thousands of dollars
> he may have been making – and this was money that was being

split nine ways to begin with – back into getting that space started. The Hotel2Tango, which is one of a number of very good,
accessible recording studios in the city, and certainly not the only
one, survives because two of the principals in that studio took
whatever success they had and with real genuine commitment
put it back into the idea of building local infrastructure. One
way that Montreal has flourished which might be different than
other places … what everybody wanted was to encourage, by example, encourage other people, even in your own town, let alone
smaller towns and other places, to build up the same kind of
thing. I think that's a huge part of how Montreal has flourished.
There's lots of indie labels [but] people are not trying to become
the top of that pyramid. The same goes with venues. There's been
a non-hierarchical kind of spirit in this city at least that doesn't
get replicated everywhere.[28]

The success of Godspeed You! Black Emperor, and the work of the
various band members to open music venues Casa del Popolo and
Sala Rossa, as well as the recording studio Hotel2Tango, are part of
the origin story and mythology of the creative flourishing of the independent scene in Montreal, but this origin story needs to be recast
as one of commitment rather than escapism. Small-scale culture does
not spontaneously thrive in the vacuum of economic investment and
pertinent cultural policies; it needs continual labour for its development and maintenance. Florida emphasizes employees in creative
sectors and the economic draw that creative cities can have, but
Ilavsky underlines cooperation, small-scale investments, and the importance of key spaces and sites for nurturing a local scene and local
development. In short, it is a bottom-up rather than a top-down
vision. Florida envisions that bohemians attract creative professionals to a city, but rather than having these "bohemians" displaced by
cycles of gentrification, Ilvasky promotes of vision of working, maintaining, and investing in small-scale culture itself. Similarly, Pied
Carré works to anchor artists in the communities they have built
rather than have them displaced by real estate speculation.

Ilavksy's vision of Montreal also differs from Angela McRobbie's
outline of current trends in the creative industries that are based in
her research in London. Surveying how artists attempt to make a
living, McRobbie states, "gone are the kinds of radical and collaborative actions of the past which drew artists closer to marginalized

or disadvantaged groups; gone too are artist community initiatives ... [Artists] are radically disconnected and dislocated from 'community.'"[29] Celebrating the utopian potential of Montreal and its cultural offerings obscures challenges and labour, but collaborative and community-based projects do exist in this city, including the M60 film festival discussed in Chapter 1 and the Indyish art relays that will be discussed in Chapter 7. They may not be "radical" but they are of and for the community, and these collaborative and community-based efforts should be included in Montreal's branding of itself as a cultural metropolis.

One promising avenue to pursue a bottom-up vision of cultural planning within *Montréal, Métropole Culturelle* is its provisions for developing "quartiers culturels," or creative neighbourhoods, which the city began working on in fall 2011. In its orientation document for public consultation, the city states the vision for these creative neighbourhoods is "to enrich the ability of [Montrealers] to appreciate art, culture and heritage throughout the city as well as in its downtown core and to build on Montreal's reputation as a cultural metropolis in keeping with the identities and environments of the targeted sectors."[30] This vision includes broad plans for borough-based cultural development by targeting areas such as local cultural activities, promotion, transportation, urban planning, real estate, and management and coordination. In response to the city's request for public consultation on this creative neighbourhoods plan, Pied Carré prepared recommendations that advocate that this local development of culture be executed in a bottom-up fashion that protects local artists and their needs by targeting zoning, permits, and artist work spaces. For example, Pied Carré recommends that as the city transfers authority for local cultural development to the boroughs, these boroughs also need to actively include local cultural producers, cultural organizations, and citizens in their development of cultural action plans; these community partners also need to be allocated resources to be able to participate in these processes.[31] Mercer discusses that moving toward a cultural planning approach involves "bringing together ... diverse interests and stakeholders,"[32] including research, industry, and government sectors, as well the community sector, which "often has the necessary 'local knowledge.'"[33] The plans for these creative neighbourhoods had yet to be developed at the time of the publication of this book, but this area is one to watch to see if municipal policies are able to include and promote small-scale culture.

POSTERING AND THE ANTI-LITTERING BYLAW:
"MAKE A POSTER, PAY A NICKEL TO PHOTOCOPY IT,
AND GET THE WORD OUT THEMSELVES"

In Montreal, legal issues around postering flared in the spring and summer of 2010, and this postering issue reveals competing stakes and investments in independent cultural production and municipal policies. Studying the events around this postering issue offers an opportunity to see the labour and commitment involved in maintaining the independent Montreal scene and provides an example of how the case for supporting small-scale culture has been made. As per municipal bylaw Regulation 21(6) (RRVM, C. P-12.2), also known as the anti-littering bylaw, putting up posters on what is known as "street furniture" is illegal and punishable with hefty fines: for an individual, a maximum of $1,000 for a first offence and up to $2,000 for a repeat offence, and for a business, a maximum of $2,000 for a first offence and up to $4,000 for a repeat offence. For many small-scale cultural producers, be they individuals or small businesses, putting up posters on lampposts, electrical poles, and mailboxes is the most attractive, accessible, and available option to advertise events. Even in an age when information is rapidly disseminated on the Internet, the physicality of visible posters is still seen as a critical promotion tool. Meyer Billurcu, who has run his promotion company Blue Skies Turn Black for ten years (which will be fully profiled in the Conclusion), notes that postering is "still the most direct way of promoting ... The Internet's great, but people get bombarded, so stuff falls through the cracks. If you have a nice poster, it can really grab attention."[34]

Similarly, Hilary Leftick, executive producer of Pop Montreal, comments on the affordability of postering as a promotion tool for small events: "When we do shows at [small venues like] Cagibi or Casa, we're not going to take out ads in the newspaper most likely; we just don't have the budget to do that, but we're not going to not advertise. And we also feel that it is beautiful and it promotes a different art form, and there's a history and etiquette to postering. It's really important that young promoters and cultural entrepreneurs have the ability to make a poster, pay a nickel to photocopy it, and get the word out themselves, and realize that that's an option."[35] Here, Hilary explains that even for a more established music festival like Pop Montreal, postering is an important means of promotion,

especially when considering budgets for smaller events that the festival produces. Hilary also invokes the vital importance of postering
for youth and for emerging cultural producers due to the low cost
and the ability to do it for oneself that postering represents. Though
postering is seen as littering at the city level, Hilary suggests that
posters are in fact not a form of garbage but can be seen as a valid
form of art, created by young cultural producers.

Postering on "street furniture" is illegal in Montreal, but the city
has designated that postering can legally take place on construction
worksites. In a report prepared about the postering issue, L'APLAS
states that DIY postering is an affordable option for small-scale cultural production, and the alternative to DIY postering, paying the
postering company Publicité Sauvage, which posters on construction
sites, is not in the means of small-scale cultural producers.

> Let's discuss the exclusivity of the company Publicité Sauvage and
> the limits that it imposes on small cultural producers and on small
> venues. Postering on worksites with this company requires using
> a minimum size of 11" by 17" and printing at least 300 posters,
> because the minimum number of posters they'll put up is 300. If
> we estimate that the fee for this postering job is nearly $1,000,
> the cost-per-poster-per-spectator, if there are 100 spectators, is
> $10. Being that the revenues from concerts are already uncertain,
> these revenues from the concert would nearly be all absorbed
> by the postering, which is a necessary part of advertising for
> a concert.[36]

In addition to the small-scale sums that postering for oneself costs,
postering is a form of small-scale employment for youth. Billurcu
explains, "we pay someone to design a poster, and we pay someone
to put up a poster." With the looming threat of stiff fines, "now I can't
do that, so I'm putting people out of work. We do 150 to 200 shows
a year, so it adds up."[37] Blue Skies Turn Black pays posterers forty
cents per poster put up, and generally puts up fifty to two hundred
posters per event. To make postering a financially worthwhile activity, a posterer will generally put up several event posters at once. As
an employment and promotion mechanism, postering is an important part of making a living for some young cultural producers.

Postering has existed as an illegal practice for decades, but
Montreal cultural producers noticed a hardening in the city's and

the police's attitudes towards this practice and increasingly received fines through 2008 and 2009. For this reason, the postering issue was foregrounded as a pressing concern for many cultural organizations that coalesced together in the spring of 2010 under the banner of COLLE (Coalition pour la libre expression). Hilary is also a spokesperson for COLLE, and she chronicles the emergence of this network as follows.

> [Pop Montreal] was talking to a couple of other festivals about starting an organization to help share resources and that organization is Le Regroupment. By winter [2009] it established a name and mandate and everything else. At that same time, there was another group of different people interested in arts and culture – Cagibi, Le Pickup, Fringe Festival – and they were really interested in coming together to do stuff around the arts and cultural spaces and different issues that affect them. They decided that their biggest concern and the first thing to tackle, a good idea would be postering. At Le Regroupment, the way it was structured at the time was that we each bring projects to the table ... and [postering] was one of the things that I felt was impacting our organization [Pop Montreal, which had received $11,000 in postering fines] a lot. So I said I would like to work on postering at the same time that this other group came up. Postering was an issue for some of us at Le Regroupment, but not all, because some of us don't poster. That's sort of how this other group came about, and we called it COLLE.[38]

Hilary cites that not all members of Le Regroupment had a vested stake in the postering issue, but she also notes the simultaneous interest in this issue from many diverse parties. When COLLE formed, it counted music and theatre festivals, an independent bookstore and record store, music and theatre venues, as well as an organization representing small venues, L'APLAS, amongst its members. Postering might be most readily associated with the promotion of music concerts; however, this list of members suggests that a more diverse array of parties were negatively affected by the city's bylaw. Though Montreal's independent music scene is characterized by Stahl as an "Anglo-bohemia,"[39] COLLE brought together not only a diverse group of cultural producers, but also an array of both anglophone and francophone organizations.

COLLE set out to lobby the City of Montreal and work towards a solution to the postering issue. First, the network aimed to gather and publicize pertinent information. Hilary narrates the group's activities: "one of the first things that we did was we tried to outreach to as many people as possible to get an idea of the needs of postering, how many posters people put up, and also to get a sense of how much money and fines, to have a more global vision. We did two general assemblies. The first one to get all the details, and a second one to present our thoughts, and a summary of all the details. We also did a press conference between those two."[40] Through these general assemblies, COLLE attempted to compile and disseminate data to chart the economic and cultural significance of the events that postering promotes. COLLE discovered that its members collectively had $215,262.76 of unpaid fines from postering infractions. The group estimated that, collectively, its members produced three hundred thousand posters annually to publicize six thousand events.[41] Even if postering itself represents a small expenditure, its widespread use supports thousands of events, which COLLE members estimate generate an annual revenue of $15 million. This collected data about the impact of the anti-postering bylaw and the widespread practice of postering was used to lobby the municipal government, including a letter to the mayor and other contact with city officials.

Hilary suggests that the COLLE group was quickly able to come together and garner attention due to "collective interest; people were keen. And the fines kept coming – the problem had to be dealt with." The network did effectively solicit the attention of the city, but Hilary nonetheless describes the process of organizing the network as a "learning curve" because "you want to keep it informal, because you don't want it to be such a formalized network that is has its own administration and more work to deal with, but at the same time, when things are informal, then there's more risk for problems. How are decisions made? Is it a collective decision? Is it a majority decision?"[42] Hilary states that the members within the group had different ideas about how to work with the city and what potential solutions to the postering problem might be, but the group publically presented a "unified vision" of its goals and beliefs.

One element of the unified vision that COLLE emphasized on their website and in a press release is the importance of mechanisms to preserve the existence of small-scale cultural production. COLLE suggested that the city promotes itself as a cultural metropolis, but this vision of culture does not include small-scale culture: "Montreal actively promotes itself as a cultural centre and regularly celebrates the justified global renown of its many well-known artists and cultural events. However, the question remains as to whether this success and notoriety can be maintained in the longer term. The city's cultural life will only renew itself if enlightened policies are implemented which foster the development of new ideas, artists, tendencies and activities. The city therefore needs to broaden its outlook and develop policies with an eye to the future by supporting the smaller members of its cultural ecosystem rather than just the large ones."[43] Here, COLLE targets the impact of policy making on cultural production, and these remarks are suggestive of the need for a creative ecology framework to register the value and importance of small-scale culture. COLLE also stresses the role that postering has to play in the continued existence of small-scale culture: "Independent venues and promoters, and certainly artists, do not have the means to advertise through newspapers, television, or radio. Most of the 6,000 shows this community holds annually are announced first by means of posters placed on street furniture. As Internet-based calendars and cultural publications do not provide an effective workable alternative, postering continues at the risk of receiving fines."[44] To this end, COLLE suggests that small-scale cultural production needs to be taken as seriously as large-scale cultural production due its economic and cultural impacts.

COLLE also targeted the legal front when making the case for postering. COLLE highlighted the 1993 Supreme Court decision in Peterborough, Ontario (*Ramsden v. Peterborough (City)*, [1993] 2 S.C.R. 1084), in which the Supreme Court of Canada overturned the City of Peterborough's anti-postering bylaws and declared them unconstitutional. Kenneth Ramsden received two postering fines and successfully fought them on the grounds that anti-postering bylaws are at odds with the freedom of expression protected in the Canadian Charter of Rights and Freedoms. In its ruling, the Supreme Court cited postering as "historically and politically significant" because of the important societal role that posters can play: "it is clear that postering on public property, including utility poles, fosters political and social decision-making."[45] COLLE made use of the *Ramsden v. Peterborough* decision in its campaigning to argue for the validity and legality of postering, as well as to call for the City of Montreal to find a means to deal with postering rather than banning it altogether.

As COLLE began working and garnering media attention about the postering issue, the city also made strides to work towards a solution to this problem. An economic adviser to the city was appointed to look into the issue, and the concept of legal postering spaces in the form of "collars" was put forth at a city public meeting on 5 July 2010.[46] In this incarnation of the legal postering proposal, rubber collars of twenty-two inches across and several feet tall would be wrapped around existing "street furniture" and on new postering pillars. The collars would be a legally designated space for postering, so the bylaw concerning the illegality of postering in other areas would remain. COLLE's position was that the legally designated postering collars were a "positive first step," but the group also raised questions about the number, location, and design of the collars, amongst other issues. Hilary states, "there's some concerns among members of COLLE that [the city] are just doing it now to get it done. How's it going to grow? What happens if they don't put the things in the right spot? The city is very concerned with how it's designed and looks – [but] what are the rules for these things? Can you post any time? Does it have to be two weeks before your event? Can you post three of the same poster on the same collar? There's all these logistical issues."[47]

Before the city had to delve into these logistical issues, another legal decision further compromised the illegality of postering. In 2000, renowned activist Jaggi Singh was fined for putting up posters for the Montreal Anarchist Book Fair. After a ten-year legal battle, on 15 July 2010, the Quebec Court of Appeal overturned the Quebec's Superior Court's prior decision to uphold Singh's penalty. Singh's argument that the fines were unconstitutional was supported by the Court of Appeal, which "declared the anti-littering bylaw 'invalid.'"[48] Hilary explains that the city acquiesced to this ruling, "and then those court decisions came out, which really kind of made [COLLE's] job a lot easier, because the city was basically mandated to find a solution, and because we had been working with the city on something, and they realized it was a problem and there was no point on spending money to fight it. They would just not fight it."[49] As a result of the Quebec Court of Appeal's decision, the legal postering collars were put in limbo. It was thought that this legal decision would create a moratorium on postering fines in Montreal due to the uncontested new legal invalidity of the bylaw against them. Many COLLE members hoped to carry on business as usual and resume their normal postering practices. On its website, COLLE member Pop Montreal reported, "postering is legit. Somewhat. It's been a while since we've updated you all on the postering issue, reason being that there are no real updates to provide. Until there are formal municipal furnishings for your posters, you can still put them up on poles."[50]

Despite the Quebec Court of Appeal's ruling, fines for postering continued. Scott Johnson Gailey, a posterer, describes continuing to receive fines and have run-ins with the police through the summer of 2010 and into 2011. With regards to postering, he states, "I thought this was okay to do." He explains, when being ticketed, "[the police] never respond as to where you are supposed to put them up … They won't tell you what bylaw they are ticketing you under."[51] When contacted to comment on this issue, the Montreal police lacked relevant information, as I was informed the ticketing was continuing while the city appealed the Quebec Court of Appeal's decision, but no such appeal is taking place. The City of Montreal referred me to borough rather than municipal anti-littering bylaws. Jaggi Singh spent ten years working on overturning the legality of municipal postering bylaws, but since 2002, municipal legislation has been shared between Montreal and its boroughs. Some Montreal boroughs have their own anti-littering bylaws or have enacted new ones. For example, the downtown Ville Marie borough, home to the Quartier des Spectacles, passed a new "cleanliness" bylaw on 13 November 2010. This bylaw, RCA-24-085, contains the same provisions against postering that were in the overturned city-wide bylaw. That this bylaw was newly enacted after the city-wide one was struck down suggests a lack of attention to the importance of small-scale culture. It also suggests that the *Montréal, Métropole Culturelle* vision for Montreal as a creative city has not adequately thought through what mechanisms and infrastructure are needed to support small-scale creative practices.

PROJECT NOISE: "TOTAL AND COMPLETE INCOMPREHENSION"

Though the Quebec Court of Appeal ruling in July 2010 initially was thought to bring a tentative resolution to the postering issue, another clash between small-scale cultural production and municipal cultural policies in Montreal occurred in the same month. In the Plateau borough, local government adopted a resolution known as Project Noise, which increased the cost of noise fines given out to bars and clubs. Formerly, these fines were in the realm of a few hundred dollars, but the Project Noise initiative increased these penalties to a maximum of $12,000. Plateau borough mayor Luc Ferrandez has stated that these new hefty fines were aimed at clubs and discotheques that pull in large revenues and that regularly incur noise fines, but choose to pay the fines rather than invest the money – upwards of $40,000 – that soundproofing requires. Amongst those most concerned and potentially impacted by these changes, however, were small venues where live music is regularly performed; these small venues do not have the financial ability to seriously invest in soundproofing or withstand these increased penalties for noise complaints. The cofounder of small venue Le Divan Orange, Lionel Fouronnet, comments, "two of these fines, and we close."[52] The closure of a small venue due to noise fines is significant because such venues serve an important role for the incubation of independent cultural production and employment.

In addition to the severity of these fines, small venues raised objections that they were not consulted or notified about Project Noise. L'APLAS (L'association des petits lieux d'art et de spectacles) is an advocacy group that champions the role that small venues play in developing small-scale cultural production; the group has worked to oppose Project Noise. In a news bulletin about the increase in noise fines, L'APLAS director Sebastien Croteau raises this issue: "Before the hardening of present noise laws and the start of Project Noise, the city and elected officials could have put a consultation process in place that included citizens and people involved with the independent music scene. From this consultation process, solutions and strategies could have emerged. The borough also could have met with interested parties and made them part of the project of dealing with noise laws, including building awareness. In brief, the city could have started a dialogue and demonstrated that it understands and takes to heart its role as a cultural metropolis."[53] This lack of notification and dialogue with pertinent parties suggests an undervaluing or misapprehension about smaller venues and the potential impacts of Project Noise on them. This lack of awareness about small venues was also suggested at the 2 October 2010 Pop Montreal symposium panel about Project Noise, as Croteau related that the police commander of the Plateau borough has stated that Société de développement du Boulevard Saint-Laurent (SBDSL) was informed about the changes in noise fines, but not all small venues are members of this organization, or are situated on Boulevard St Laurent.

While the Project Noise fines seemed to be a serious and daunting problem facing small venues, Croteau suggests that noise fines are only "the tip of the iceberg" of the problems that threaten these venues and small-scale culture in general. In order to avoid these hefty new fines, many small venues would have to invest in soundproofing, but this is beyond their financial means. In a L'APLAS news bulletin, Croteau explains that larger venues receive public support in the form of funding and subsidies for equipment, programming, and promotion, but small venues do not. Small venues often rent rather than own the spaces that they operate in, so they cannot access public funding. Because of the difference between renting and owning, investing private funds into a building that a venue is renting from is not a logical choice. As Croteau states, "a small venue that is not the owner of its building would never risk investing large sums of money in soundproofing. Why not? With the non-renewal of its lease, the small venue could find itself having uselessly invested this money. This 'risky renewal' argument is also used by funders to justify not supporting small venues."[54] To combat this problem of the possible non-renewal of leases and the futility of investing in a potentially vulnerable space, Croteau suggests that mechanisms need to be put into place so that small venues have the means to access ownership of the spaces that they operate in: "Where should we start? Through access to ownership of the property? Support for programming? Soundproofing? Equipment? Probably on all fronts at once because these elements are interrelated. Therefore, it's the ensemble of problems that we have to consider if we really want to help small venues. We cannot only pay attention to one of these elements (noise) and hope to solve the problem with a single attempt."[55] According to Croteau, supporting small-scale culture means tackling this complex mix of underlying issues and their interrelated nature.

Croteau also highlights the impact of gentrification on small venues, as they are vulnerable to complaints from neighbours and landlords who may want them out of the spaces they occupy to make way for more lucrative new condos and residential developments. For this reason, noise complaints may not all be warranted. At the Pop Montreal symposium panel about Project Noise, Alexandre

Lemieux, who formerly ran the small venue ZooBizarre, discussed his decision to close his venue after being targeted by frequent noise complaints.

> We closed out of our own choice, but because we had too much pressure. Pressure from the police and from the neighbours about the noise. So we decided to close because we weren't necessarily in a solid enough place to go to battle. The first two years of the business went very well, and we had a good relationship with our neighbours. Then one day, a new neighbour moved in and decided to declare war. He took his battle to the borough, and the borough mayor made a personal case out of it for political gain. They sent the police and the police started to hassle us. ZooBizarre is a venue that has a capacity of 120 people. Sometimes the police would show up for a noise complaint when there were only eight people present. They would come in with their flashlights during a poetry reading. It became like that every week – every week, our neighbour called the police and more and more police showed up. So we gave into the pressure.[56]

Lemieux related that it is at the individual and subjective discretion of the responding police officer to decide if a noise complaint is warranted. To add to this discussion, Croteau stated at the symposium that these noise complaints, even if unwarranted, accumulate in a complaint file compiled on the venue in question. Although ZooBizarre closed due to Lemieux's decision to not continue to fight the police and the city, Croteau explained that accumulated noise complaints can cause the non-renewal of a small venue's liquor license, which would mean the end of a small venue, as they tend to almost exclusively operate on the funds made at the bar.

In Montreal, venues other than ZooBizarre have been adversely affected by noise complaints and have developed different solutions to deal with this problem. At the Pop Montreal symposium, Croteau gave the example of the Bobards venue on St Laurent, which was initially surrounded by commercial spaces. A developer bought up these spaces, and they were rezoned as residential and converted into condos. While the new residents were ostensibly conscious that they were moving into a space next to a music venue, noise complaints about Bobards started to accumulate, and the owner of the club decided to rent the apartment beside his venue to avoid some of these complaints. Croteau stated that this type of problem emerges because it is too easy to convert a commercially zoned area into a residential one to the detriment of small venues. Rather than rely on small venues to come up with creative solutions to these changes or perish, Croteau suggested a new "cultural zoning" designation to preserve the precedent of existing small-scale cultural infrastructure. He commented that small venues, like Casa del Popolo or Le Divan Orange, may not be able to survive a move, as they are tied to the particular spaces that are situated in.

> Small venues develop the culture of their neighbourhoods and it's very important that they can stay where they are. For example, I don't know if Casa del Popolo or Le Divan Orange could survive a move. Often, there's no financial support for that. So it's very important to work to anchor these venues in their communities. One of the only ways to anchor them is to make it so that they can access owning the building that they rent from. There's presently nothing to make this happen. These venues develop a whole infrastructure – a whole life forms around these venues, and they are negatively affected by laws and rules. They are certainly affected by the complete lack of public financial support and subsidy.[57]

Venues are not only tied to their neighbourhoods, as they also play a vital role in developing their neighbourhoods. Rather than having them fall victim to changing property values and zoning designations, and subsequent eviction out of their spaces, Croteau suggests developing means to anchor these venues in their neighbourhoods.

All of the complex problems enmeshed in the noise issue that Croteau identifies would take considerable time to remedy. In the short term, Croteau advocates that police use sound-level meters so that objective measures of noise are registered in decibels. At the symposium, he stated that some of the venues represented by L'APLAS are afraid of objective evaluation of noise levels, but he countered that without them, small venues will constantly be fighting their infractions, and wondered, "Do owners of businesses have the time to contest [their infractions] each time in municipal court?"[58] Croteau further argued that there are objective measures and instruments to evaluate drunk driving and speeding and a similar approach should be adopted towards noise violations, or small venues will always be at the mercy of the subjective judgment of the responding police officer. Beyond this short-term solution, L'APLAS attempts to raise the visibility of small venues so their importance as incubators of culture is understood. Due to the absence of pertinent quantitative data about small-scale culture, Croteau has initiated a study with Université de Montréal to quantify the impact that small venues have in terms of numbers of concerts, revenues, employment, etc. However, he also recognizes that it is difficult for artists and other stakeholders involved with small venues to get involved in such initiatives because they are constantly in "survival mode" and do not have a developed reflex towards mobilizing and pursuing collective action regarding issues that concern them. At the symposium, he asked, "Do people like Alexandre [Lemieux, ex-owner of ZooBizarre], who do the administration, the bar, the booking, and the mopping have the time to participate or do that kind of thing?"[59] Those involved with small-scale cultural production often take care of many different aspects of their enterprises; as such, they may be particularly vulnerable when they do not have the time to fight against incidents that arise. In addition to developing quantitative data to demonstrate the significance of small venues and the value of supporting them, L'APLAS has also spearheaded other initiatives, such as organizing a mini-bus tour of small venues and producing a map of small venues to be distributed by Tourism Montreal.

At the Pop Montreal symposium, Croteau opened by characterizing a "total and complete" lack of comprehension of municipal administrators about the "underground" scene. Nonetheless, he disputed some commentators who have suggested that the Plateau borough mayor has declared open war on the independent Montreal scene. Croteau cited the mayor's awareness and clemency towards the many small venues that are operating with a bar or restaurant permit instead of the required salle-de-spectacle permit. Through his participation in borough-initiated public meetings about measuring noise levels and subsidizing small venues' soundproofing costs, Croteau comments, "Right now, I have complete faith in [the borough's] willingness to solve the problem ... They are walking the walk and talking the talk, so it's fine."[60] While there may have been a little progress with the Plateau borough and the Project Noise issue, the series of events with the postering and noise problems suggest a pattern of calamitous events impacting small-scale cultural producers, agitation, and later response from the city and boroughs rather than developed or existing underlying support and awareness.

This agitation needs to be registered when envisioning the independent cultural production scene in Montreal, not to merely suggest a city of strife, but to record the labour involved in maintaining favourable conditions for cultural production and to work towards safeguarding these conditions through supportive cultural policies. Tracking these small details – permits, posters, sound levels – provides a way to register the challenges faced by emerging cultural producers and enhances the picture of their navigation and negotiation process of making a career. To cast Montreal's independent scene only as an escapist utopia limits the ability to register this process of navigation and negotiation and, in turn, limits the ability to make a case for supporting young cultural producers through these challenges. COLLE and L'APLAS offer case studies of how community members may create their own initiatives to facilitate this navigation and negotiation process, and in Part Three, I turn to a more detailed examination of the role of youth artist networks in supporting youth cultural production.

PART THREE

Initiatives

7

Beyond Subculture

The Role of Networks in Supporting Youth-Led Initiatives

As we have seen in Part Two, youth working in the creative industries are impacted by structures and policies that both enable and circumscribe their activities. In Chapter 6, we saw how youth create initiatives to respond to some of these constricting structures. Part Three continues this examination of how youth develop initiatives to assist their navigation and negotiation of the creative industries and investigates youth organizations. "Youth-led" refers to organizations that "maintain 51 per cent or more of the decision-making power in the hands of youth and young adults," and "youth-involved" refers to "organizations which involve youth and young adults to varying degrees in their decision-making processes."[1] This chapter examines youth-led networks and their roles in facilitating youth cultural production.

DEFINING NETWORKS

As those working in the fields of youth culture and subculture studies move away from characterizing youth subcultural activities as necessarily oppositional in nature, the term network has been used as a means to capture and discuss the infrastructure of grassroots youth movements. Henry Jenkins discusses old theoretical models of subcultural innovation and mass media co-optation and attempts to think of better ways to characterize grassroots activities: "The old rhetoric of opposition and co-optation assumed a world where consumers had little direct power to shape media content and faced enormous barriers to entry into the marketplace, whereas the new digital environment expands the scope and reach of consumer activities. Pierre Lévy describes a world where grassroots communication is not a momentary disruption of the corporate signal, but the routine way the new system operates: 'until now, we have only reappropriated speech in the service of revolutionary moments, crises, cures, exceptional acts of creation. What would normal, calm, established appropriation of speech be like.'"[2] Jenkins's work and comments here draw on media and media making in relation to communication, but these remarks are useful for conceptualizing other kinds of youth activities, digital or not. Though Jenkins highlights the expansion of consumer activities through the digitization of media, investigating the mechanics of networks can also be a way to foreground cultural production. As a concept, networks might be a way to register "normal," "calm" grassroots activities and foreground the mechanisms and infrastructure that are needed for these activities to maintain a sense of normalcy and calm. The term scene might also be able to do this type of theorizing, but this chapter expands this examination to networks, as this is a term that some youth groups have chosen to describe their activities. In the era of social media, networks may have become ubiquitous, and accounts such as Jenkins's may sometimes be overly celebratory of the utopian potentials of digital technologies and the networks they enable. Conversely, this chapter foregrounds the challenges, contexts, and material conditions in which specific youth artist networks occur.

Networks may be "calm," but this tranquility does not necessarily mean that the activities in question are apolitical. For example, the riot grrrl movement of the early 1990s involved a subcultural infrastructure that, while initially centered around Olympia, Washington, diffused nationally and internationally. Doreen Piano comments that the DIY feminism that was central to this movement and its forms of cultural production "can be seen in the emergence of a polymorphous infrastructure of grrrl-related cottage industries that include the production of not just music, but zines, stickers, crafts, mixed tapes, and alternative menstrual products."[3] The diffusion of the riot grrrl movement out from its origin point and its focus on cultural production can suggest the need to re-evaluate the traditional theorizing of subcultures that early Centre for Contemporary Cultural Studies (CCCS) work characterized as localized and symbolic in nature. In opposition to these types of conceptualizations, Piano comments on "the political praxis of resistance being woven into low-tech, amateur, hybrid, alternative subcultural feminist networks" in the riot grrrl movement.[4]

Here, the lens of the term network may allow for an investigation of the mechanisms through which low-tech amateur movements can disseminate and low-tech amateur skills are developed, shared, circulated, and mobilized. Chapter 6 discussed that scenes have been most often conceptualized as music scenes, and while the concept of scenes may also be useful to conceptualize other cultural formations, networks do not necessarily have these resonances of music-based cultural production. In *Beyond Subculture: Pop, Youth and Identity in A Postcolonial World*, Rupa Huq introduces new terms that perform theoretical work "beyond subculture," or terms that are used to denote practices, affiliations, and formations that the term subculture is said to not adequately capture. In discussing the feminist formation of riot grrrl, Huq forwards the term network, as does Piano. This term draws on Gilles Deleuze and Félix Guattari's concept of horizontally rooted rhizomes, and Huq deems it useful to describe riot grrrl's exploration of other forms of cultural production besides music, such as fanzines, and to suggest a dispersed geographic base behind a subculture.

The youth-led organization Ignite the Americas, which will be discussed in detail in Chapter 8, defines networks as "groups of individuals or organizations who share information, ideas and resources in order to accomplish individual or shared goals. Networks usually possess a common interest or concern, while maintaining flexible connections amongst their members."[5] Though the language above is generic and neutral, Ignite the Americas is not an apolitical organization, as it is interested in establishing infrastructure for youth artist networks to move towards positive social change by including youth in community building and government decision-making processes. The term network is able to suggest the amorphous and flexible boundaries of an organization, but is also able to capture the purposeful, action- and goal-oriented mandate of many groups that come together under the rubric of a network. These goal-oriented mandates may also differentiate networks from some of the more "ephemeral" qualities of scenes.[6]

LIMITATIONS OF NETWORK AS A CONCEPT AND A TOOL

The concept of the network is not only used by theorists and youth organizations to characterize youth activities. Kate Oakley notes that this concept has been taken up by the British government in its conceptualization of people's involvement in the creative industries, and she argues that the government's leveraging of this concept does not work towards social inclusion and equity. Oakley explains,

> New Labour [creative industries policy] was focused firmly on the creative individual or independent. It accepted that such people were, or at least thought of themselves as being, highly individualistic, anti-authoritarian, and in some cases, anti-corporate. The "downsizing" of the 1980s had convinced them that the job for life was unattainable and possibly undesirable and that work could be about self-expression, as well as personal enrichment ... Not only was New Labour interested in re-designing the role of public services to aid individual empowerment, but it was also keen on encouraging new forms of collaboration. The site of this collaboration had changed, the network rather than the trade union, say.[7]

Networks may be prized as a new site of social organization, but they do not and cannot perform the same work as trade unions in terms of safeguarding employment and other rights of labourers. Youth affiliations seem to be moving away from trade unions, but this points to the need for continued work to develop mechanisms and policies that intervene in areas of inequity and vulnerability. In the British context, New Labour's championing of networks moves away from a definition that suggests formalized youth-led organizations; its meritocratic discussion of "networking" and "collaboration" assumes youth have informal contacts they can mobilize for self-advancement, which differs from the above discussion of network as a concept. This slippage in terms is not innocuous, and though the British government's rhetoric of networking assumes that the "'creative economy' [is] one in which everyone could play,"[8] there is a lack of equity in black and ethnic minority participation in the creative industries. Despite the rhetoric of access for all, emphasis on "networking" and "collaborating" is exclusive rather than inclusive, as it relies on informal mechanisms that people from disadvantaged backgrounds may not have access to and may reproduce hegemonic power structures. In order to work away from a celebratory usage of "networking," this chapter makes a distinction between formalized youth networks and informal networking.

Oakley problematizes the British government's take up and celebration of networking, but surveys of youth and their development of professionalization in the creative industries also cite networking as an area of need. In the *Next Generation of Artistic Leaders and Arts Audiences Dialogues* report, networking was identified as an important tool for artists but also as an area of unequal access.

Networking was described as the ideal way to foster information and resource sharing between arts communities. It also had potential benefits in terms of fostering creative collaborations and cross-disciplinary activities. Many participants, particularly those in urban locations, said they informally network but in an unstructured fashion. Artists and arts professionals from rural and isolated communities struggle to network with other artists outside their immediate worlds, and, as a result, felt they could benefit from more formal networking activities. Some participants drew analogies between the culture of networking in the business world and that of the arts scene and felt there was a strong need to create, foster and maintain more networks for young and emerging arts practitioners in Canada, either online or face-to-face. In particular, participants from rural and isolated communities said they would benefit from more networking and collaborative opportunities with urban artists.[9]

In the Canadian context, the divide between urban and rural areas means a divide in access to informal networks that often form in urban centres. Formalized youth-led networks may be on the rise, but an increase of youth at the helm of organizations may not correlate with correcting this problem of inequities in networking. A report supported by the Laidlaw Foundation about the emergence of youth-led work, *Foundations & Pipelines*, notes the difficulties that even those involved in youth-led work have networking with others: "The current situation does not provide a strong mechanism for youth organizers to connect with each other and access the mentors, partners, training and resources and networks that can enhance their work. Sustained support is needed to ensure ongoing development at the individual, group, and community level in youth organizing work."[10] Nonetheless, networks remain an important area to investigate when mapping youth activities and the logistics of careers in the creative industries. The organization that is profiled in this chapter, Indyish, has elected to use the term network to describe the nature of its activities, and I chronicle the activities of this youth network and investigates the role it plays vis-à-vis the professionalization of youth cultural production.

INDYISH: BACKGROUND AND OVERVIEW OF ACTIVITIES

One of the founders of Indyish, Risa Dickens, describes it as "a network of independent artists who co-author a website ... We do collaborative events together ... [It is] a mass of artists, mostly local, musicians, fashion designers, jewellery artists, independent publishers, writers, visual artists, filmmakers."[11] The name of this network, Indyish, invokes the "Independent" demographic that Charles Leadbeater and Kate Oakley discuss and the "indie" prefix that is often used to denote small-scale forms of cultural production, but the move from "indie" to "indyish" is suggestive of interpenetrations between art and commerce and entrepreneurial models of youth creative work. While Indyish operates online, it is also organized locally in Montreal around events and collaborations between artists. Risa explains the importance of collaboration and personal networks in getting the Indyish project off the ground: "I harassed a few friends in each [of the above stated] areas, and other people that I knew – [after that] I'm very interested in working through the links in a network. [All of the people that I knew] had huge artist networks ... I just started working through those networks." Through these informal networks of personal contacts, Risa has created a more formalized structure that is based out of pooling the contacts, knowledge, and opportunities that individual members have access to.

Indyish has a boutique to sell cultural products on its website, but Risa suggests that the purpose of Indyish is not to merely allow artists greater opportunities to make a living, but is also to allow for more opportunities for collaboration. She states that "the idea is not just to use the site to sell the stuff, but to co-author the site, and to want to work together at some point ... when we do projects like The Assembly, it's open to wider [participants] than just the artists who are on the site." The Assembly was an Indyish art relay project that took place between 10 February and 10 March 2007. To begin, writers wrote scripts using Celtx.com, a free open-source film and theatre pre-production software. After the writers uploaded their scripts to Celtx, filmmakers downloaded the scripts and put together a short film, and finally musicians added a soundtrack. Using the Celtx software allows for ease in the relay process and for artists from dispersed areas to work together on the same project.

These collaborative and interdisciplinary events are at the heart of what Indyish aims to do. When its website was being launched, Indyish hosted a music video making contest in which bands donated a song and up-and-coming young videographers made a video for the song over a twenty-four-hour period. Risa describes that, during the same period,

> we got factory seconds donated from the local garment area where we were doing all these events, and we gave them to designers who signed up and they made clothes for twenty-four hours. There was a local design collective who judged, and they were only slightly more established than the young designers who came out for it, so the judging was really more like meeting them, and talking to them – it was a really positive experience for some of the emerging designers. We threw a big event where you could see the art and see the bands and we projected the music videos.[12]

Indyish also started hosting a monthly "Mess" in 2007, which Risa characterizes as a "curated variety show," but "instead of [the performers] being just very different acts, we'll curate them around a theme ... We try to bring people together around who would be inspired by a topic." Messes have included musicians, dancers, circus performers, film screenings, comedians, and also academics, authors, and other speakers. The Messes have had eight to fifteen acts each, which means that at its biggest, the Mess has had sixty different performers and ten staff, all working on a volunteer basis. Risa states that the principle behind the Mess is that "we operate on zero budget and don't do things that can't pay for themselves." As the motivation behind the Mess is not to make a profit (admission is pay-what-you-can), Risa and the Indyish staff are free to select smaller and fringier acts, which provides opportunities for emerging artists.

These types of events create end products that get showcased, but these initiatives also act as support mechanisms that foster the professionalization of youth cultural production. Connections are fostered between participants at events who otherwise may not come in contact with one another. Risa speaks of the "loose positive effects" of Indyish and gives the example that bands that played together at the Messes and have later gone on tour together. Because the Messes are purposefully curated to include different types of performers from different scenes, performers also often gain new audiences outside of their usual circles. In order to offer further support to emerging artists, Indyish maintains a web presence, and staff "work hard on getting traffic to the site through search engine optimization – technical stuff that helps people get noticed." The site also includes a blog that chronicles local events, and Risa states that "artists will get in touch because we've written about them and play a future show or join the network or come to a show." Through these mechanisms, Indyish offers points of entry for collaboration and growth to young cultural producers.

CHALLENGES

While it may be easy to celebrate the creation of collaborative and interdisciplinary events and the support and opportunities that they offer for emerging artists, this work is not without its challenges, beginning with space. Risa explains that "trying to find venues that are the right fit for us is really hard." Not-for-profit community events require spaces to house them, and the rental fees associated with even small venues may be beyond the budgets of these events. Additionally, Risa notes difficulties with securing long-term funding because a network is neither exactly a business nor a not-for-profit organization: "We've tried for a couple of grants, but really found the grant process distracting and demoralizing. I just don't feel like grants are targeted at us. We tried and we looked and we always felt like we were doing yoga back bends to fit ourselves into what they wanted. We don't fit … We run a very strict, tight, little, specific thing. If we're going to grow, it's going to be somehow in that. I feel like there was [the suggestion from granters to] 'become a small business.'" Here, Risa addresses the limited models that are available to categorize youth creative practices in the current granting system. Risa also comments that current models of best practices in the arts are often structured around growth, which may pose problems "for being intentionally small."

> Not that I want a pat on the back. For example, we do these
> art relays, there were sixty people all around the world, passing
> scripts. We didn't print anything. It was entirely web-based. The

company that supported it gave us USBs, so everyone was trading stuff on USBs. There was zero paper trail for this project that lasted two months and had hundreds of people involved by the end. There's no backwards environmental "you didn't create waste." We biked for the whole project ... Everything is set up from the perspective if you're this big and you create this much waste and you reduce it by 10 per cent, congratulations! We never got that big; we didn't make that big mess. We're just trying to do small community things: there should be something more to support it.

Contemporary youth cultural production may be entrepreneurial but also community-oriented, and current funding structures have difficulty registering the hybrid and intentionally small-scale nature of some contemporary youth cultural production.

In addition to these challenges of space and funding, Risa also foregrounds the struggles associated with needing to formally legitimize the network through business registration. This registration is based on the notion of profits and revenues and, as such, might not be appropriate for youth cultural production in its emerging phase.

If you're going to do anything entrepreneurial at all, you need to register yourself immediately and start paying taxes four times a year and start jumping through what feels like at the time scary scary paperwork hoops, where you're like, "we're not making any money, so how can I ... and I'm spending all of my time and I'm working another job to do this ... Why would I register?" Why does this need to be a business? So they can have a number to track us? I can't take all of that on for something [incorporating] that doesn't give me anything. Especially for youth projects – we have so many people coming to us, saying, "you've started a cooperative, tell me how I can go about it" ... The first thing they want to do is register ... You can get obsessed on how to do that starting detail right, and you get on the other side of it and you have no idea. You have to still work every day to figure out what your business is going to be and how it's going to work, and you should get to do that for a couple of years before you're killing your brain trying to file these taxes for money you haven't made.

Risa characterizes the requirement to officially legitimize youth practices through registering as a small business as not only distracting from the start-up work of getting projects up and running, but also at odds with the needs of contemporary youth as they engage in the creative industries. Her comments suggest that different streams of policy may be more appropriate for youth small-scale practices in the creative industries.

[There should be] some type of other policy that addresses those types of projects, and funds them, and gives them grants. Like a start-up project. You can run a start-up project for three years, register for twenty dollars instead of eighty dollars, get a number, if you make over X amount, then you send the thing in and you come and now you start paying taxes, but until then, now you're one of *these other things*. Those other things, well, there's special programs for them, especially if you're making it into a job for yourself. If it's just paying you, then you don't need to do all the other [stuff]. If you're going to do the simplest possible thing, that's ok, and we'll help you. Maybe that exists?

Risa's remark about "these other things" illuminates the qualities of some forms of contemporary youth cultural production – "other" to recognized forms of business and cultural production and currently unnamed and unrecognized in policy structures. Her statements about the challenges surrounding the expectation to incorporate are echoed by other youth organizers. In the *Foundations & Pipelines* report about youth-led organizations, one respondent comments, "Could small groups rather than be incorporated or have a trustee, work in an infrastructure – how do these groups have a safe space to try their idea, get charitable dollars, get access to administrative infrastructure, mentoring, capacity building support from someone before they are expected to be a legal entity? Do they even need to become a legal entity?"[13] Greater knowledge about the boundaries of contemporary youth practices may be a starting point to appropriately deal with "these other things" and put some of these recommendations into practice.

Need for Support for Youth Spaces

One policy challenge that Risa highlights above is the need to find suitable spaces to house youth activities. Indeed, Rinaldo Walcott comments on the importance of youth having spaces in which to do cultural and community work: "In my view what we need are programs that will allow young people to engage with and make sense of the ways in which they can contribute to the culture of their communities and beyond. Such an approach means providing young people spaces where they can offer a critique of the culture and society and offer up alternatives."[14] The challenge, then, is to create infrastructure that includes physical spaces where this work can take place. Academics such as Walcott discussing this need for physical spaces marks a departure from the emphasis on youth subcultures symbolically "winning" spaces that emerged from early CCCS work.

The desire for more physical space is often foregrounded by youth cultural producers and youth arts organizations. The Canadian Youth Arts Network held town hall meetings in Toronto in 2008 to survey needs and desires of youth cultural producers. Concerning space, the document that was prepared following these focus groups, *So Much Things to Say: Report II*, states,

> It's no secret that the youth art sector not only desires, but also requires physical space. It was felt that a central network with regional locations is vital in order to strengthen the youth arts sector. In addition, it was widely understood that a strong sense of legitimacy is gained when energy is collected under one roof. Many of the youth that were invited to participate in the focus groups were between the ages of 19 to 25. Therefore, most of the participants understand this issue first hand, as they are currently out of school and no longer have an institution to house their work. Space that has been made available is normally borrowed. Therefore, you are always working within someone else's limitations.[15]

This report cites that the need for space is particularly acute amongst emerging youth cultural producers who are transitioning between the fields of education and work and who are beginning the process of establishing themselves in the creative industries. One proposed solution was exchanging and sharing space between youth arts organizations. According to Kehinde Bah of The Remix Project, "a co-operated space would also encourage shared resources. [During the town hall meeting] it was stated, 'A lot of time you buy the equipment and do the project and then it just sits there. I think it would be cool to have a centralized spot. Let's say you want to do a photography project, now you don't need to put that in the grant.'"[16] Shared spaces could allow for the sharing of resources and for collaboration and networking. As such, physical spaces may be able to play a supporting role in the professionalization of youth creative practices beyond housing and facilitating individual cultural production.

When the Arts Network for Children and Youth (ANCY) produced their *Undervoiced Voices: Strategies for Participation* report, they set out to gather information about what kinds of changes youth arts organizations would like to see in current funding structures; they found that these organizations desire physical infrastructure to facilitate programs with youth. Respondents noted that the programs most frequently requested by youth are those that are arts and culture related, such as music, theatre, and dance, and that these types of activities "require a significant amount of space and that busing the youth to locations outside the neighbourhood doesn't work, as, 'they simply don't show up.'"[17] One of the strategies that the *Undervoiced Voices* report cites for "improving mechanisms to enhance undervoiced racialized youth participation" is increased funding for space: "serious funding consideration must also be given, in collaboration with corporate partners who have appropriate real estate holdings, to developing and improving infrastructure / creative spaces for youth arts programs."[18]

Physical infrastructure was also targeted by ANCY in its proposal, *Creative Spaces for Children and Youth*, which was submitted to the Ministry of Finance for the 2009 stimulus budget. The first recommendation of this report is for the creation of a "Creative Spaces Children and Youth Infrastructure Fund," which would require "a beginning investment of $50 million to be used for pilot infrastructure projects in urban, rural, and remote and First Nations communities."[19] Targeting rural, remote, and First Nations communities is important to work towards greater equity in creative industries participation, as these areas receive less support than major urban centres. The Canadian government allocated $60 million to cultural infrastructure in Budget 2009, but these funds were not specifically earmarked for spaces for youth, as was requested by ANCY. This organization cites that the youth-specific spaces that are currently being built are correctional institutions and mental health facilities rather than creative infrastructure. The *Creative Spaces* report elaborates that this creative infrastructure could include "small neighbourhood art / creative centres"; "multi-disciplinary art / creative centres with artists, equipment, and supplies"; "new green multi-disciplinary facilities where training is included in the construction"; "facilities specifically designed for older youth"; and "facilities in rural, remote, and First Nations communities."[20] ANCY suggests that the creation of these types of facilities "will ultimately not be a drain on public funds" as this investment will provide a return through "costs savings to other sectors, job creation, and most importantly, the improved overall health of our children and youth."[21] A creative ecology framework could be useful to advocate for the creation of these spaces, as it forwards connections across sectors and can make links between the creation of youth spaces, youth engagement, employment, and community development.

Difficulties with Grant Writing and Limitations with Funding Streams

The second policy challenge that Risa suggests, in her comment that her experience of applying for grants was like doing "yoga back bends to fit ourselves into what they wanted," is the limitations of current cultural funding. Risa's experience of attempting to find funding for her network but having difficulty in matching her initiatives with funding streams is a common experience for many youth cultural producers. In the *Next Generation* report, "some participants who work in multidisciplinary practices said they were confused about which funding streams are appropriate for their work."[22] To this end, one of the "future directions" that was recommended for arts funders was an awareness of the "multiplicity" of contemporary young artists: "Increasingly arts funders will need to recognize that arts practitioners are not solely invested in singular aspects of creative practice or sectoral employment. Many participants have multidisciplinary orientations and work many different types of jobs to support their creative work. This is of particular relevance when discussing categorization of practice, eligibility criteria and assessment of artistic achievement with arts funding bodies."[23] These comments foreground the need for more awareness about the characteristics of contemporary youth cultural production. These characteristics might include interests across different funding silos and for-profit and not-for-profit streams as well as pursuing unrelated paid work outside of creative pursuits.

Like the *Next Generation* report, the *Undervoiced Voices* report also contains a myriad of recommendations about grant application, including streamlining application processes, requiring less detail, allowing for alternative application formats, having staggered and flexible deadlines, and increasing allowable expenses to include food and public transit tokens.[24] Rather than address the concern of multiplicity from the perspective of interdisciplinary work, the *Undervoiced Voices* report foregrounds diversity from the perspective of youth from ethnic and minority backgrounds and suggests that the grant application process needs to be altered to allow for more equitable distribution of funds to youth arts organizations and youth from marginalized backgrounds. One way that the *Next Generation* report suggests altering the grant application process is through coordinating funding applications of municipal/provincial/federal levels, as there is no cohesion between the various levels of government and their arts programs. The *Next Generation* report recommends "allowing for sufficient space between different deadlines (so that organizations can have enough time to prepare strong applications), or by allowing organizations to apply all at once for different funders using a standard application form."[25]

Lack of Support for Small-Scale and Emerging Youth Practices

The third policy challenge that emerges in Risa's comments is a lack of support for small, emerging community-based projects. In the *Next Generation* report, many young artists describe that contemporary models of youth cultural production do not follow standard models of growth and specialization: "many participants believe that the existing arts infrastructure, which emphasizes specialization, linear career development and clear role delineation, is not reflective of their current reality."[26] These emerging artists felt that the different pathways and characteristics of their work needed more recognition: "participants generally agreed that young and emerging arts practitioners represent a distinct community and that arts funders need to do more to understand the attitudes and pressures they face."[27] Many participants also cited limited levels of experience with the granting process as young emerging artists and voiced concerns about the genre of grant writing. They felt that funding may be allocated to those who have the best grant writing skills, which are skills that many emerging artists do not feel fully confident with. This concern is present amongst young artists and arts organizations. The *Undervoiced Voices* report recommends "establish[ing] a funding graduation process, recognizing emerging and established organizations. Three specific funding categories are suggested: a) emerging with one primary service, b) established with one primary service, and c) established with multiple services."[28] This report also recommends establishing small-scale funding, such as "a program of small grants ($500–$2,000) aimed at individual youth or emerging collectives of youth."[29] This desire for support for small-scale practices harkens back to Charles Leadbeater and Kate Oakley's suggestion that emerging "Independents" in creative fields need access to small sums or "micro-credit."[30] The challenges that Indyish and other youth arts organizations face illuminate the shortcomings of presenting the value of the arts through underscoring their economic significance, as not all arts organizations are working towards becoming economically significant, and this is especially true when dealing with youth practices in the creative industries.

Lack of Available and Accessible Information

When Risa wonders, "maybe that exists?" after she articulates a model to better support artist networks, she raises a fourth policy challenge: more access to information about support structures for youth cultural producers. While Risa has navigated available grant channels, and is correct that there is a lack of available funding streams that speak to her organization, she is not sure if there are or are not funding categories that cover "these other things." Some streamlined information does exist in websites like www.canadaart.info, which provides an overview of federal and provincial grants, but Risa voices uncertainty about which grants or funding categories would be appropriate for her project. In the *Next Generation* report, many participants voiced confusion about funding streams and available programs. It should be noted that these youth responders were selected to participate in the study from a "long list of candidates culled from records of grant applicants, community contacts, suggestions from arts organizations, service organizations and schools."[31] This would suggest that the young artists who were selected were amongst the most aware and engaged with the infrastructure of funding programs, yet

> many artists said they are unsure or unaware of many of the services and funding streams that are offered to them. In many

cases, artist recommendations for improving existing programs
or creating new programs were similar to those already offered
by various funders, or by other government funding streams.
This was especially true with regards to funding streams for multidisciplinary works, collaborative projects, and those directed
specifically at young and emerging artists. Participants were also
largely unaware of existing online directories and resources currently available on arts funders' websites. Young and emerging
artists said they are at a disadvantage and lacked access to informal information-sharing networks that funders use to disseminate information.[32]

A proposal that emerged out of the Canadian Youth Arts Network
town hall meetings was to create a centralized hub to better share
information concerning the arts, as "youth know that the resources are out there," but these resources are "scattered and isolated."[33]
The hub was envisioned as "an umbrella organization [that] provides the youth art sector with the connections, resources and expertise to strengthen the community rather than fragment it."[34]
Information about resources need not only come from experts or
from a centralized hub, as youth at these town hall meetings also
desired forums to facilitate "informing one another about what is
being done. Opportunities need to be designed that allow the network to share their stories."[35]
   As we have seen, youth-led artist networks offer unique opportunities for youth to set their own agendas and work towards better
facilitating youth involvement with the creative industries and the
professionalization that this entails. However, youth artist networks
are not a cure-all to gaps in cultural policies and narrow funding
streams. Nor are they a solution to problems of unequal access to
employment in the creative industries. The existence of youth networks demonstrates the ability of youth to create initiatives and
infrastructure to support their own practices in the creative industries and demonstrates the need for resources and information-
sharing, as this is what many networks aim to provide. Chapter 8
furthers this discussion of the possibilities and limitations of youth
networks by profiling an international youth artist network and
examines not only how this artist network sets its own agenda but
also how it attempts to partner with governments to work towards
better supporting youth creative work.

Community-Based Models of Youth Involvement with the Creative Industries

Ignite the Americas and The Remix Project

Youth involvement with the creative industries may not always register in academic research or in government policies, but this lack of presence of youth does not preclude the possibilities of youth–government partnerships that have yet to fully materialize. This sort of partnership offers one potential avenue for better supporting youth involvement in the creative industries, and Ignite the Americas is one youth-led network that takes up this possibility. In 2008, I observed the Ignite the Americas conference that was held in Toronto and brought together youth delegates from North, South, and Central America. The initial Ignite conference in 2007 was Toronto-based and gave rise to the idea of a national youth network, the Canadian Youth Arts Network, which is now on hiatus; the scope of Ignite the Americas is international, as it operates in conjunction with the Inter-American Committee on Culture (CIC) of the Organization of American States (OAS). The overt purpose of the 2008 conference was for the youth delegates to prepare a presentation of recommendations in the areas of toolkits, policy, and networks to bring to a meeting with ministers of culture and authorities of the OAS at the Royal York Hotel on 19 September 2008. This meeting was conceived as a first step in possibly creating a broader partnership. As the post-forum report states, "the purpose for coinciding Ignite with the CIC meeting was to lay the foundation for stronger and enduring partnerships between young people and government, so that arts and cultural policy can be better informed by local realities. In concrete terms, the main goal for this meeting was: To explore how young peoples' voices/experience can contribute to decision-making."[1] Though many youth arts organizations have raised the desire for more youth involvement in decision-making processes that affect them, the Ignite the Americas conference offered the possibility to take up this desire in a tangible way.

The 19 September 2008 meeting was the first occasion of youth being invited to an OAS meeting and, as such, marked a unique opportunity for youth–government dialogue. Speaking to the youth delegates a few days before their meeting with the OAS, Canadian Governor General Michaëlle Jean commented, "this unprecedented, and dare I say revolutionary, partnership between the OAS and the pan-American youth arts sector is really laying the groundwork for movement that can not only ignite but also shake up the Americas."[2] Jean's comments suggest that this partnership between youth and government already signifies real change in the ways in which government organizations conduct their business and that this partnership will continue to affect change in the world. Although Jean's rousing rhetoric suggests that positive social change is not only desired but has already and will continue to happen, we need a closer examination of the possibilities and challenges of youth engagement with their governments. If current cultural policies do not reflect contemporary youth realities, can youth themselves participate in creating a more youth-centered agenda for government? Can youth agendas be heard by governments? Can youth initiatives be transformed into government policies, and can these policies be put into practice? These questions are ones that Ignite is grappling with, asking policy-related questions in their documents, including "What roles [have] arts and culture ... already played in building community at both a local and national level? What kind of role can Government play in the growth of the culture industry? What should a partnership between government and young people look like?"[3]

IGNITE THE AMERICAS: MISSION AND RECOMMENDATIONS

Ignite the Americas operates on the principle that art is a vehicle for social change and youth engagement. The organization maintains a heavy focus on the role of youth in social cohesion, but it equally underlines the economic impact of the arts and their contribution to community development and makes connections between these areas of youth inclusion and economic/community development. Ignite's website underscores the "increasingly important role that arts and cultural expressions play as an engine for economic growth,"[4] and the Ignite conference *Policy Primer* suggests that good governmental policy links economic growth with sustainable community development, and sustainable community development includes youth engagement: "Funders should encourage their grantees to understand and articulate how their services/project fits into larger community development goals. They should be challenged to ensure that they are working with various approaches that engage diverse youth populations, particularly those who are marginalized."[5] One way the organization suggests that economic development can be linked with youth engagement and community development is by using the arts to combat the violence and crime that many youth face in impoverished areas. Ignite's website states, "arts and cultural activities can and do significantly contribute to economic growth, the reduction and the prevention of violence by strengthening human potential, generating resilient community ties, augmenting self-esteem, and developing skills in young people that can allow them to secure decent jobs."[6] These links between youth engagement and employment through the arts, economic growth via development of the creative industries, and sustainable communities are consistently found throughout Ignite's documents. The organization's post-forum document states, "when young people feel excluded from meaningful opportunities in society, there is a greater risk of them leaving the mainstream for the murkier waters of crime and violence. However, the arts engage young people and combat social exclusion by providing them with a constructive outlet for their frustrations, while also providing a way of transforming those frustrations into positive, tangible and sustainable economic activities. Globally, arts and cultural expression have proven to be effective vehicles in facilitating integral development strategies within our societies aimed at building healthy individuals, communities and economies."[7] Due to this articulation of youth, the arts, the economy, and communities, Ignite the Americas holds a unique vision of the purpose of the arts and the role that youth have to play within economic and community development.

The commitment to youth cultural production as a viable economic and community development model is not the only noteworthy characteristic of Ignite the Americas; the organization also presses for more statistical research in the field. One of Ignite the

Americas' key principles is the need for accurate data to demonstrate the social and economic impacts of the arts. The organization's executive director, Che Kothari, was invited to speak at a follow-up meeting to the Ignite conference in September 2008 at the Fourth Ministerial Meeting of Cultural Ministers and Highest Appropriate Authorities in Bridgetown, Barbados on 21 November 2008. His summary of the youth delegates' recommendations at the OAS meeting in September included the need for adequate data collection in the arts. He stated,

> Our case for culture becomes infinitely stronger as a unified force; so, these impacts must continue to be mapped, measured and then shared across the Americas. We must build this as a movement. We must also remember to not only focus on the quantitative data, but all of the qualitative impacts that are much harder to measure, but really help tell Culture's story. We must work together on all levels to get this message out to everyone: that culture is a leading solution, which is not being given the attention and support it deserves ... We must work together to effectively measure the impact that Culture is having across the Americas by continuing to develop Cultural Information Systems. By doing so, we will be building the extremely needed case for Culture. This information needs to be derived from all levels, from grassroots arts movements to fine arts practices. There is a plethora of examples that I can provide of youth arts organizations that effectively combat violence or that have built their own local cultural industries.[8]

Kothari cites both quantitative and qualitative data as part of making the case for culture, and though many may individually know "a plethora of examples," mapping and collecting these stories in "Cultural Information Systems" is proposed as a way to strengthen the case for culture. Some academics as well as organizations like the Canadian Conference for the Arts (CCA) and L'APLAS have pointed to the need for more data collection and mapping of the creative industries. Kothari extends these calls to also advocate for maps of youth engagement with the creative industries. After CCA director Alain Pineau held national forums to consult the public about how to best make the case for culture, the CCA published a report that included a call for better data collection.

Everywhere, people agreed that there is a need for more data and analysis concerning the arts and culture sector. There is currently a certain quantity of research done by various government agencies, administrative tribunals, universities and by some arts service organizations. Most of the time this work is done to satisfy punctual requirements. However, hardly any of this research is done in a coordinated fashion and it is almost impossible to know what is available. Even more importantly, years of successive budget cuts at Statistics Canada have meant that less and less fundamental data is made available to the sector to present fact-based arguments in its attempts to make its case to the various levels of government.[9]

When the CCA calls for more data collection in order to make the case for culture and develop a "national cultural advocacy strategy," it does not foreground the role of youth in making this case; conversely, Ignite the Americas always includes the role of youth when strategizing how to make the case for culture.

Another significant aspect of Ignite the Americas' mandate is its desire to have youth involved in decision-making processes that affect them. In many cases, youth organizations voice a desire for youth to participate in funding juries' decision-making processes. In the *Next Generation of Artistic Leaders and Arts Audience Dialogues* study, participants stated that "arts funders should create a separate system or pool for first-time applicants. First-time applicants should be assessed by a jury of emerging artists."[10] This desire is also foregrounded in the *Undervoiced Voices: Strategies for Participation* study of youth arts organizations. The recommendations include "establish[ing] an adjudication process which would include decision-making power for funders, youth and young adults" and "improv[ing] the structure and effectiveness of the individual and collective funding bodies by amplifying diverse, racialized youth voices in decision-making contexts such as juries and boards of directors."[11] Ignite the Americas goes past the desire for youth inclusion in funding decisions, as the organization hopes that youth can be involved in shaping the direction of cultural policies through their involvement in decision making of this sort.

During the conference in September 2008, the youth delegates suggested that the recommendations they were putting forth required a shift in the way art is sometimes conceptualized, and many attendees voiced that a model of advocating the intrinsic value of "art for art's sake" must be broadened in favour of a model of art as a vehicle for social change. As such, they desired that the OAS validate and dignify the important and transformative role of art in society. They also desired that the ministers of culture from their respective countries open channels of communication with youth. Delegates commented that youth are too often seen as the source of social problems, but if they were asked to work with governments, they could be part of the solution to these problems. Ignite the Americas suggests that change needs to happen so that these goals can be reached, not only with a redefinition of art's role in society, but also with what is included in governments' definitions of art. One of the organization's preparatory materials for the youth delegates, the *Policy Primer*, states that "there is a need for governments to recognize various non-traditional forms of arts,"[12] citing examples of "street art forms" and "amateur arts." Underlying this broadened definition of art is the need for more recognition and validation of youth cultural production, as youth are often involved with emerging and non-traditional forms of art.

The recommendations that youth made during the conference were informed by their involvement with the arts, both as practitioners and as organizers. For example, Choc'late Allen, the youth delegate from Trinidad and Tobago, and the youngest youth delegate to Ignite the Americas at the age of fifteen, is both a reggae recording artist and an activist, and works to integrate art more fully into curricula in Caribbean nations. Allen works with Caribbean Vizion, a group of young artists and educators that use performing arts to sensitize youth about issues such as teen pregnancy and drugs. This work has been officially endorsed by the Caribbean Community (CARICOM) secretariat, UNESCO, UNICEF, as well as many regional heads of governments. Many of the youth delegates at Ignite do similar kinds of work, and in a debriefing session the day after the meeting with the OAS, many youth delegates expressed that the most powerful thing that they took away from the conference was the contacts that they had made with like-minded people across the Americas who do work that is similar to their own. Many delegates also discussed a strong desire to maintain the contacts and network that they had formed during the conference to be able to share struggles and best practices.

IGNITE THE AMERICAS:
CONFERENCE PROCEEDINGS

During the week-long conference, Ignite the Americas' youth delegates developed a series of recommendations that were presented at the OAS meeting and later published in a post-forum report. In the area of toolkits, youth desired templates for starting a small enterprise or a community initiative, for finding funding and finances, for communicating and working with governments, and for general mentorship and guidance. They also desired toolkits that included a central funding calendar and case studies/stories that share successes and challenges. In the area of networks, the delegates sought the development of a Pan-American Youth Arts Network that would "advocate for youth arts across the hemisphere; serve as a forum for exchanging best practices and promoting inter-cultural dialogue; [and] improve/sustain government and NGO relations."[13] Delegates desired that this network would have regular face-to-face meetings, an interactive website/portal, radio/television/web broadcasts, and a quarterly magazine to ensure dissemination of information for those, especially in rural areas, who do not have Internet access. In the area of policy recommendations, the youth delegates made proposals in five main areas: "incorporate the voice of youth in governmental decision-making processes; encourage evaluation and demonstrating value of arts & culture through promising programs; strengthen arts education; build capacity & develop and share resources; support ongoing local, regional, national, and hemispheric meetings for practitioners and practitioners + governments."[14] While Ignite the Americas may seem unique in its conception and vision, none of these recommendations are radical in nature: the commonplace nature of these recommendations points both to the lack and need for infrastructure for youth in the creative industries.

At the OAS meeting, the presentations of these recommendations went smoothly, but many youth delegates later voiced disappointment with the lack of response that they received from the OAS delegates who were present. This lack of response seemed to suggest a gap between the official invitation to be present, and the actual reception of the youth, and may also suggest that the "revolutionary" change that Michaëlle Jean spoke of in her address to the youth delegates has not yet materialized. Youth delegates were seated with the oas delegates from their countries, but only about half of the oas delegates attended the meeting, as it was a preparatory meeting for a ministerial meeting in November 2008 in Barbados. Many youth felt that their proposals had a lukewarm reception and wanted more dialogue with the ministers present. Generally, those ministers who did speak said that the proposals made were good ones, but the youth delegates commented that they did not want to be congratulated on their efforts; they were seeking feedback and engagement with their ideas. Several ministers commented that the delegates' proposals were valid for all artists, not just youth artists. Although these comments were delivered in encouraging tones, they also disparage the youth-specific challenges in the creative industries that the youth delegates were attempting to address and may suggest the difficulty of getting a youth-specific agenda put into policy. Some ministers also stated that several policies and tools that the youth were recommending already exist in some countries, but these remarks ignored the recommendation to create databases that compile existing programs and best practices across the Americas, such that youth can be more aware of these existing structures.

During the meeting, a discussion emerged about funding, as some oas representatives expressed that the youth delegates' proposals required funding that governments either did not have or that would take time to procure. Some youth delegates chafed at this suggestion, commenting that governments have money for war, but not for art. One delegate commented on the August 2008 cuts to Canadian art programs (PromArt and Trade Routes) and suggested that these cuts to Canadian arts funding send a negative message to developing nations where there are still struggles to have the importance of arts education understood. According to Anna Upchurch, Canada has indeed played a leading role in commitment to cultural policy and infrastructure.

In the international field of cultural policy, Canada has often assumed a leadership role in the decades since the Canada Council was established. It was a charter member of the United Nations Educational, Scientific and Cultural Organization (unesco) when that body was established in 1946, and it has consistently taken an activist position in definitional debates and trade issues around cultural diversity. The Canada Council organized the first world summit of arts councils in December 2000, with its major objective "to lay the groundwork for an effective and sustainable global network of national arts councils and arts funding bodies"; the International Federation of Arts Councils and Culture Agencies (IFACCA) evolved from this summit.[15]

With Canada's 2008 cuts to its arts programs, delegates were unsure if Canada actually retained this leadership role.

The OAS representative from the United States asked the youth delegates what could be immediately done by the OAS to support youth practices that would not require funding. Answers to this question included greater youth involvement in planning processes, greater recognition of freedom of expression and youth creative practices (e.g., recognition that graffiti is a form of artistic expression, not a crime), greater involvement of experienced artists in running programs for youth, greater recognition of the arts as a vehicle for social change, and greater recognition of the arts in education systems (e.g., the Jamaican delegate desired a public performing arts high school, and a public museum of reggae). Ignite delegates also desired to be formally recognized as youth ambassadors for culture. At the meeting itself, these desires were neither accepted nor rejected, as they did not get any direct response. Although the Ignite the Americas conference was intended to be a partnership between youth-led initiatives and governments, some delegates felt wary of working with governments altogether, later stating in a debriefing session that governments want to keep citizens under control, not create change. Some youth delegates felt that their efforts should be directed towards mobilizing citizens instead of governments. Discussing models of governance and government engagement with non-governmental actors, Caroline Andrew and Monica Gattinger foreground the challenges for governments "in thinking about appropriate structures and processes" but also the challenges for the public: "if citizens and civil groups want to have influence, they have to make use of techniques that governments can understand."[16] The challenges of youth–government partnerships may not only emerge from resistance or reluctance on the part of government, but may also emerge from reluctance to engage on the part of youth, or inability/lack of desire to use rhetoric and strategies that are government-friendly, such as refraining from critiquing governments' engagement in war when requesting funding.

IGNITE THE AMERICAS: THE AFTERMATH
AND THE COMPLEXITIES OF POWER AND PRIVILEGE

In a debriefing session the day following the meeting, many delegates discussed further challenges that arose in the process of working towards engaging with a governmental body. Some youth stated that during their week in Toronto, they felt too bogged down with working on the recommendations to bring to the OAS meeting and did not have enough time to share their experiences with one another. Delegates were asked to bring examples of their cultural production or community involvement in the arts with them, but there were few opportunities to share these works with one another. Due to the short time in which the conference was organized, pre-conference communication was limited, and some delegates were unaware of the actual purpose behind travelling to Toronto. Some expressed a desire for more preparatory materials before they arrived. Some delegates noted that the rigid schedules they had to follow and output they had to produce were at odds with their cultural backgrounds and desired more informally structured time to connect with one another. There was also some miscommunication and confusion about industry leaders who were brought in – successful young people who work in the creative industries – and who were given cars, twice the per diems than the youth delegates, and were lodged in a nicer hotel (many delegates voiced concerns over the cleanliness of the hostel they were lodged in). The role of these industry leaders – experts to consult – was not made transparent, and some youth delegates questioned that an industry leader was chosen as one of the representatives to make a presentation at the OAS meeting: the youth delegates did not know that this industry leader was not in fact one of them.

Some delegates forwarded these concerns not only in terms of organizational problems, but also in postcolonial critiques of power and voice. Due to the predetermined task of putting together a set of recommendations for a meeting, the Ignite the Americas conference organizing team hired professional facilitators to work with the delegates. Many delegates voiced satisfaction with their overall experience, including that with the facilitators, and found the opportunity to meet with government officials and communicate their concerns and desires to be empowering. However, many delegates also critiqued the facilitation process. One delegate commented that she resented being told by facilitators that she didn't understand the themes that were meant to be discussed. Another stated that he felt he was being asked to paint inside the lines that someone else created. He suggested that a colonial mindset was in evidence through the facilitation process, highlighting the symbolism of inviting in four white people as facilitators when the delegates were predominantly black and Hispanic. After this discussion, one of the conference coordinators commented on the complexities of power and privilege and asked everyone to continue to be aware of this. Even after this dissatisfaction with the facilitation process was expressed, the facilitators returned to do a final closing activity. Delegates were asked to write down their goals and commitments for the following two weeks, two months, and two years concerning how they would carry on their work at the conference in their home countries. There was some opposition to working with pens and paper, and some youth wanted to talk about their commitments instead of writing them down. The activity proceeded anyways, and the youth delegates wrote down their commitments to be kept on file. This final activity of the official proceedings of the conference revealed a disconnect between the official purpose of the organization to be a youth-led initiative that works with government and the reality of being required to complete an activity by an outside body. These issues around power and voice represent another layer of challenges when working towards youth-government partnerships.

IGNITE THE AMERICAS:
MODELS OF YOUTH ARTS

The Ignite conference may not have ended on a note of overwhelming success, but the group will continue to attend OAS meetings, and the potential for effective youth-government partnerships remains. Certainly, Ignite's unique vision of the role of the arts is one to retain. Other organizations make connections between youth arts and employment or discuss youth engagement through the arts, but Ignite offers a more holistic vision. The Grassroots Youth Collaborative's study, *Youth on Youth: Grassroots Youth Collaborative on Youth Led Organizing in the City of Toronto*, surveyed youth-led organizations operating out of Toronto about struggles and best practices. This report showcases some youth organizations that make links between youth creative activities and economic development, but these links are more limited in their conception in comparison to Ignite the Americas. For example, the *Youth on Youth* report gives an overview of the ways in which one youth organization, Regent Park Focus Youth Arts Media Centre, has been able to create employment opportunities for the youth involved in its creative projects, as organizations such as Canadian Union of Public Employees have hired the Regent Park Focus youth to make videos. However, these connections between youth creative activities and economic opportunities are not an explicit part of Regent Park Focus's vision. Their website emphasizes the primary mandate of youth engagement through the arts: "Regent Park Focus is a not-for-profit organization located in Regent Park, Toronto. Regent Park Focus is motivated by the belief that community arts and participatory media practices play a vital role in building and sustaining healthy communities. Regent Park Focus seeks to increase civic engagement and inspire positive change by giving youth the tools and support to create artistic works and media productions."[17] While youth engagement through the arts may occasionally produce economic opportunities, youth creative employment is not specifically targeted in this model.

In contrast to Ignite the America's broad mandate, this focus on the psychological/individual development aspects of the arts is more often seen in youth arts organizations. For example, the rhetoric of self-expression and voice is evident in the remarks of the program co-coordinator at Regent Park Focus: "Media is an outlet that is different because a lot of youth don't have outlets where you can express how you feel and have people actually listen to you. So when you are on the radio or on video you just feel more important ... We try to encourage this through the video and radio show, to identify issues that relate to youth. We hope that they are making videos about real issues that they are facing in their lives."[18] For many community youth arts organizations, the foreseen end result of their programs is that youth will have gained opportunities to express and empower themselves. Bronwen Low argues that "giving voice" through media production has been seen as a mode of empowering youth: "Hopes of 'giving voice' to the disempowered have also long driven documentary film production more generally. Recent decades have seen this commitment take the form of increasingly participatory structures in which filmmakers give cameras to those who have traditionally been objects of others' representation and interpretation. Much of this work takes place within community-based media programs in which the education and empowerment of the filmmakers-in-training is the foremost objective."[19] Low problematizes the vision that the access to the tools of media production automatically equates with youth empowerment as this "vision glosses over the intricate politics of representation, of speaking and of listening, which inevitably shape all forms of cultural production and reception."[20] Though "giving voice" might often be cited as a way to empower youth, Low suggests that the politics of "giving" this voice involves complexities of power that are often not grappled with. Digital technologies may be democratizing in terms of allowing access to the tools of cultural production, but these tools themselves cannot grapple with the politics of representation.

Elsewhere in the *Youth on Youth* study, the economic and career potentials of youth arts are questioned by those working in the field, and this suggests the challenges behind Ignite the Americas' mandate. One interviewee, commenting on youth arts programs, states, "I think that it's really popular and it's using popular culture to attract youth ... I guess what is a concern to me however is that the Caribbean background youth aren't [going into] other career skills development programs ... They are getting involved in music production and DJ-ing, anything around music ... and I think the music industry has targeted [Black] youth as well [i.e., by reproducing the Blacks as entertainers and entertainers only stereotype]. That's what concerns me about that."[21] Here, the arts as an employment pathway is portrayed as potentially limiting for black youth, but this view perhaps does not see cultural production skills as viable long-term employment skills. This bifurcation of cultural production from viable skills is echoed elsewhere in the *Youth on Youth* study. One interviewee states, "We teach them more life skills and experiences and dealing with business situations and dealing with people and overall communication skills and leadership skills. That's more important than them becoming a better rapper because the chances of being a rapper is slim."[22] The implication here is that communication and leadership skills are transferrable skills that can be taken to other non-creative industries or lines of work. This view does not take into consideration that the "life skills" developed in the process of learning to become a "better rapper" might also include acquiring skills that are necessary to navigate the mechanisms of employment in the creative industries themselves. Drex, one of the coordinators of The Remix Project, emphasizes that through the process of pursuing a music career as a performer, other kinds of employment within the creative industries might be found because there are "job opportunities within these industries that people might not even realize are there that might be interesting to them and more realistic."[23]

The *Youth on Youth* study also cites a similar concern about the viability of creative industries employment from the parents of participants in youth arts programs.

> One difficulty faced by organizations deploying the arts as a medium of youth engagement concerned the devaluation of art as a worthwhile activity, based primarily on its perceived inability to in any way further the career potential and/or marketable skills of youth. Parents and youth "don't think of the arts as a way to continue their schooling," Adonis Huggins, Program Co-coordinator at Regent Park Focus for instance contended of the challenges of using arts as a youth engagement tool. Staff working in communities with high concentrations of immigrant and/or working-class youth also spoke of the tendency of immigrant/working-class parents to prioritize and support more traditional educational forms of programming with seemingly more fungible skills transfer, over the arts, which was sometimes perceived as a luxury ill afforded to those already facing systemic barriers to full entry into the Canadian workforce.[24]

These systemic barriers to employment are important to recognize. In the *Youth on Youth* study, these criticisms about the value of the arts are answered by forwarding that art programs do facilitate entry into the workforce through fostering social skills that are integral to job readiness. The arts are seen to teach "tangible and intangible career and life skills"[25] and are valued for their "indirect" benefits. One youth arts program coordinator comments that the arts are "an opportunity to gain life skills, like problem solving, working together, creativity, decision making … employment, setting goals."[26] The indirectness and looseness of these links between cultural production and employment might mean that these programs do not fully serve the youth who attend them, as these youth may have a clear and direct conception of their desired involvement in the creative industries. Many youth are seeking out channels to make careers for themselves in the arts rather than channels of self-expression and job readiness by attending youth arts programs. Robin Wright, Lindsay John, and Julia Sheel's *Edmonton Arts & Youth Feasibility Study* profiled youth arts programs and notes that "youth were interested in media and in anything to do with making their own music videos, filming, singing, hip hop/breakdance – all activities directly part of their own youth culture. Youth expressed interest in making careers in these fields."[27] Careers in these fields require more than training in the skills of artistic production; for example, training in the "business of art" is often highlighted in studies of youth needs in the creative industries. The *Next Generation* study found that "small business expertise was considered a key need for emerging artists and participants. Most wanted to see more support for the development of these skills among young and emerging artists."[28] Because of this disconnect between youth desires and the rubrics under which some youth arts programs run, organizations like Ignite the Americas offer opportunities to study and explore different models of the role of the arts in the lives of youth.

YOUTH ARTS AND CAREERS IN CREATIVE INDUSTRIES: THE REMIX PROJECT

Ignite the Americas makes interesting connections between youth engagement and creative industries employment in their mandate, but they are not the only organization that makes these links. For example, The Remix Project is a Toronto-based program that assists youth in entering into careers in the creative industries, describing itself as a "youth program that acts as an arts and cultural incubator." The Remix Project's programming is specifically employment linked, and creative career development is foregrounded in its program description: "Young people aspiring to start careers in the urban arts sector drive the program by developing personal six- month plans for success."[29] Here, The Remix Project underscores urban arts, and the description of the program's history on its website explains the importance of hip hop in its origins: "carry on tradition. From its roots in the South Bronx, hip hop is a movement driven by community, passed down from generation to generation. Our intent is no different. Started in the fall of 2006, The Remix Project is a program designed to help youth develop their careers in the hip hop/urban culture industry. We draw on the support of Toronto's own cultural industries and institutions, to provide them with all of the knowledge they need to be successful."[30] While hip hop is described here as an integral part of The Remix Project, hip hop and music production are not the only components of the program. One of The Remix Project's founders, Derek Jancar, also known as Drex, describes Remix's facilities, in particular its recording studio with "top of the line" equipment, as the "sexy" part of Remix.[31] Similarly, cofounder Gavin Sheppard refers to music and art as the "Trojan horse" that intrigues youth to come to The Remix Project and gets them to open their "gates."[32] Once these gates are open, youth learn life skills, and Gavin outlines that the "three exit strategies" of The Remix Project are "education, workforce, entrepreneurship."[33]

Origins, Early Days, and Growth

The Remix Project makes direct and explicit links to cultural employment and entrepreneurship, and the history of this youth program demonstrates the need for these types of support systems for youth who want to make their way in the creative industries. The Remix Project originally began as Inner City (I.C.) Visions in 2000, when Gavin and Drex started a "hip-hop recreational centre"[34] funded by the Lakeshore Area Multi-Services Project in the South Etobicoke area of Toronto. Gavin describes I.C. Visions as a "drop-in program, where it was turntables for public use, open mics, graffiti walls, and stuff."[35] Originally run in the basement of a community centre, the program grew, and Gavin and Drex sought out ways to expand its facilities and services as they noticed a desire from the youth frequenting the program to move forward in their careers.

> People who were winning these MC battles, they would come here and be like, "Ok, I'm winning these battles but I have no idea how to get myself out there." We were like, "we don't know either." And so we started to bring in industry professionals to talk about the industry and how it was working and where it was going and what not. And then people were like, "Ok, so I'm getting some notoriety in the neighbourhood for winning the battles, I'm learning about how to promote myself and build press kits and grassroots marketing and what not, I still can't afford to get into the studio." So people had found out that Drex had started a studio at his home, and all started going to his

house. And we were literally getting thirty, forty people coming to his house, which was crazy.

As I.C. Visions accumulated more participants, this growing process involved grappling with how to assist youth with the logistical and economic sides of cultural production. Because of the demand from youth coming to his house, Drex decided to start a more formal recording studio. Gavin states,

> Again, we moved – to the basement of a small business centre – and we started getting kids from as far east as Ajax, all throughout Scarborough, Jane and Finch, Regent Park, but then, Rexdale, Brampton, everywhere, coming in. It was insane. And we would have fifty, sixty kids showing up on a Sunday afternoon to drop in to use the studio and we could probably accommodate about twelve. And it was madness in there. We had two part-time staff [Gavin and Drex]. It was a very small operation, literally self-funding the studio side of it. We would take the money we made through our part-time salary and pay the rent for the studio, and, after hours, we would work the studio to make our own money to live off of. So it was a really insane time. The most frustrating aspect of all of that, though, for us, was having so many young people coming in, and but then having some really talented, gifted young people who could use that extra support, and who we thought could really do something and go somewhere, but not being able to give it.

These numbers – forty youth showing up to someone's home recording studio, and sixty youth coming from across Toronto on any given Sunday – demonstrate the desire for access to facilities and support systems for youth who are pursuing cultural production not just as a hobby, but are looking for the means to develop careers from their creative enterprises.

The many youth deaths from gun violence in Toronto in the summer of 2005, known as "the summer of the gun," marked a change in government funding for programming targeted to "at-risk" youth, and also increased the support and facilities that I.C. Visions was able to provide. Gavin chronicles the effects of the summer of 2005 on youth programming.

There was this massive outcry and then political response, but without actual direction to the political response and funders as well … saying, "we need to do something, we need to do something, we need to do something," but what? And because of the work we'd been doing since 2000, I.C. Visions had been uniquely positioned as a leader working with the target demographic of youth who'd been labeled "at-risk" and been labeled all sorts of things … When there was that call for something, a guy named Kehinde Bah came to check us, who was on the mayor's advisory panel, and he knew about I.C. Visions, and thought there was an opportunity to take what we were doing and scale it up. He presented us as a best practice and then together we started on this idea that became Remix, which was basically born out of the frustrations of seeing so many talented young people and not being able to really work with them to cultivate those skills to get to that next level.

Due to this increase in funding, I.C. Visions was able to evolve and remix into The Remix Project, which began in 2006 in new and expanded facilities. This funding was of great benefit to the services that Gavin and Drex were able to offer, but Gavin explains that the sudden increase of funding in 2005 was not handled in a sustainable way. He remembers "a plethora of youth groups … got started all across the GTA with this huge influx of money but that influx of money wasn't sustained. It was a one-time gift." This sudden influx and evaporation of funding for youth programming points to the need for a larger vision and a sustainable youth-oriented policy framework. Although the government responded to youth in crisis by allocating more funding to these organizations, a more comprehensive policy structure could also address youth and youth cultural production at times other than when youth are seen as a social problem.

Programs and Pedagogy

While Gavin narrates that I.C. Visions increasingly responded to hip hop MCs who were seeking out ways to further their careers, The Remix Project's focus on "urban arts" is quite loosely defined and the programming itself does not necessarily have any inherent connection with hip hop. Other types of music are made by youth in the recording arts stream, and this stream is one of three, which also include creative arts and the art of business. Recording arts targets youth who are seeking out careers as "recording artists, producers, and audio engineers." In this stream, youth learn how to make sound recordings, and also learn how to assemble press kits and write grants. The creative arts stream is intended for youth who have interests in "Graphic Design, Illustration, Fashion Design, Videography, Photography, Writing." The art of business stream has served "managers, publicists, community workers, party promoters, and magazine editors" as well as "fashion and consulting entre-preneurs." Youth put together business and marketing plans in this stream, and take workshops on topics that include copyright law, managing credit, and financial planning. In many ways, The Remix Project offers many of the elements that researchers and community arts organizers have identified as important directions for policy makers to take up and support: Remix is housed in a facility that offers a wealth of services, including recording and photography studios, graphic design and video editing suites, and also offers in-dustry professionals who mentor youth one-on-one. Additionally, "Remix works with young people to identify grants, bursaries, and loans to help them get their businesses and ventures started. Remix has started-up a brand new micro-credit program which will be able to lend loans of $300 to $1,000."[36]

As a result of the mentorship in not only creative but also industry fields, Gavin says that youth exit The Remix Project "already hitting the ground running with these kinds of skills and contacts."[37] They may have come into the program with a creative project in mind, but, according to Drex, do not have "the resources to do it, don't have the networks to do it."[38] One way that alumni of The Remix Project "hit the ground running" after the completion of the pro-gram is through continuing to be involved with the for-profit side of The Remix Project, called Remix Projects, which is a boutique cre-ative agency. Staffed by alumni of The Remix Project and housed in the same facility, this creative agency specializes in branding identity, imaging, and special events, and has worked with clients such as TIMEX Group, BMW Group, and the City of Toronto. Youth em-ployed by Remix Projects are paid standard industry rates for their work, and the profits that the agency makes are folded back into the not-for-profit side, The Remix Project. Remix Projects also operates by leasing the facilities of The Remix Project after hours. When the recording studio and photography studio are rented out, alumni studio engineers and photographers who are carrying out the jobs receive half of the hourly charged rate, and the other half is reinvested in The Remix Project as means for it to become self-sustaining. The Remix Project facilities also now house *Pound* magazine, a nationally distributed urban lifestyle magazine whose owner and publisher sits on Remix's board of directors and has bequeathed the magazine to Remix. The magazine has become youth-run and youth-led, with "all young people, young writers, young photographers, designers, layout, everything, continuing to profile people doing it here on the local scene, but also internationally as well."[39]

Alumni of The Remix Project also continue to be involved with the program with what Gavin calls the "each one teach one" system of alumni returning to mentor current youth participants. Gavin gives the example of alumni Will Nguyen, a photographer with a renowned blog, *Lost in the Wilderness*, who "then ... turns around and launches the photography program, because he notices there's a gap within what we're doing. Because that was only one small section, photography, for our overall creative arts. We'd have maybe two spots for it."[40] The development of this photography program suggests the ways that Remix is able to grow and expand by adapting to the needs of its participants. Through this close community that Remix fosters, some youth come back to Remix in various capacities after they finish the program, while others transition into the worlds of employment and education.

The support and guidance that youth receive at Remix stems from a learner-centered pedagogical model based in close contact between participants and project leaders. Youth are taught through one-to-one mentorships and in small group settings. Each stream of the program has ten participants and is run by one educator, in addition to close contact with industry mentors. The first stage of The Remix Project involves building the confidence of the participants "because so many young people are here because they haven't done well in the formal education system."[41] On the first day of the program, participants are congratulated for being chosen, as 250 youth might apply for each session and thirty are admitted after an interview process. Gavin comments, "We walk in and we're like, 'congratulations, you made it. You're the best of the best.' We do this whole thing, and really try to instill some pride and some confidence in the young people for making it that far ... So we start on that high note, then we try to maintain it throughout." The Remix Project operates with "self-generative curriculum," and in the initial two weeks, youth participants develop a six-month plan based in small goals: "it's simply, 'in the next six months, what do you want to leave here with? What do you want to accomplish, and where are you trying to go?' And so we say, if you are trying to be here, by point G and we're starting at A, then we have to do A, B, C, D, E, F, G to get there, and we start laying out small goals, a manageable plan, but with smaller goals inside of it to start building that confidence, snowballing into larger and larger successes at the end of the six-month plan." In addition to the self-directed learning that happens through developing and following this six-month plan that is supported by program and industry mentors, youth are required to attend some mandatory workshops on subjects that relate to the creative industries, such as credit. Remix participants cite acquiring this knowledge of the logistical aspects of cultural production as an important factor of the program. One Remix participant, Kyauna, explains she "had no clue about what type of artist I was, where I wanted to go with my music. Now I know what I want to do, I have a plan for everything I want to do; I know who to talk to."[42] Another Remix participant, Roxanne, foregrounds the importance of having opportunities to connect with like-minded youth and being around "people who believed it and lived it and were successful from believing it."[43]

Though The Remix Project differs from the formal education system in that it develops closer relationships with participants and has a self-generative curriculum, the program makes use of rhetoric adapted from traditional educational models, with the goal of building the confidence of participants and equipping them to potentially return to school. At The Remix Project, youth choose a program (either creative arts, recording, or business), develop a major in this program, and work on completing a thesis project over their six-month semester. Gavin describes that this language is introduced gradually.

> Let's say they go to apply to Humber College to get into photography and they've never even graduated high school, but they're applying as a mature student now, then they can say, "Well, I went to The Remix Project, I was in the creative arts program, I majored in photography and my thesis project was this portfolio that I brought here to you today." That idea of language is so

important and so powerful, and recognizing also the success and
the things that we accomplish, so it's putting it into that framework and it also makes the formal world that they might be entering into – whether it's academic or professional – a little less
scary because they are starting to become accustomed to that
language.[44]

In addition to acquiring familiarity and ease with the rhetoric of the
academic and professional worlds, The Remix Project participants
receive formal recognition of completing the program. Gavin states
"we do a whole diploma series." These mechanisms allow for disen-
franchised youth who have creative or entrepreneurial ideas to build
confidence as they develop their projects and learn to communicate
these projects to the outside world. However, The Remix Project
moves beyond a youth engagement model as it emphasizes the development of creative careers themselves in addition to these life skills.

Challenges

Remix is, in many cases, a model program and has received a Habitat
Programme award from the United Nations for excellence in community safety and crime prevention, but it also faces its own set of
challenges. Gavin explains that, initially, putting forward hip hop-
oriented urban arts programming required an "education piece about
urban music and culture and how it can be harnessed." Though the
pedagogical potential of hip hop is now more widely recognized and
understood, Gavin notes that this was not the case when I.C. Visions
began, "and we were trying to say … this is a means, this is an avenue of communication, this is an entry point, this is the most authentic way to communicate with young people, but a lot of our funders
were from different generations … It was a huge process for us to
not only apply for funds, which is already a hard thing to do with
any youth organization, but on top of applying for funds, starting an
education campaign to educate while we're applying about why, so
it was almost double the workload that we started with." In addition
to the work of initially having to educate funders while applying for
funds, securing sustainable funding has been a challenge for Remix,
as it is for many youth programs. In June 2009, The Remix Project
started its now annual funding drive, called Give Money Make
Change, as its main funder, National Crime Prevention Canada, had
funded the project for its first three years as a pilot project only.

Gavin states that "core sustainable funding … is kind of that unicorn that we are all chasing." The Remix Project has been successful in securing core funding from the Ontario Arts Council: "It's a relatively small percentage of our budget, but it's core, so that's great. And Toronto Arts Council, we're currently applying for the same, which would be even smaller, but again, if it's core, that's fantastic." With its funding drive and with Remix Projects, the program is also moving past the model of exclusively depending on government funding and towards a more entrepreneurial vision.

Beyond these funding challenges, Remix also faces the problem of space. In 2006, The Remix Project moved into a building with a three-year lease, as the building was scheduled for demolition in 2009. Searching for a new space after this point included the challenge of "finding a landlord and then neighbours who not just respect what we're doing, but can live with it. So a lot of people respect what we're doing, but the majority of those people … doesn't mean that they can live with it. They absolutely hate the idea of young people being in the space … you know, it's all great to be 'we support at-risk youth,' except not here. We found that a lot in our different incarnations over the last ten years." After leaving their initial space at 110 Sudbury Street in Toronto, The Remix Project looked into a new space that the landlord would have to develop to make suitable for use: "he was going to get the space ready, bring it up to code, put in floors, then put in a second floor, and then we were going to build from there." Months of delays meant that The Remix Project was closed for much longer than initially foreseen when moving between spaces, and the delays eventually produced the revelation that the landlord did not have adequate funds to transform his building into a workable space. After months of wrangling and being misled by the landlord, Gavin comments, "I think we kind of got played for simple, because we're youth-led as well, so [The Remix Project coordinators are] young people ourselves." After this difficult experience, The Remix Project finally found a new home that has 4,800 square feet of space on two floors and that is well-situated: "[It's] right in Liberty Village [in Toronto] … This neighbourhood is kind of known as a creative hub for the city and it's one of the creative districts … [There are] major music labels within two blocks, major video and film production rental houses, design firms, television stations like YTV. We're already finding partners within walking distance that are already taking our young people on in different small contracts or internships as well as partnering with us to do different projects." Here, Gavin suggests the importance of well-suited spaces for youth programming and the increased opportunities that can come with these well-suited and well-situated spaces.

Through all of these struggles and successes, Gavin is optimistic about where young people of his generation have arrived after, in his case, ten years of youth-led work. Referring to his year of birth, 1982, and his partner Drex's year of birth, 1981, Gavin states, "one, two rules the word right now." He explains that the work and movements that the young people of his generation have been a part of are now beginning to be recognized and seen as legitimate.

> We're starting to get into places – we're not in the places of decision making yet – but we're starting to get into really interesting places now. Even as a cultural movement, and it doesn't just mean hip hop culture, but just our culture and what we recognize as popular culture, and then the subcultures that used to be a part of that, are now raised to this place of just – it's understood, and you're operating. Where before you were educating, educating, now we just operate on the level that we all get it and we can move forward from here. It's become a lot easier.

Youth may create their own initiatives, and may have developed increased ease with their work, but a more comprehensive youth policy framework to continue to support and develop the important work that is being done could further expand and equitably distribute this ease.

While many community programs offer exciting avenues and examples of positive work with youth, it is as important to note the challenges and limitations of this work as it is to celebrate its possibilities. Community programs may offer sites of learning for youth outside of the formal education system, but these sites encounter their own challenges and complexities of power and privilege in working towards affecting change and engaging with youth. Nonetheless, programs like Ignite the Americas and The Remix Project offer interesting models of how to foster youth involvement with cultural policy making and the creative industries. These two projects offer examples of what a creative ecology framework could look like in execution in individual projects, as these projects are conceptualized through a connection between youth, employment, creative industries, and community and economic development.

Towards a Comprehensive Youth Policy Framework to Support Youth Cultural Production

The film *Almost Famous* is Cameron Crowe's semi-autobiographical tale of a fifteen-year-old high school student, William Miller, who goes from a bedroom-based rock music super-fan to an internationally travelling music correspondent for *Rolling Stone* magazine.[1] Through William's journey, Crowe suggests that successfully implanting oneself in the creative industries is a matter of pluck, ingenuity, and faith. William's first entry into the field of rock journalism happens after meeting rock critic and *Creem* magazine editor Lester Bangs at the local radio station where Bangs is being interviewed. After the interview, William chats Bangs up and is given an assignment: write a review of the local Black Sabbath concert. Without a press pass, William unsuccessfully attempts to be let in backstage, but eventually gains access when the up-and-coming opening act, the fictitious band Stillwater, arrives late, and William refers to the band members by name and praises their latest recordings. In these opening scenes, William's journey towards rock journalism is mapped out as a matter of being in the right place at the right time and knowing the right thing to say. William's review of the concert is a success. Soon after, he is contacted by *Rolling Stone* to write a piece profiling Stillwater, and in order to do so he goes on a cross-country tour with them. William effortlessly goes from attending high school and obsessively listening to records in his bedroom to regularly conversing on the phone with a legendary rock critic and receiving work requests from an important music magazine. As William embarks on an adventure-filled cross-country tour, high school quickly becomes unimportant and is left behind: his mother attends his high school graduation, but William does not. When William eventually sends

Rolling Stone a tell-all piece with the nitty-gritty details of his time spent with Stillwater, the band denies the story and it goes unpublished; by the end of the film, though, Stillwater's lead singer is in William's bedroom making amends for his conduct and calls *Rolling Stone* to give the go-ahead for William's tell-all cover story, seemingly cementing William's nascent career as a music journalist.

The film did not meet with great box office success but it received good reviews, Oscar nominations, a win for best screenplay, and kudos from Roger Ebert as the best film of 2000. The coming-of-age story of the local boy who makes good seems have a powerful hold over our imaginations, but the ease with which William moves from ordinary high school kid to published journalist obscures the challenges that accompany the desire to be employed in the creative industries. The film highlights the importance of personal contacts and perseverance for success in the creative industries, but also masks the logistical struggles that many youth encounter in the process of securing sustainable employment in creative fields. For William, the challenges that the film presents are only those of dealing with the personalities and shenanigans of the rock stars he is following; important contacts with key figures are instantly created, and William's integrity and honesty are repaid with career success. Although there is certainly something engaging about this type of narrative, we need to better map the experiences of youth as they go from high school students to making their way in the creative industries. Mapping these youth experiences could pave the way for developing better support systems, such that William's experience of the inconsequentiality of his formal education vis-à-vis his career ambitions does not need to be the normative experience of youth in education systems as they seek out work in the creative industries.

This mapping project could be of specific use to policy communities. Stéphanie Gaudet notes that, "as social roles vary based on social and historic contexts, policy can quickly become unsuited to the changing realities of populations."[2] This changing reality is particularly true for contemporary youth, and, as we have seen, many current policies are unsuited to the contemporary realities of ad hoc, small-scale, and self-generated youth work in the creative industries. In this book, I have begun to map the experience and processes of youth as they forge small-scale careers for themselves in the creative industries and have identified themes of interdisciplinarity, the interpenetration of art, commerce, and community, and the importance of recognizing small-scale practices, amongst others. These themes are ones for further investigation and mapping to get a broader sense of the parameters of contemporary youth creative practices and to also get a sense of how current structures may sometimes hinder or harm these practices. This concluding chapter looks ahead towards what more suitable cultural and educational policy structures might look like for the contemporary youth population and then closes with the life stories of two Montreal-based music promoters that illustrate contemporary youth realities.

MOVING TOWARDS A CANADIAN COMPREHENSIVE YOUTH POLICY FRAMEWORK THAT SUPPORTS SMALL-SCALE AND SELF-GENERATED YOUTH ACTIVITIES

Chapter 3 outlined the scattershot nature of federal cultural policy and its inapplicability to some contemporary youth realities in Canada. In this current scattershot system, it is sometimes difficult to register where out-of-date and out-of-touch policies are. Joyce Zemans explains that cultural programs are often municipal and provincial responsibilities in Canada, and though the country "has yet to develop a true cultural participatory model ... national policies in countries such as the Netherlands, Sweden, France and Australia have been successful in stimulating development in this field."[3] Including cultural production and youth cultural production in models of cultural participation may be an important part of better engaging the contemporary youth population. Unlike the above-named countries, Zemans suggests that jurisdictional issues in the Canadian context have "precluded the collaboration necessary to develop national strategies, allowing governments to share research and resources. By working in cooperation with the provinces, the potential exists to create a coherent communications, education and arts and cultural policy ... situated in the Department of Canadian Heritage."[4]

Presently, policy structures exist in both of the areas of youth and culture, but these structures exist in isolated silos that do not work towards shared goals or visions and do not have mechanisms for communication and coordination across sectors.[5] For example, while the Department of Canadian Heritage does not have a youth arts sector, it does fund youth arts programs under the rubric of "youth participation," but programs in this sector are not geared towards cultural employment, or employment of any kind, as employment falls within the purview of Human Resources and Skills Development. Sandra Franke explains that, at the federal level in Canada, "approximately ten departments and agencies have well-defined youth responsibilities particularly with respect to justice and crime prevention, employment and training, civic participation, health, culture and international development."[6] In practice, this means not an abundance but a lack of attention to the real needs of youth; as discussed in Chapter 4, youth are often only targeted as an at-risk population when they are addressed by federal policy.[7]

Franke states that this disjointed policy structure also exists at the provincial level in Canada, as there are policies that are directed towards youth in a number of provincial policy sectors, including education, health, employment, and participation. It should be noted that at the provincial level, British Columbia has had a youth policy framework since 2000, as has Quebec, since 2001. The Secrétariat à la Jeunesse comments that Quebec's youth policy has "piqued the interest of other Canadian provinces and foreign delegations from Europe, South America and Africa. Some of them even intend to base their youth strategies on Québec's."[8] Despite the existence of these provincial frameworks, further federal work could offer more support and coherence. Quebec's Secrétariat à la Jeunesse notes the overlap between provincial and federal programs directed towards youth: "In actions aimed at young people, the federal government administers its own youth programs, which to varying degrees cohabit with Québec's. In certain cases, agreements between the federal and Québec governments have led to the creation of joint programs. Overlapping, though, is visible in other areas, notably in employment, education, and health care. The Québec youth policy is an opportunity to ensure that Québec maintains a consistent position on young people, thus bolstering the Québec government's scope for initiative and reaffirming its priorities when acting on youth issues."[9] Though there may be consistency within Quebec in terms of its youth programs, the overlap and gaps between provincial and federal programs suggests that a broader federal policy structure that coordinates with both provincial and municipal policies could allow these policy levels to more effectively target local youth needs. Indeed, Joyce Zemans and Amanda Coles argue that "without a national policy framework that facilitates an understanding of the ways in which their policies and programs share strategic directions and goals, the ability for partners to efficiently share critical research, knowledge and resources is considerably limited. This has the effect of producing a complicated sectoral landscape for youth arts in Canada marked by both overlap and significant gaps in support mechanisms."[10] More research needs to done to map this "complicated landscape" of municipal, provincial, and federal cultural policy layers so that the interactions of these layers are clearer, and the overlaps and gaps in these layers can begin to be addressed.

One mechanism to address these gaps is what has become known in policy circles as "joined up" policy, or policy that groups together disjointed structures under one umbrella; in this case, a comprehensive federal youth policy could begin to address the gaps and overlaps in youth policy. According to the Commonwealth Youth Programme, a youth policy framework could be defined as "a practical demonstration and declaration of the priority and directions that a country intends to give to the development of its young women and men. A [youth policy framework] specifically represents an inclusive statement that encapsulates the elements of vision, framework and realistic guidelines from which strategies and initiatives can be developed to facilitate meaningful youth participation and development."[11] Youth participation is specifically mentioned here, but small-scale youth cultural production could also be targeted and supported by a national youth policy framework. This policy framework could allow for mechanisms to coordinate services for youth across government sectors and create "institutional arrangements" to "integrate youth policy into federal, regional, and community planning, and assist in the coordination and funding of all related activities."[12] In this way, youth needs could be addressed across sectors to both ensure consistency and that these needs are being met. The recognition of the distinct needs and practices of youth vis-à-vis policy is important; while policy can call permanence into being, youth activities may be transient and transitional and have a model of success that is not tied to growth and expansion. Discussing changes to copyright policy, Tina Piper notes that "community interest, inclusion, altruism and action out of a non-monetary interest play little role" in copyright laws,[13] but these concepts may be important to a small-scale mode of youth cultural production. The challenge, then, is to create a comprehensive youth policy framework that recognizes this mode of production, allows for flexibility rather than permanence, and is able to register development rather than growth.

A starting place for a comprehensive youth policy framework could be a clear vision of its goals and functions. As discussed in Chapter 4, Canada currently lacks an overarching vision of the role and functions of culture, and thinking through the desired role of Canadian culture could be a further starting place for conceptualizing the relationship between youth and culture in policy structures. A comprehensive youth policy could mean that services are integrated and coordinated across government sectors to "contribute to long-term positive outcomes for youth."[14] In terms of youth involvement in the creative industries, these outcomes for youth might include more stability in their lines of work, more knowledge about how to access resources, more equity in gaining access to resources, and more of an opportunity to make a living wage from self-generated small-scale creative industries practices. To be appropriate to contemporary youth needs, a vision for a comprehensive youth policy framework might underscore awareness of self-generated youth activities and include provisions for interdisciplinary and small-scale work – whether in cultural production or in other fields. If we do not foreground the differences and validity of youth practices, it is difficult to register the bedroom economies of small-scale cultural production because, as discussed in Chapter 2, most definitions of the creative industries revolve around industrialized forms of production that do not speak to contemporary youth activities.

This vision for a comprehensive youth policy framework would move beyond the youth engagement model that currently has traction. Once youth are registered as active – rather than "at-risk" or potentially / latently criminal, as they are seen in a deficit model – it is foreseeable to create mechanisms that include youth in decision-making processes and to work towards more sustainable long-term funding for community organizations that work with youth. This lack of sustainability in funding for projects that target youth has emerged in this book; indeed, for "youth-serving programs, youth-led projects and higher level youth organizing, concerns have been raised about the lack of structural sustainability and the strain that is becoming evident based on a patchwork approach of project-by-project funding and the absence of supportive policy frameworks."[15] Without structural sustainability, youth organizations compete with one another for funding rather than cooperate to work towards positive outcomes for youth. To be appropriate to local and specific youth needs, a comprehensive youth policy framework might also foster community development emerging from a bottom-up view of cultural planning, as discussed in Chapter 4.

SHIFTING EDUCATIONAL MODELS TOWARDS THE CREATION OF LEARNING COMMUNITIES

Developing a comprehensive youth policy framework would mean getting in touch with the realities of contemporary youth, including grappling with what post-secondary education means for youth today. As Gaudet notes, "a recent OECD report (1999) states the importance of adapting educational systems to the new exploratory paths of youth. In fact, countries tend to favour an idealized and fairly linear educational model that stands in the way of youth taking trajectory changes."[16] As discussed in the Introduction, these trajectory changes may mean the prolongation and redefinition of youth. It is also important to recognize that trajectory changes for youth might take them away from the formal education system altogether. Many policy structures are directed towards the idea that youth in what has come to be known as the "emerging adulthood" phase of life are pursuing post-secondary education; for example, provincial and federal levels of government offer loan programs for post-secondary studies. However, not all youth pursue post-secondary education, and some might need other kinds of institutional support, especially in the development and generation phase of work in the creative industries. In *Almost Famous*, creative industries work and the formal education system quickly became separate and non-intersecting trajectories. Many of the youth interviewed in this book have post-secondary degrees, but these degrees often have little bearing on their present involvement with the creative industries. Chapter 3 outlined the ways in which post-secondary education can act as an incubator of creative careers, not because it has any direct connection with these careers, but because it allows youth time for personal development and the creation of contacts. This model of the post-secondary institution as an incubator for cultural production suggests a disconnect between the actual content of post-secondary education and some youths' creative pursuits. Though this might be a functional model, a vision of post-secondary education that posits that the formal education system can have direct relevancy in youths' development of their creative practices might be more productive.

This separation of education systems and creative industries work also suggests that formal education systems might need to be reconceived away from idealized and linear pathways, such that they can accommodate back-and-forth and exploratory movement. Franke states, "one useful approach would be to document the best practices of flexible education systems that support multiple trajectories, easy navigation between different pathways, and progressive pathways ... What is important is no longer the basic academic education but the ability and opportunities for updating learning and skills on a lifelong basis. In this context, other forms of capital (financial, cultural and social) are equally vital to navigating easily among different learning systems and to accommodating the requirements of lifelong education."[17] As we have seen, creative industries employment may require a lifelong reeducation circuit. Youth with differing levels of financial, cultural, and social capital may have differing abilities to access and navigate a flexible education pathway, and greater openness in post-secondary education may allow for more equity in this navigation process. Canadian cultural policy may envision that youth who want to pursue careers in cultural production will study extensively in their fields, but Chapter 3 outlined the lack of appropriateness of the national training centre model for many contemporary youth practices in the creative industries. A comprehensive youth policy framework might be underscored by a understanding of contemporary youth as producers and creators such that it can include a vision of training for artists that positions youth as actively generating and developing their own artistic practices rather than training in established forms. Chapter 3 outlined Ruben Gaztambide-Fernandez's alternate vision of artistic training, and what is key in this vision is the openness of the artistic training institution and the connections between the institution and the surrounding community. Some of the youth in this book have mentioned the need for further training in the logistical, business, and legal aspects of the creative industries but do not cite the formal education system as a means to acquire this training. Conceptualizing institutions of higher learning as open public spaces may facilitate some of this back-and-forth movement in and out of post-secondary education and allow for a vision of post-secondary education that is supportive of the development of youth cultural production.

As discussed in Chapter 2, current academic research in media education may advocate for this vision of schools as open public spaces and favour small-scale collaborative creative projects. Further connections between schools and outside institutions are necessary to put this vision and these types of learning activities into practice. Providing youth with opportunities in the formal education system to navigate the aspects of their own projects, supported by institutional connections, could assist them in learning to take active roles in creating their own projects and working with others. The formal education system does not need to directly instruct these logistical aspects in its program content, but designing curriculum that gives youth opportunities to actively seek out and complete their own projects could better equip them for a future in small-scale self-generated careers.

In addition to the vision of institutions of education as open public spaces, another useful model of the educational institution is the hub school. As discussed in Chapter 5, the British policy document *Creative Britain: New Talents for a New Economy* promotes moving towards the school-as-hub model by fostering connections between elementary and secondary schools and institutions of higher learning through the sharing of curriculum, industry contacts, and facilities, and by providing mentoring for students and exchanges for staff. This model could be useful to support youth involvement in the creative industries as it could allow students to work on projects that have some connection with the outside world rather than being assignments for school credit alone. Further research could be done to see what this British model of the hub school looks like on the ground, and if it has potential applications in the Canadian context.

In Quebec, this vision of the school as a hub rather than an isolated unit is not directly spelled out in educational policy, but the vision of teacher education set out by the Ministère de l'Éducation, du Loisir, et du Sport's (MELS) official teacher training document calls for strong partnerships between post-secondary teacher training programs and local schools: "[Teachers in training] will work in collaboration with the other members of teaching staff and cooperate with the school team, parents, and various social partners, in attaining educational objectives."[18] In order to achieve this collaboration,

MELS states that "partnerships between the university and the school system must be strengthened and extend beyond the organization of practical training."[19] The field of education can share expertise in this area of partnerships between the university and the school system with its model of teacher training in the professional development school, which envisions teacher education taking place in schools that are partnered with universities. In this model, teacher education happens predominantly on-site at schools, and academic research takes place in classrooms. In this last regard, academic research in youth culture and practices could move towards more concrete, empirical, and ethnographic studies, as youth culture research has often been lacking in these areas, as discussed in Chapter 2. Above all, youth could benefit not only through connections to outside expertise in their classrooms, but also through academic examinations of contemporary youth needs and practices that could lead to a better formulated comprehensive youth policy framework.

This book closes with the narratives of two Montreal-based music promoters whose experiences are suggestive of the future of work in the creative industries and illuminate the gaps between policy and youth realities. In order to close these gaps, this book has suggested that we need a better picture of current youth realities as they face the creative industries, and the life stories of these two youth map out some of these realities. These life stories chronicle the origin of these two youths' creative practices and the challenges they have faced, and though these narratives tell the story of two particular experiences, they also resemble experiences that are common to many youth in the creative industries.

NOAH BICK AND PASSOVAH PRODUCTIONS

While Noah Bick's experiences in the world of music promotion are not those of William Miller, his youthful enthusiasm, combined with his ability to create personal contacts, are somewhat reminiscent of parts of the *Almost Famous* narrative. He outlines how he first came into contact with the movers and shakers of Montreal's music scene in a way that recalls William's first entry to the Stillwater concert in the film.

Me and two of my still best friends ... I think I was sixteen at the time and we wanted to go see Islands perform at Les Saints.

Me and two of my friends are standing outside, we're like, "What the fuck are we going to do? It's eighteen plus, they're not letting us in." So eventually we're waiting around for two hours, and Graham walks out, and I have no idea who Graham Van Pelt is, but my friend had just been at Osheaga [a Montreal music festival] a month earlier and remembered the guy from Think About Life, and I figured out that he was opening the show. "Hey, Graham from Think about Life," says my friend to Graham. "Could you try to get us in?" And he says, "Yeah, sure." So he pretends that we're his crew. His load-in crew! Three sixteen-year-old boys helping Fort Miracle, the one-man act, load his non-existent drum kit out of Les Saints ... So the bouncer doesn't buy it; we go home. The three of us become really good friends after that, and then the next night we went to see Think About Life, and then Graham tells the story to the crowd, then I'm like, "[Pop Montreal] is a cool music festival, if things like that happen." I think I sent an email, it might have been to info@popmontreal.com, some sort of question involving an Arcade Fire concert, and then from there I think Dan Seligman, who runs the festival, told me about the secret [Arcade Fire] con- cert that happened ... in a church basement. After that I offered to help out. It became once in a while for the past two summers, and now it's kinda like part-time volunteer. Whenever they need an extra hand for something, I'm always down.[20]

Through his volunteerism at the Pop Montreal office, Noah has gained an informal internship or apprenticeship in the business and logistics of music promotion and production. He states that the staff members at Pop Montreal, "each in their own respect," have be- come mentors for him. Noah describes his time with Pop Montreal as a learning experience in which he has learned "everything. How a concert's settled, how it's run, how you email people, how you treat certain people certain ways. Recently, I started booking tours. Dan [Seligman] has been very helpful in explaining to me ... Basically, he sends me templates of a contract and I just edit it to suit my needs." That learning, mentorship, and apprenticeships happen through informal means away from the education system is com- mon to youth in the creative industries and, as we have seen, may necessitate investigating how to develop more equity in access to creative industries employment.

Noah continues to work at Pop Montreal and is increasingly brought into assisting in producing the festival in aspects that include artist selection. He also runs his own music promotion company, Passovah Productions, which he started when he was seventeen with the same friends from his Think About Life anecdote. With Passovah Productions, Noah puts on small local shows in Montreal, and Noah displays his abilities to mobilize his personal network to further the goals of his production company: "I've started to build up more of a team. My best friend David is kinda like the number two. Especially if I become more involved in the booking aspect of this organization, he's going to help [with] the local production kind of work. I have someone in charge of the blog, which is becoming a website, which is more money, which is money we don't have. So I have a production member of the team, then I have an Internet member of the team. I'm friends with a graphic designer who's going to take care of all the graphics." Here, Noah comments on the importance of collaborating with other like-minded people, but this version of doing-it-with-others (as opposed to doing-it-yourself) differs from the industrialized model of David Hesmondhalgh's "project team," discussed in Chapter 2, in that it is small-scale, grassroots, and self-generated. Noah also describes expanding his personal contacts across Canada through his experiences of booking shows for local bands when they tour: "Now I know people in Thunder Bay, people out in Regina. And a lot of these people are people that I've got in contact with through bands that I've done shows for that have been [from] these towns. The Di Ninno brothers in Medicine Hat. People like that are just gems. Or Marshall Burns from Regina. It's a beautiful network." Though Noah is speaking to the importance of informal personal networks to sustain small-scale production, formalized networks, seen in Chapter 7, are an initiative that youth have taken up to develop and safeguard their creative industries involvement, and registering both informal and formal networks is an important part of mapping youth cultural production.

Noah's passion for what he does and his willingness to carry out these activities without direct financial rewards come across when he talks about the projects he is involved with, but he also highlights the challenges of this work. One of these challenges is balancing school work with his production company. At eighteen, Noah entered his second and final year of a demanding college program: "I put on a lot of concerts in May and June, and now July, I'm kinda

easing up on the booking now, especially because I have a big semester coming up ... I've had nights where it's an 8 a.m. class and I get
home at 2 a.m., and I've been out the whole day. I'm trying to avoid
that this coming semester. In the school year, it [has been] about two
shows a month, and in the summer it's about five shows a month
and I think I'm going to bring it back down to one from August to
December [the length of the CEGEP semester]."[21] In addition to jug-
gling these two different aspects of his life, Noah also discusses the
challenges of learning the legal and business parameters of music
promotion. He describes reinvesting the money his company makes
to further expand what he does, but feeling uncertain about the legal
parameters of the mechanisms he makes use of: "When we do make
a bit of money, it goes into this company account that I've set up,
which is not fully legal. I'm kinda halfsies on the legal aspects of this
thing. I think in the first year and a half we made $300 total. I spent
almost 100 per cent of that. I bought this Zoom H4 recorder, which
is a mobile four track and you can plug it right into the soundboard.
It has two XLR inputs ... Now we get crazy quality rips of every
show! I want to start putting them out. And now that we're buying
a website, we can post our own stuff." This set of challenges, of
negotiating the legal and business ends of the creative industries, is
something that many youth grapple with. Noah states, "I really
don't want to go into management and all that stuff. I might have to
take a course or two eventually, to cover my legal ass." Here, Noah
references a desire to perhaps take some business courses, but to not
enroll in a management program, and reconceptualizing educational
systems might be a means to better accommodate these pursuits.

Like many youth, Noah is exuberant about the potential of working long-term in the creative industries, which he thinks is "totally"
feasible: "I feel like if I could pay rent and eat. Imagine existing, and
by existing and I mean eating and paying rent ... If you could do
that by doing something you want to do, that's the name of the
game." These modest aspirations – ability to pay one's rent while
pursuing fulfilling work – are common to youth attempting to make
careers in small-scale and self-generated ways, and many youth
share this ambition of making a living by "doing something you
want to do" in the creative industries. For many, this involves grappling and navigating and sometimes fumbling their way through
the logistical aspects of their ambitions. Rather than relying on the
William Miller narrative that success comes to those who happen to

be in the right place at the right time and know the right people, a policy framework that is able to respond to the needs of youth could allow for more equitable and sustainable success in the creative industries.

MEYER BILLURCU AND BLUE SKIES TURN BLACK

Now thirty-five, Meyer Billurcu has been involved in various aspects of the music industry since he was eighteen. Like Noah, Meyer is committed to being a music promoter for the long term, and states that he "can't imagine not" running his production company, Blue Skies Turn Black. After ten years of operating this company, Meyer displays a seasoned realism about the risky nature of creative industries enterprises.

> Being a promoter is being a risk taker. It's gambling. You're making an offer and you're hoping for the best. Just because you think something is a 90 per cent sure sell-out [show] doesn't mean it is. There's a show that we did a few months ago where we lost thousands of dollars on it. But meanwhile, on the rest of the tour, that band sold out [their shows]. It was just Montreal that was a bad city … We've been doing this nine years, it's going to be ten years. There's always going to be part of us [that thinks] maybe we should quit. You have a string of bad shows or something's not working. But you'll have a string of really good shows, and you're "this is why we got into this."[22]

Meyer speaks to the constant instability in his line of work due to the uncertainty of audience attendance for music concerts, but this instability is found across many types of creative industries work. Despite this instability, Meyer has been able to get to a place where he is able to support himself solely from his production company and no longer holds employment other than Blue Skies Turn Black.

Like Noah, Meyer describes the importance of fandom and mentorship in his own origin story of his route towards becoming a music promoter.

> The genesis of it was Brian [Neuman, Meyer's partner in Blue Skies Turn Black] and me went to Washington, DC … and we wanted to visit the Dischord Records [a seminal punk label]

house. The address is on the back of all the Dischord CDs. It
was a big influence, for both of us. So we went to this house, we
went to the address and rang the doorbell and an old woman answered. We were like, "This must be the wrong house … There's
two streets with the same name." So we just asked her, "Is this
the Dischord house?" We didn't know what else to do! She said,
"Oh yeah, you found the right house. I'm Ginger MacKaye, I'm
Ian MacKaye's mother" … We were kind of blown away. They
had a letter for anyone who visited the house that said, "Hi, wel-
come to the Dischord house. This is where Ian lived until he was
19. He doesn't live here anymore, but we kept the Dischord address here because he wasn't sure where he was going to be living
at any time. While in DC, you should visit these record stores and
these venues." We were kinda really blown away, because you
hear about DIY and underground, for us it was still a big thing,
but then when you realize it's really like a mom-and-pop operation, it kind of changed our perspective on a lot of stuff. It inspired us to want to do something similar in Montreal. For us,
[Ian MacKaye's band] Fugazi was still a *big* band. Any band that
plays Metropolis, to us, is a *big* band … When you realize that,
holy shit, they are doing everything themselves, and they've hired
their friends to work, it's not a real corporation … [Rather] it's a
real community thing. I was like, "hey, we should do something
like that in Montreal."

Witnessing a viable small-scale model of production led Meyer to
want to take up his own small-scale, community-based enterprise.
As such, Meyer chronicles the importance of existing examples of
grassroots and DIY culture to encourage youth to start their own
initiatives. Founded in 1980, the independent record label Dischord
has been able to survive and maintain its DIY principles in increasingly challenging times for the record industry. Support for these
types of small-scale practices might also be a means to motivate
and assist the entry of the next generation of youth into the creative industries.

Prior to the inception of Blue Skies Turn Black, Meyer remembers
a feeling of frustration that bands he was a fan of would not come
to Montreal on tour, or if they did come, their shows would often be
poorly attended due to lack of promotion. Through the 2000s, Blue
Skies Turn Black was instrumental in working towards building

support systems that allowed a thriving independent music scene to develop in Montreal. Meyer explains that his process of starting to work in the creative industries initially involved pursuing a range of projects. First, Blue Skies Turn Black put on a screening of the Fugazi film *Instrument* in Montreal: "We just started reaching out to different media outlets. We put up posters all over the city. The two of us did everything ourselves, and we ended up having one of the most successful screenings that they had." After this point, Blue Skies Turn Black was interested in becoming a record label and was mentored by a local small record label owner and promoter.

Like Noah, Meyer notes a disconnect between his formal education and his career ambitions, but also describes mobilizing the knowledge and skills he gained in art school when he started his production company.

> I was in art school at the time, but it wasn't really gelling for me. I wasn't finding what I wanted to do or meeting people. I liked art but I was more into lowbrow art like comic books and stuff, and my teachers and me were on different wavelengths. They weren't really interested in what I was doing, didn't really offer any real help. I was really into music, but I wasn't a really good musician, neither was Brian, which is how we got involved in this. Once Blue Skies started, I just decided, "Fuck it, I'm going to use what I learnt in school, apply it to this company." First, I self-published a few comic books. That was the first time we used the name Blue Skies Turn Black, for those comics. I started promoting a few shows … I made posters. In school I did drawing classes, silkscreening classes. And then we met a couple local bands. And I'm like, "Fuck it." I wasn't interested in doing anything else with silkscreening than making record covers. So I started making record covers. So I was using my education, or using my time in school to kickstart Blue Skies. I was doing computer classes – I did our first website from what I learned in computer classes.

Meyer not only describes feeling disconnected from his schooling, but also describes a disconnect from more traditional forms of employment. Starting Blue Skies Turn Black was an alternative to his own seemingly pointless experiences in art school and an alternative to meaningless work for his partner Brian.

Meyer chronicles acquiring knowledge and skills that relate to running a production company through on-the-ground experience, as neither he nor Brian "have any business training." He remembers being "really ambitious in the beginning, but really naïve." Though the Blue Skies Turn Black record label initially released five records in the span of a few years with an ethos that "good music sells itself," Meyer realized "it does take a lot more work than that to really push records," and eventually the record label aspect of Blue Skies Turn Black ended.

> [To promote a record] you really need to try to get radio play with the college radio; you should do ads in various zines and magazines. We started learning that we have to do a little bit more for the records than just putting them out. It got to the point where most of the bands broke up and/or we were more interested in pushing their record than they were. Some bands didn't really want to tour … I kind of ended the label for a couple of years and that's when the promotion side took over. To me, the term "promoter" was like industry and scumbags. I was like, I run a record label that happens to do shows. And then a few of years go by and no one even knows that we had a label. Most people were like, "Oh, you had a label? I thought you were just promoters."

Meyer's experiences of navigating and negotiating his way through the creative industries rather than setting out on a clear career path are common to many youth, as is the growing awareness of the interplay between seemingly "commercialized" (music promotion) and "authentic" (DIY record label) aspects of the creative industries.

> So we started doing more promoting and press. How we started is bands would contact us direct, [play] our show, cover our expenses, and any money after we would just split with the band. Then, when we started dealing with booking agents, it became a whole different ballpark. Agents were like, "Send us your offer." And this to us was like, "I don't get what that means." What do you mean send an offer? You tell me how much you want for your band. But we started learning how things were done. We asked some people who had been booking shows, "What does an offer mean?" "Well, you make a budget, and you offer them a

certain amount of money, it's a guarantee." This blew our minds.
We were just used to door deals. We started learning how to
make offers and what "break even" was and what "promoter
profit" was. Our first couple of offers, I don't think we had promoter profit, so we weren't really making a lot of money. One
agent was like, "Hey, you guys didn't put your promoter profit
in there." She was really nice; she helped us out a lot. It really
became more business-y. We really were starting to learn all the
tricks of the trade … After a certain while, you learn how to do
things. [Now], we have a much better idea of what a band is
worth, for a lack of a better word. When a band comes to town,
we're like, "This is probably how many people we'll get [at the
show]." You have to think what size venue is good, how much
you're going to pay in rent, how much you're going to spend on
promotion. If you do a show for a band at Metropolis you can't
just put up a hundred posters in the [Mile End] neighbourhood.
You've got to put ads in the paper. We've definitely become a lot
smarter about things.

Here, Meyer narrates his experiences of learning concert promotion as a trial-and-error process that gradually became more
professionalized.

Unlike the William Miller model of near overnight success, Meyer
went through a ten-year development process with Blue Skies Turn
Black. While he has become an established presence in the Montreal
independent music scene, this wasn't always the case.

When we started, no one wanted to give us the time of day. Most
booking agents didn't want to talk to us; some labels wouldn't
talk to us. But once we started proving ourselves, some agents
were great and they were willing to give us a shot, and things
went really well, and other agents kind of fell in line, like, "Hey,
those guys are doing pretty good." I think the turning point came
for us four years after we started and we did a Modest Mouse
show at the Rialto. I remember this one agent wouldn't even talk
to us, and then he saw that we did that show, and then started
offering us some of his bands.

Blue Skies Turn Black has grown into an entity that is taken seriously, but this company is not an inherently lucrative scheme. Meyer
remarks, "you can make $2,000 or $3,000 one day but you can lose

$6,000 the next day." He has tried to pursue more stability through finding government grants, but music promotion is something that falls outside of the boundaries of ventures that are supported by government funding structures.

> When we started, we were not really a label and not really ... we've tried [to apply for grants] but we've never got any. Now that the label's done and we're pretty much just promoters, it's really hard to get grants. There's grants you can get as a band, there's grants you can get as a label, but a grant as promoters? We've tried to find a way that is was possible but we haven't found it yet. When we started, Blue Skies was totally funded by Brian and me, and whatever little money we had saved up, and now things are a little different. There is a bank account [but] we've never received any [government] funding.

Rather than pursue the government funding route, Meyer and Brian, along with other partners, opened a music venue, Il Motore, in the summer of 2008 because bar sales provide more stable revenues.

THE ROAD AHEAD: "IT STARTED AS A HOBBY, BUT NOW IT'S A REAL BUSINESS"

Though fourteen years separate them, Meyer and Noah share common experiences, and these experiences are also common to many youth as they attempt to make careers from creative enterprises. Meyer explains that his production company "sort of turned itself into a career" over the course of ten years. Meyer's and Noah's experiences both illuminate themes of professionalization of one's creative enterprises while also bleeding together work and leisure, as well as themes of the continued importance of small-scale production and the constant navigation and negotiation learning process that is required to sustain a career in a creative field. This book concludes on these notes, as they are themes that have been heard across this book, and are important ones to register to be able to get an accurate picture of youth cultural production today.

When asked to reflect back on their experiences, both Meyer and Noah comment on the professionalization that they have recently undergone in their creative practices. Noah describes this professionalization process as one that he has absorbed through his continued work experiences at Pop Montreal: "In May, I started working twenty hours a week and it became forty by the end of the summer for Pop Montreal. The job was a lot heavier on the responsibility thing so I've been learning a lot more about the bureaucratic, paper side of the music business. I'm also learning a lot more about how to interact with people known in the world. You do it more professionally than I've been doing for the last three years."[23] Meyer also highlights the required professionalism in his line of work, suggesting that there is a misperception of the creative industries and the music industry in particular as "there's a lot of people out there who aren't serious and don't see this as work ... There should be a certain level of professionalism ... So many people just don't get that. They just think it's about free drinks and guest list." These perks may stand out and be part of the reason why creative industries employment is seen as desirable for some, but bureaucratic and logistical elements often weigh more heavily when considering steady employment. Meyer discusses that grappling with bureaucracy eventually meant a restructuring and professionalization process that he undertook in 2010 to ensure the sustainability of his production company.

> You have to stay relevant. This year, we had so much change. We took control of our affairs. We hired an accountant. We're like, "hey look, we're a business now." We formed a partnership and we got an accountant and found out we did a lot of things wrong. That made us be like, "ok, we can't just concentrate on the shows." We have to take control of everything. Now I spend a lot of time going over the finances and doing the accounting because I want to make sure everything is done right. And we have a much clearer idea of where we are, and we can use that information to see where we're going and where we've been. It's sustainable, but it's just like anything – you have to be smart about it. I've hired an assistant because it's just too much for me to do by myself. That was one thing that we did this year; we organized ourselves to be able to handle all this stuff. I got an office for the first time in ten years. I used to work at home, and that just doesn't work after a while. It started as a hobby, but now it's a real business.[24]

In this sense, over the course of ten years, Meyer has indeed gotten out of the basement – or out of his bedroom home office – and this movement and longevity has been due to his growing ability to tackle the business end of his creative practices.

As much as youth are increasingly grappling with the logistics of professionalization of their cultural production, the creative industries are also characterized by the bleeding together of work and leisure for many youth. Noah comments that he's "chummy with a lot of people that [he does] business with" and suggests that his personal investment and connections with other like-minded people is something that sustains his interest in creative industries work.

> One reason why I stuck around for the past couple of years is because of the people ... A lot of my friends now are five to ten years older than me. I like the people, specifically the Montreal scene, because it's all I know. A lot of my good friends are people from Blue Skies, people from Pop [Montreal], [people from] bands that I've worked with. It's dangerous. Sometimes when that line [between work life and social life] gets blurred it's a little dark, but other times it's the greatest. Sometimes I'm sitting at the door [of a music venue], and I'm sitting with a friend who's playing in a band. Everyone gets paid at the end of the day; everyone is happy, drinking beers. Other times, though, when you pay a friend twenty-five dollars, it's kind of dark. Or when you feel slighted because a friend chooses to go with someone else.[25]

The intermingling of work and leisure might mean enjoyable and expressive work – beers and buddies – but it also means that leisure time becomes increasingly taxing. In his discussion of the music industry, David Hesmondhalgh notes that "in both major and independent companies, there is a stressful continuum between leisure and work. Evenings are often spent attending live concerts in order to stay aware of new developments and to maintain contacts. In independent record companies, there are additional burdens. The people working together are often friends, and relationships are put under great strain by new and unexpected roles."[26] Even outside of the music industry, many youth work long hours through their leisure, sometimes in uncomfortable and compromising situations, in order to create small-scale careers for themselves.

Creative industries labour might mean that a night of work brings in twenty-five dollars. Though the nature of these small-scale profits is hardly desirable, Noah and Meyer both espouse a commitment to developing and expanding a small-scale model of cultural activity. Meyer states,

We're not going to do a Bell Centre [a Montreal arena] show:
that's not who we are, that's not what we set out to do. We're
sort of a niche promoter in a sense, and it's very broad. Like last
night would be a good example. We had one indie rock show. It
was at Casa, which is a small room, but it was packed. Another
show, which was more weird, arty, kind of punk rock, and there
were six hundred people at that show. When I say niche, we deal
within various genres of music but I think we are able to reach
the people we need to reach to make sure the right people hear
about the right shows.[27]

Meyer's production company may put on multiple small concerts
in different genres on any given evening, but he does not desire to
replace this small-scale model with a larger scale, in his case, arena-
scale model. Behind this small-scale model, Meyer discusses a business practice based in a small-scale ethos. He characterizes his
employees as "all music lovers" and comments, "that's why I think
the company has been able to stay relevant and people really like the
company because it's not a faceless corporation. Everyone knows
who works at Blue Skies." For Meyer, this small-scale model is one
of human interaction and community. For Noah, this small-scale
model means restricted production and personal investment in what
he chooses to pursue. He describes restricting the production of his
own company, Passovah, as he became employed by Meyer's company, Blue Skies Turn Black.

In terms of my company, it's been an interesting year because I
got employed by Meyer's company. In terms of my own company, at the highest point, I was booking shows out of town and
booking about four concerts in Montreal per month. Since I've
kind of gotten absorbed by, not really absorbed, but a lot of my
time is spent working for Meyer now, I usually do no more than
two a month instead of four. And usually one, if not two, of
those shows are collaborations with Blue Skies. Right now I'm
trying to make it more boutique-y in a way. I want to only work
with bands that I actually feel passionate about. I want to represent bands that I like or that I feel that really need this push at
the right time.[28]

Here, Noah envisions his role as curatorial rather than strictly entrepreneurial, and the reference to his passion and desire to assist other

bands is reminiscent of the other community-based aspects of creative industries work seen in this book.

Finally, both Noah and Meyer highlight a learning process of constant navigation and negotiation. They describe learning through doing, and that this constant learning curve is not necessarily something that is undesirable as it allows for continued growth. Noah comments on the immersion, learning-through-doing process that occurred as he became employed by Blue Skies Turn Black: "Blue Skies has been a great learning experience. At first, the other person who was running production went away to the States for about two months. Instead of picking up more and more work as I became more seasoned at the job, I kind of got thrown into doing it five nights a week at the beginning because the other employee was away." Many youth are plunged into – or plunge themselves into – work in the creative industries that is often unfamiliar. Discussing his future in the music industry, Noah relates that he is unsure about what exact role he would ultimately like to pursue, but states, "there's nothing else that I'd rather be doing in terms of work." He is mindful of negative aspects of producing concerts, and "being at a show every night and having horrible sleep." He also has considered tour managing, but is aware that tour managers "have a lot of stress and they have to deal with a promoter in every town ... [and] adapt to a brand new climate every night." He describes himself as "sticking [his] feet in all different kinds of waters" in the music industry as he is unsure about continuing in his present line of work of producing concerts; he remarks, "maybe the challenge will die and I'll want something brand new. So the idea of managing a client, and maybe switching clients, and trying to build clients is something that I find the most promising and interesting right now."

For his part, Meyer describes the navigation and negotiation process of figuring out how to sustain and continue operating Blue Skies Turn Black. After examining the ways he had been doing business for ten years, he realized that some of his business practices had become outdated and began "looking at our smaller shows, looking at our bigger shows, trying to make budgets that made sense for a particular show instead of using the standard template we had created for many years." Part of Meyer's restructuring process was hiring new employees who brought "new ideas" with them. He comments, "I think the way for this company to survive is to always have new blood working with it so that we can stay relevant and stay up to speed." Despite the uncertainty that is inherent in the creative industries due to their transitional nature and the need for constant renewal to stay relevant, Meyer expresses optimism about his continued existence in this field. Referring to 2010, he states, "business is up across the board, from the big shows to the small shows." Many have raised alarm bells about the decline of profits in the music industry, but Meyer sees the change and restructuring of this industry as providing new opportunities for new business and new audiences. Citing the influx of new audiences at the concerts he promotes, Meyer suggests, "it's a new generation. It's not the kids who just want to listen to the record at home. They weren't brought up with records; they were brought up with going to shows. A whole generation of people that for them music is about the live experience and if they like it they'll download the mp3, maybe buy a record, most likely they'll buy a t-shirt, because record sales aren't what they used to be."[29] Meyer notes not necessarily a decline in revenues in the music industry, but a restructuring in how revenues are made. The process of figuring out where these new revenues are and how to pursue them can be found across the creative industries, and it is a process that many youth are grappling with.

Youth are most present in discussions of creative work when they are seen as a social problem, and creative activities are foregrounded as a remedy for risky behaviour. But youth cultural production is not a remedial pursuit. It takes place on a somewhat quieter scale, at home, in bedrooms and basements, in front of computers, guitars, cameras, and sewing machines. Though the field of education recognizes that youth bring skills from home into the classroom, it does not put enough stock in the fact that these skills return back home after graduation. These bedroom economies need to be taken seriously if we want to get an accurate picture of youth life pathways and of economic trends, and this warrants more empirical attention to how youth navigate and negotiate multiple streams of work and grants in order to generate income and make their way out of the basement while engaging in personally meaningful activities.

Notes

INTRODUCTION

1 McRobbie, *In the Culture Society*, 26.
2 McRobbie, "From Holloway to Hollywood," 97.
3 Sean Michaels, "Ice-T tells Soulja Boy: You Killed Hip-Hop," *Guardian*, 19 June 2008, http://www.guardian.co.uk/music/2008/jun/19/news. culture1.
4 "Soulja Boy Response to Ice-T," YouTube, 20 June 2008, http://www.you tube.com/watch?v=OYsytJvYJzw.
5 Ibid.
6 Ibid.
7 Canadian Youth Arts Network, *The Final Report*, 7.
8 Megan Twohey, "West Suburban Teen Runs Style Rookie Fashion Blog," *Chicago Tribune*, 30 December 2009, http://articles.chicagotribune. com/2009-12-30/news/0912300157_1_high-fashion-blog-suburban.
9 Sarah Nicole Prickett, "Interview: Tavi Gevinson," *Eye Weekly*, 23 March 2010, http://archives.eyeweekly.com/citystyle/article/86201.
10 Twohey, "West Suburban Teen."
11 Prickett, "Interview."
12 Twohey, "West Suburban Teen."
13 Peter Rowe, "Father's Day Odd Couple," *San Diego Union Tribune*, 20 June 2010, http://www.signonsandiego.com/news/2010/jun/20/fathers- day-odd-couple/.
14 Cited in Molgat and Larose-Hébert, *The Values of Youth in Canada*, 22.
15 Secréteriat à la Jeunesse, *Bringing Youth*, 42.
16 Beaujot and Kerr, *Emerging Youth Transition*.
17 Coles, "The Transformation of Youth Labour Markets," 119.

18 Gaudet, *Emerging Adulthood*, 11.
19 Molgat and Larose-Hébert, *The Values of Youth in Canada*.
20 Banks and Hesmondhalgh, "Looking for Work," 417, 418.
21 Ibid., 420.
22 McRobbie, "From Holloway to Hollywood," 97.
23 Canadian Conference of the Arts, ABC *on the Status of the Artist*, 2.
24 Ibid.
25 Franke, *Current Realities and Emerging Issues Facing Youth*.
26 Throughout this work, the term "infrastructure" is used to refer to "hard" infrastructure, such as physical spaces, but also to refer to "soft" infrastructure, such as policies and programs. I argue that both are needed to support youth cultural production.
27 Duxbury, *Under Construction*, 9.
28 Ibid., 34.
29 Mercer, "From Indicators to Governance," 5.
30 Ibid., 12.
31 Hoechsmann and Low, *Reading Youth Writing*, 6.
32 See, for example, Buckingham, *Media Education*; Giroux, *Fugitive Cultures*; Hoechsmann and Low, *Reading Youth Writing*; Jenkins, *Confronting the Challenges*; Sefton-Green, *Young People, Creativity, and New Technologies*; Willis, *Common Culture*.
33 Florida, *The Rise of the Creative Class*.
34 Ibid., 45–6.
35 Statistics Canada, *Industry – North American Industry*; Statistics Canada, *Occupation – 2001 National Occupational Classification*.
36 McRobbie, *In the Culture Society*, 26.
37 Risa Dickens, interview with the author, April 2009.
38 DECODE, *Next Generation*, 8.
39 Ibid., 14.
40 Ibid., 35.
41 Hill Strategies Research Inc., *New Report Reveals 10 Key Facts*, 3.
42 Ibid., 3.
43 Ibid.
44 Statistics Canada, *Industry – North American Industry*.

CHAPTER ONE

1 Goodley, Lawthom, Clough, and Moore, *Researching Life Stories*, ix. Regarding the use of life stories and turn to narrative and oral history

research in the social sciences, see Bertaux, *Biography and Society*; Plummer, *Documents of Life*; Parker, *Life after Life*; Riessman, *Narrative Analysis*; Smith, Harré, and Van Langenhove, *Rethinking Methods*; Atkinson, *The Life Story Interview*; Booth and Booth, *Growing up with Parents*; Denzin and Lincoln, *Handbook of Qualitative Research*; Erben, *Biography and Education*; Goodley, *Self-Advocacy in the Lives of People*; Chamberlayne, Bornat, and Wengraf, *The Turn to Biographical Methods*; Miller, *Researching Life Stories*; Clough, *Narratives and Fiction*.

2 Van Manen, *Researching Lived Experience*, xi.

3 McRobbie, *In the Culture Society*, 27.

4 Cited in Mercer, "From Indicators to Governance," 13.

5 Haraway, "Situated Knowledges," 296–7.

6 Maxwell, "Designing a Qualitative Study," 87.

7 Daniel Terdiman, "My Left Arm for a Gmail Account," *Wired*, 20 May 2004, www.wired.com/culture/lifestyle/news/2004/05/63524.

8 McRobbie, *In the Culture Society*, ix.

9 Tom McNihol, "25 Best Blogs 2009," *Time*, 2009, http://www.time.com/time/specials/packages/0,28757,1879276,00.html.

10 Sean Michaels, interview with the author, July 2009.

11 Spencer, *DIY*, 11.

12 McRobbie, "Second-hand Dresses."

13 Michaels, interview.

14 Drew Nelles, "Issue 37 Launch: Interview with Sean Michaels," *Maisonneuve*, 15 September 2010, http://maisonneuve.org/pressroom/article/2010/sep/15/interview-37-launch-interview-sean-michaels/.

15 John Seroff, "Meeting the Neighbors," *Tofu Hut*, 9 September 2004, http://tofuhut.blogspot.ca/2004/09/holtzclaw-is-dead-long-live-holtzclaw.html.

16 Michaels, interview.

17 Amy Johnson, interview with the author, June 2009.

18 Secréteriat à la Jeunesse, *Young People*, 27.

19 Johnson, interview, June 2009.

20 Amy Johnson, interview with the author, September 2010.

21 *WORN Fashion Journal*, "About," http://www.wornjournal.com/about/.

22 Serah-Marie McMahon, interview with the author, March 2007.

23 Serah-Marie McMahon, interview with the author, November 2010.

24 Serah-Marie McMahon and Gwen Stegelmann, "Dear Readers," *WORN Fashion Journal*, Fall/Winter 2011, 4.

25 McMahon, interview, March 2007.

26 McMahon, interview, November 2010.

CHAPTER TWO

1 Caves, *Creative Industries*; Leadbeater and Oakley, *The Independents*; Lloyd, *Neo-Bohemia*; McRobbie, *In the Culture Society*; "Second-hand Dresses."
2 Galloway and Dunlop, "A Critique of Definitions," 17.
3 Ibid.
4 Cunningham, "The Creative Industries after Cultural Policy," 106.
5 Hesmondhalgh, *The Cultural Industries*, 227.
6 Ibid., 14.
7 See Hesmondhalgh, "The British Dance Music Industry," "Indie: The Institutional Politics," and "Post-Punk's Attempts" for his discussions of some of the parameters of the independent music industry.
8 Galloway and Dunlop, "A Critique of Definitions," 19.
9 Banks and O'Connor, "After the Creative Industries," 367.
10 Florida, *The Rise of the Creative Class*, 31.
11 Ibid., 32.
12 See Florida, *The Rise of the Creative Class*, fig. 4.3, 75.
13 Ibid., 71.
14 Dubinsky, "In Praise of Small Cities," 85.
15 Throsby, "Modelling the Cultural Industries," 229–30.
16 McGuigan, "Doing a Florida Thing," 295.
17 Oakley, "The Disappearing Arts," 410.
18 Williams, *Culture*.
19 Hesmondhalgh, "Bourdieu, the Media and Cultural Production," 214.
20 Ibid., 229.
21 McRobbie, *In the Culture Society*, ix.
22 Ibid., x.
23 Ibid., 26.
24 Ibid., 27.
25 Hannah Seligson, "No Jobs? Young Graduates Make Their Own," *New York Times*, 11 December 2010, http://www.nytimes.com/2010/12/12/business/12yec.html?pagewanted=1.
26 Ibid.
27 Lloyd, *Neo-Bohemia*, 17.
28 Ibid., 239.
29 McRobbie, "Second-hand Dresses."
30 Caves, *Creative Industries*, 29.
31 Hesmondhalgh, *The Cultural Industries*.
32 Ibid., 200, 229.

33 Ibid., 229.

34 Ibid., 221–2.

35 Huq, *Beyond Subculture*.

36 Andrew Nosnitsky, "Lil B," *The Wire*, May 2010, 16.

37 Zach Baron, "'You Know Who I Feel Like? I Feel Like I'm Motherfucking Mel Gibson!': The Ten Greatest Things Lil B Said Saturday Night at Santos Party House," *Village Voice Blogs*, 26 July 2010, http://blogs.villagevoice. com/music/2010/07/you_know_who_i.php.

38 Nosnitsky, "Lil B."

39 Ryan Dombal, "tUnE-yArDs Sign to 4AD," *Pitchfork*, 15 July 2009, http:// pitchfork.com/news/35934-tune-yards-sign-to-4ad/.

40 Tyler Grisham, "Guest Lists: Diamond Rings," *Pitchfork*, 20 October 2010, http://pitchfork.com/features/guest-lists/7874-diamond-rings/.

41 Bill Brownstein, "Don't Sell This Other Festival Short," *Gazette* (Montreal), 3 July 2009, http://www2.canada.com/montrealgazette/columnists/story. html?id=52080ecf-29b9-4b84-b43b-4e6cb8a092ac.

42 Bill Brownstein, "Some Like It Short. Really Short," *Gazette* (Montreal), 9 September 2009, http://www2.canada.com/montrealgazette/columnists/ story.html?id=cb8afd5d-0d2d-4753-9b98-544ebe657265.

43 Sefton-Green, "Introduction: Evaluating Creativity," 4.

44 Ibid, 2.

45 Buckingham, *Media Education*, 128.

46 Sefton-Green, "Introduction: Evaluating Creativity."

47 Jenkins, *Confronting the Challenges*, 32.

48 Sefton-Green and Reiss, "Mulitmedia Literacies," 3.

49 Jenkins, *Confronting the Challenges*, 3.

50 Ibid.

51 Ibid., 51.

52 Levine, "A Public Voice for Youth," 119.

53 Hesmondhalgh, *The Cultural Industries*.

54 Levine, "A Public Voice for Youth," 131.

55 Ibid., 131, 132.

56 Buckingham, *Media Education*, 137.

57 Ibid., 134.

58 Ibid., 131.

59 Jenkins, *Confronting the Challenges*, 6.

60 Hesmondhalgh, *The Cultural Industries*, 214.

61 Jenkins, *Confronting the Challenges*, 3.

62 Ibid., 18.

63 Clarke et al., "Subcultures, Cultures, and Class," 32.

64 McRobbie, *Feminism and Youth Culture*, 26.

65 McRobbie, *Postmodernism and Popular Culture*, 159.

66 Clarke et al., "Subcultures, Cultures, and Class," 35.

67 Ibid.

68 Giroux, *Fugitive Cultures*, 90.

69 Ibid., 3.

70 McRobbie, *Postmodernism and Popular Culture*, 156.

71 Giroux, *Fugitive Cultures*, 10.

72 Muggleton and Weinzierl, "What is 'Post-subcultural Studies' Anyway?," 13.

73 Huq, *Beyond Subculture*, 41.

74 Willis, *Common Culture*, 9.

75 McRobbie, *In the Culture Society*.

76 Willis, *Common Culture*, 82.

77 Thornton, "The Social Logic of Subcultural Capital."

78 Reddington, "'Lady' Punks in Bands: A Subculturette?," 246.

79 McRobbie, *Postmodernism and Popular Culture*, 161.

80 Ibid.

81 Ibid., 159.

82 Ibid., 162.

83 Ibid., 167.

84 Ibid., 160.

85 McRobbie, *In the Culture Society*.

86 Jenkins, *Confronting the Challenges*, 4.

87 Cited in Volkerling, "From Cool Britannia to Hot Nation," 439.

88 Oakley, "Include Us Out," 263.

CHAPTER THREE

1 Foote, *Federal Cultural Policy in Canada*, 8.

2 Zemans, "Where Is Here?," 16.

3 Foote, *Federal Cultural Policy in Canada*.

4 Schafer and Fortier, *Review of the Federal Policies*.

5 Foote, *Federal Cultural Policy in Canada*.

6 Schafer and Fortier, *Review of the Federal Policies*, 22.

7 Baeker, "Back to the Future," 279.

8 Zemans, "Where Is Here?," 6.

9 Paul Litt, "Canada's Highbrow Bastion," *The Beaver*, February–March 2007, 14–15.

10 Schafer and Fortier, *Review of the Federal Policies*.

11 Baeker, "Back to the Future," 280.

12 Ibid., 285.

13 Saskatchewan Arts Board, "About Us," accessed 15 October 2012, http://www.artsboard.sk.ca/about-us.

14 Baeker, "Back to the Future," 280.

15 Meisel, "The Chameleon-like Complexion of Cultural Policy," 71.

16 Ibid.

17 Foote, *Federal Cultural Policy in Canada*, 4–5.

18 Ibid., 5.

19 Ibid., 17.

20 Jeffrey, *Youth Policy*.

21 Cultural Human Resources Council, "Becoming a YIP Intern," accessed 15 October 2012, http://www.culturalhrc.ca/YIP/intern-become-e.asp.

22 Steven Greenhouse, "The Unpaid Intern, Legal or Not," *New York Times*, 2 April 2010, http://www.nytimes.com/2010/04/03/business/03intern.html?pagewanted=all.

23 McRobbie, *In the Culture Society*.

24 Bennett, "Putting Policy into Cultural Studies," 23.

25 See, for example, Banks and Hesmondhalgh, "Looking for Work"; Leadbeater and Oakley, *The Independents*; McRobbie, *In the Culture Society*; "Clubs to Companies"; "From Holloway to Hollywood"; "Making a Living."

26 Banks and Hesmondhalgh, "Looking for Work," 428.

27 Ibid., 429.

28 McRobbie, *British Fashion Design*, 18.

29 Leadbeater and Oakley, *The Independents*, 12.

30 McRobbie, *British Fashion Design*, 12.

31 McRobbie, *In the Culture Society*, 29.

32 McRobbie, *British Fashion Design*, 11.

33 Straw, "Pathways of Cultural Movement," 183.

34 Ibid., 187.

35 Ibid., 191–2.

36 Robertson, *Policy Matters*, iii.

37 Ibid.

38 Ibid.

39 Ibid.

40 Canadian Conference of the Arts, *A Canadian Cultural Policy*, 1.

41 Department of Justice Canada, *Status of the Artist Act*.

42 Gaztambide-Fernandez, "The Artist in Society," 239.

43 Ibid., 240.

44 Arnold, "Sweetness and Light," 31.

45 Ibid., 29.
46 Gaztambide-Fernandez, "The Artist in Society," 244.
47 Ibid., 248.
48 Ibid., 250.
49 Ibid., 253.
50 Ibid., 251.
51 Department of Justice Canada, *Status of the Artist Act*.
52 Ibid.
53 Neil, *The Status of Status*, 3–4.
54 Gaztambide-Fernandez, "The Artist in Society," 244.
55 Leadbeater and Oakley, *The Independents*, 11.
56 DECODE, *Next Generation*, 55.
57 Ibid., 13.
58 McRobbie, "Making a Living," 133.
59 DECODE, *Next Generation*, 55.
60 Neil, *The Status of Status*, 7.
61 Ibid., 13.
62 Foote, *Federal Cultural Policy in Canada*, 8.
63 Matt Shane, interview with the author, November 2010.
64 Jeannotte and Straw, "Reflections on the Cultural and Political Implications," 274.
65 Shane, interview.
66 Leadbeater and Oakley, *The Independents*, 20–1.
67 Creative Skillset, *Strategic Skills*, 21.
68 Higgs, Cunningham, and Bakshi, *Beyond the Creative Industries*, 93.
69 Ibid., 95.
70 Leadbeater and Oakley, *The Independents*, 26–7.
71 DECODE, *Next Generation*, 3–4.
72 Leadbeater and Oakley, *The Independents*, 29.
73 Eliot Van Buskirk, "Dumb Labels, Laws (Not Google) to Blame for Music Blog Deletions," *Wired*, 12 February 2010, http://www.wired.com/epicenter/2010/02/dumb-labels-laws-bots-not-google-to-blame-for-music-blog-deletions/.
74 Sean Michaels, "Google Shuts Down Music Blogs without Warning," *Guardian*, 11 February 2010, http://www.guardian.co.uk/music/2010/feb/11/google-deletes-music-blogs.
75 Van Buskirk, "Dumb Labels."
76 Patrick Duffy, "R.I.P. Pop Tarts Suck Toasted," *Pop Tarts Suck Toasted* (blog), 3 June 2010, http://poptarts.tumblr.com/post/660119812/r-i-p-pop-tarts-suck-toasted.

77 Michaels, "Google Shuts Down."
78 Ibid.
79 Cited in Michaels, "Google Shuts Down."
80 Michaels, "Google Shuts Down."
81 "Musicblogocide 2K10: La vie continue," *Masala* (blog), 12 February 2010, http://www.masalacism.com/2010/02/musicblogocide2k10-la-vie-continue/.
82 Ibid.
83 Ibid.
84 Patrick Duffy, "Response to 'Blogger Shuts Down Mp3 Blogs,'" *Pop Tarts Suck Toasted* (blog), 10 February 2010. http://poptarts.tumblr.com/post/382580784/theunderrated-stereoactivenyc-soupsoup.
85 Gollmitzer and Murray, *From Economy to Ecology*, 2.
86 Standing Committee on Canadian Heritage, *A Sense of Place*.
87 Ibid.
88 Gaztambide-Fernandez, "The Artist in Society," 252–3.
89 Ibid., 235.
90 Ibid., 255.
91 Ibid.
92 Leadbeater and Oakley, *The Independents*, 21.
93 Ibid., 42.

CHAPTER FOUR

1 Gregg, "Reframing the Case for Culture," 74.
2 Ibid., 76.
3 Fix and Sivak, "The Growing Case," 145.
4 Hebdige, *Hiding in the Light*, 17.
5 Gregg, "Reframing the Case for Culture," 78, 79.
6 Americans for the Arts, "About Us," 5 October 2012, http://www.artsusa.org/about_us/.
7 Gollmitzer and Murray, *From Economy to Ecology*, 18.
8 Throsby cited in Gollmitzer and Murray, *From Economy to Ecology*, 18.
9 Stanley, "Introduction," 8.
10 Ibid., 14.
11 Meisel, "The Chameleon-like Complexion of Cultural Policy," 66.
12 Murray, "Cultural Participation," 37.
13 Ibid.
14 Oakley, "The Disappearing Arts," 411.
15 Ibid.

16 Throsby, "Modelling the Cultural Industries," 222.

17 Galla cited in Mercer, "From Indicators to Governance," 14.

18 Ibid.

19 Donald and Morrow, *Competing for Talent*.

20 Baeker cited in Donald and Morrow, *Competing for Talent*, 18.

21 Ibid.

22 Mercer, "From Indicators to Governance," 16.

23 Throsby, "Modelling the Cultural Industries," 230.

24 Ibid., 225.

25 Slaby, *Making a Single Case*, 10.

26 Ibid.

27 Oakley, "Not So Cool," 71.

28 Bennett, "Putting Policy into Cultural Studies," 23.

29 Robertson, *Policy Matters*, 6.

30 Canadian Conference of the Arts, "CCA Bulletin 49/08 – The Economic Meltdown."

31 CBC News, "Ballet BC Lays Off All Dancers, Most Office Staff," *CBC*, 25 November 2008, http://www.cbc.ca/news/canada/british-columbia/story/2008/11/25/bc-ballet-layoffs.html.

32 Daniel J. Wakin, "Sudden Finale," *New York Times*, 22 June 2009, http://www.nytimes.com/2009/07/26/arts/dance/26waki.html?_r=1&hp.

33 Government of Canada, "Protecting Canada's Future."

34 Ibid.

35 Gollmitzer and Murray, *From Economy to Ecology*, 3.

36 Government of Canada, "Protecting Canada's Future."

37 Sutherland and Straw, "The Canadian Music Industry," 153.

38 Maxwell, *The Place of Arts and Culture*, 33.

39 Cited in Henighan, *The Presumption of Culture*, 15.

40 Robert Benzie, Bruce Campion-Smith, and Les Whittington, "Ordinary Folks Don't Care About the Arts: Harper," *The Star* (Toronto), 24 September 2008, http://www.thestar.com/FederalElection/article/504811.

41 Margaret Atwood, "To Be Creative Is, In Fact, Canadian," *Globe and Mail*, 24 September 2008, http://www.theglobeandmail.com/news/politics/article 712137.ece.

42 Canadian Conference of the Arts, "CCA Bulletin 52/08 – The Cultural Sector."

43 Department of Finance Canada, *Canada's Economic Action Plan*, 174.

44 Canadian Conference of the Arts, "CCA Bulletin 03/09 – The 2009/2010 Federal Stimulus Budget."

45 Canadian Conference of the Arts, "CCA Bulletin 04/09 – More Budget Details."

46 Department of Finance Canada, *Canada's Economic Action Plan*, 177.

47 Ibid., 175.

48 Canadian Conference of the Arts, "CCA Bulletin 04/09 – More Budget Details."

49 Creative City Network of Canada, "About the CCNC," accessed 8 November 2012, http://www.creativecity.ca/about-the-network.php.

50 Creative City Network of Canada, *Making the Case*, 2.

51 Ibid., 6, 7.

52 Albright, *Creative Spaces*, 2.

53 Ibid., 3.

54 Hughes cited in Fix and Sivak, "The Growing Case," 146.

55 Zemans and Coles, "One Hundred Musicians," 2.

56 Coles, *Focus on Youth*, 2.

57 Department of Justice Canada, "Arts and Recreation Sector."

58 Rea McNamara, "The Youth Program That Worked," *Eye Weekly* (Toronto), 7 November 2007, http://www.eyeweekly.com/city/features/article/8596.

59 Offishall cited in Coles, *Focus on Youth*, 3.

60 Wright, John, and Sheel, *Edmonton Arts*, 4.

61 Ibid., 7.

CHAPTER FIVE

1 For a full discussion of the British influence on the inception of Canadian cultural policy, see Gattinger and Saint Pierre, "Can National Cultural Policy," and Upchurch, "Linking Cultural Policy."

2 Oakley, "Not So Cool Britannia," 68.

3 Ibid., 69.

4 Department of Culture, Media and Sport, *Creative Britain*, 4.

5 Ibid., 6.

6 Ibid., 7.

7 Ibid.

8 Banks and Hesmondhalgh, "Looking for Work," 418.

9 Department of Culture, Media and Sport, *Creative Britain*, 7.

10 Ibid., 21.

11 Ibid., 22.

12 "The Music Industry: From Major to Minor," *The Economist*, 10 January 2008, http://www.economist.com/node/10498664?story_id=E1_TDQJRGGQ.

13 Jeff Leeds, "The Net is a Boon for Indie Labels," *New York Times*, 27 December 2005, http://www.nytimes.com/2005/12/27/arts/music/27musi.html? pagewanted=all.

14 Department of Culture, Media and Sport, *Creative Britain*, 5.

15 Ibid., 21.

16 Ibid., 20.

17 Banks and Hesmondhalgh, "Looking for Work," 423.

18 Department of Culture, Media and Sport, *Creative Britain*, 12.

19 Ibid., 19.

20 McRobbie, "From Holloway to Hollywood," 101.

21 McRobbie, "Clubs to Companies," 518.

22 Beat of Boyle Street, accessed 18 November 2012, http://www.beatofboyle street.com/.

23 Hamilton, *Undervoiced Voices*, 25.

24 Warner, *Youth on Youth*, 47.

25 Ibid., 48.

26 Ibid., 54.

27 Ibid., 55.

28 Hamilton, *Undervoiced Voices*, 7.

29 Department of Culture, Media and Sport, *Creative Britain*, 17.

30 Ibid., 6.

31 Ibid., 20.

32 Ibid., 6.

33 Banks and Hesmondhalgh, "Looking for Work," 426.

34 Department of Culture, Media and Sport, *Creative Britain*, 6.

35 Ibid.

36 Illiot cited in Frederika Whitehead, "It's the (Creative) Economy, Stupid," *Art Monthly*, July/August 2008, 47.

37 Morris cited in Whitehead, "It's the (Creative) Economy, Stupid," 47.

38 Conference Board of Canada, *Valuing Culture*.

39 DECODE, *Next Generation*, 47.

40 Ibid.

41 Albright, *Creative Spaces*, 2.

42 Canadian Conference for the Arts, ABC *on the Status of the Artist*.

43 Gattinger and Saint-Pierre, "Can National Cultural Policy," 344.

44 Ibid.

45 Secréteriat à la Jeunesse, *Bringing Youth*, 9.

46 Ibid., 7.

47 Ibid., 28.

48 Ibid.

49 Secréteriat à la Jeunesse, *Investing in Youth*, 72.

50 Ministère de l'Éducation, Loisir, et Sport, *Québec Education Program*, 67.

51 Ibid., 333–4.

52 Ibid., 67.

53 Ibid., 5.

54 Ibid., 376.

55 Ibid., 67.

56 Katherine Peacock, interview with the author, June 2009.

57 Emploi Québec, "Jeunes volontaires."

58 Ibid.

59 Peacock, interview.

60 Creative Skillset, *Strategic Skills*, 22.

61 Peacock, interview.

62 The Mittenstrings, "About," accessed 10 November 2012, http://www.mittenstrings.com/about.php.

63 Lily Lanken, interview with the author, September 2010.

64 The Mittenstrings, "About," http://www.mittenstrings.com/about.php.

65 Lanken, interview.

66 Etan Muskat, interview with the author, September 2010.

67 Dan Beirne, interview with the author, September 2010.

68 Muskat, interview.

69 Chris Barry, "The Joke's Online," *Montreal Mirror*, 24 September 2009, http://www.montrealmirror.com/2009/092409/news2.html.

70 Q, CBC Radio, "Jian Ghomeshi Interviews The Bitter End," 3 December 2009, http://podcast.cbc.ca/mp3/qpodcast_ 20091203_23990.mp3.

71 Beirne, interview.

72 Muskat, interview.

73 Q, CBC Radio, "Jian Ghomeshi Interviews The Bitter End."

74 Ibid.

75 Barry, "The Joke's Online."

76 Ibid.

77 Ibid.

CHAPTER SIX

1 See, for example, Rodrigo Perez, "The Next Big Scene: Montreal," *Spin*, February 2005, 61–5 ; David Carr, "Cold Fusion: Montreal's Explosive Music Scene," *New York Times*, 5 February 2005, http://www.nytimes.com/2005/02/06/arts/music/06carr.html?pagewanted=print&position=.

2 Straw, "Scenes and Sensibilities," 248.

3　Straw, "Cultural Scenes," 412.

4　Straw, "Scenes and Sensibilities," 249.

5　Straw, "Cultural Scenes," 412–13.

6　Stahl, "Tracing out an Anglo-Bohemia," 118, 100.

7　Stahl, "Musicmaking and the City," 145.

8　Ibid., 143, 145.

9　Perez, "The Next Big Scene: Montreal."

10　Carr, "Cold Fusion."

11　Denny Lee, "36 Hours in Montreal," *New York Times*, 12 August 2010, http://www.nytimes.com/2010/08/15/travel/15hours.html.

12　Straw, "Cultural Scenes," 412.

13　Ibid.

14　Susan Semenak, "Handmade Montreal," *Gazette* (Montreal), 10 December 2010, http://www.montrealgazette.com/entertainment/Handmade+ Montreal/3958636/story.html.

15　Ibid.

16　Ibid.

17　Straw, "Scenes and Sensibilities," 245.

18　Pied Carré, *Mémoire sur les Quartiers Culturels*.

19　Robyn Fadden, "Casa del Popolo's New License to Rock; Small-Scale Spectacle," *The Hour*, 3–9 September 2009, 8.

20　All translations in this chapter are the author's own. Croteau, Sebastien, "Montreal: City of Noise, Silence and Culture," panel discussion, Pop Montreal, Montreal, 2 October 2010. "Je vous mets au défi d'essayer de trouver sur le site [Internet] de la Ville de Montréal, comment obtenir ce type de permis là et les règles qui entourent la question de ce type de permis là. C'est vraiment pas évident. On a beaucoup de petits lieux de spectacle qui ont ouvert et qui ont fait à peu près toutes les démarches qu'il faut pour ouvrir un lieu de façon légale. Et à un moment donné, un inspecteur de la Ville est passé et a dit, 'Bien, tu n'as pas ton permis d'occupation. Tu as ton permis de restaurant, mais tu n'as pas ton permis pour faire des spectacles.' Et ces gens là au départ n'avaient aucune idée que ça prenait ce genre de permis là."

21　Fadden, "Casa del Popolo."

22　Ville de Montréal, *Montréal, Metropole Culturelle*.

23　Kelly Ebbels, "Drawn and Quartered," *Maisonneuve*, Fall 2009, 47.

24　See, for example, Bradford, *Creative Cities*; Donald and Morrow, *Competing for Talent*; Gertler, Florida, Gates, and Vinodrai, *Competing on Creativity*; Gertler, *Creative Cities*; Stolarick, Florida, and Musante, *Montréal's Capacity for Creative Connectivity*.

25 Duxbury, *Creative Cities*, 5.

26 Ville de Montréal, *Montréal, Metropole Culturelle.*

27 Duxbury, *Creative Cities*, 4.

28 Ian Ilavsky, "Ecology of a Scene: Indie Culture from Stockholm to San Paulo," panel discussion, Pop Montreal, Montreal, 3 October 2009.

29 McRobbie, "Making a Living," 141.

30 Ville de Montréal, *Cultural Quarters*, 7.

31 Pied Carré, *Mémoire sur les Quartiers Culturels.*

32 Mercer, "From Indicators to Governance," 13.

33 Ibid., 12.

34 Billurcu cited in Malcolm Fraser, "Going Posters," *The Mirror* (Montreal), 29 April 2010, http://www.montrealmirror.com/2010/042910/news3.html.

35 Hilary Leftick, interview with the author, December 2010.

36 L'ALPAS, *Quand L'Affichage Devient Sauvage!*, 3. "Revenons sur l'exclusivité de la firme Publicité Sauvage et les limites qu'elle impose aux petits producteurs et aux PLAS [petits lieux d'art et de spectacles]. Une campagne d'affichage sur palissades impose un format d'affiches d'au moins 11" par 17" et l'impression d'un minimum de 300 affiches, puisque la mise en place débute à 300 affiches. Si nous estimons que les frais pour répondre à cette exigence s'élèvent à près de 1,000$, l'amortissement de cet investissement représente à lui seul 100 spectateurs à 10$ chacun. Les revenus de prestation étant déjà très incertains, cela suppose que les revenus générés par un spectacle seraient presque entièrement engloutis dans ce nécessaire exercice de visibilité."

37 Billucru cited in Fraser, "Going Posters."

38 Leftick, interview.

39 Stahl, "Tracing out an Anglo-Bohemia."

40 Leftick, interview.

41 COLLE, "About," accessed 10 November 2012, http://collemontreal.org/about.

42 Leftick, interview.

43 COLLE, "About," accessed 10 November 2012, http://collemontreal.org/about.

44 Ibid.

45 Cited in COLLE, "Legal Information Sheet," 19 May 2010, http://colle montreal.org/wp-content/uploads/2010/05/LegalInformationSheet.pdf.

46 This concept was tested in a pilot project in downtown Montreal in 2005. Though this project was deemed successful, it was not renewed. See L'APLAS' report, *Quand L'Afflichage Devient Sauvage!* for a full account of the history and the particulars of the postering issue in Montreal.

47 Leftick, interview.

48 CBC News, "Montreal Postering Bylaw 'Invalid': Court of Appeal," CBC, 20 July 2010, http://www.cbc.ca/canada/montreal/story/2010/07/20/montreal-poster-bylaw-jaggi-singh.html.

49 Leftick, interview.

50 Pop Montreal, "Postering is Legit. Somewhat," Popmontreal.com. 19 December 2010, http://web.archive.org/web/20101219224426/http://pop montreal.com/en/pop/news/postering-legit-somewhat.

51 Scott Johnson Gailey, interview with the author, November 2011.

52 Patrick Lejtenyi, "Live, Loud, and Scared," The Mirror (Montreal), 23 September 2010, http://www.montrealmirror.com/wp/2010/09/23/news/cover-live-loud-and-scared/.

53 L'APLAS, "L'APLAS du Bruit à Montréal," 9 September 2010, http://www.aplas.ca/tiki-index.php#L_APLAS_du_bruit_Montr_al_.1. "Avant le durcissement de la présente règlementation sur le bruit et le début de l'opération NOISE, la Ville et les élus auraient très bien pu en place un veritable processus de concertation incluant les citoyens et les intervenants du milieu de la musique indépendante. De cette concertation aurait pu émerger des pistes de solution et à partir de ces dernières, une stratégie d'ensemble aurait pu être élaborée. L'arrondissement aurait pu aussi rencontrer les principaux intéressés et leur faire part de son projet de réglementation et bâtir des outils de sensibilisation. Bref, elle aurait pu amorcer un dialogue et démontrer qu'elle comprend et prend à coeur son rôle de métropole culturelle."

54 L'APLAS, "Bruit de Fond," 16 September 2010, http://www.aplas.ca/tiki-index.php#Bruit_de_fond, 3. "Un PLAS qui n'est pas propriétaire de son bâtiment ne se hasardera jamais à investir des sommes importantes en insonorisation. Pourquoi? Advenant le non-renouvellement de son bail commercial, le locataire pourrait se retrouver à avoir investi inutilement cet argent. Cet argument du 'renouvellement hasardeux' nous est d'ailleurs servi par les bailleurs de fonds pour justifier le fait de ne pas investir d'argent dans les PLAS. "

55 Ibid., 4. "Par où faut-il commencer? Par l'accès à la propriété? Le soutien à la programmation? L'insonorisation et les équipements techniques et sonores? Probablement sur tous les fronts à la fois. Comme vous le voyez, tous ces éléments sont interreliés. C'est donc l'ensemble des problèmes que connaissent les PLAS que nous devons considérer et examiner si nous voulons véritablement les aider. On ne peut pas porter notre attention sur un seul de ces éléments (le bruit) et espérer régler le problème d'un seul coup."

56 Lemieux, "Montreal: City of Noise." "On a fermé de notre plein gré parce qu'on avait trop de pression. Trop de pression de la police et du voisinage

pour le son. Alors on a décidé de fermer parce qu'on n'avait pas nécessairement les reins assez solide pour mener cette bataille là … Les deux premières années ça allait très bien, on avait une bonne entente avec nos voisins et un jour, un nouveau voisin est arrivé et a décidé de nous faire la guerre. Il a mené son combat jusqu'à l'arrondissement, et le maire de l'arrondissement en a fait un cas personnel. Ils se sont fait un peu de capital politique sur notre dos. Ils ont envoyé ça à la moralité et la moralité a commencé à nous harceler. Le ZooBizarre est une salle qui a une capacité de 120 places, parfois les policiers arrivaient pour des plaints de son à 8. Ils entraient avec leur flashlight dans une soirée poésie. C'était devenu comme ça à chaque semaine, à chaque semaine notre voisin s'efforçait d'appeler la police et les policiers se présentaient toujours en plus grand nombre. Et nous, on a cédé a la pression."

57 Croteau, "Montreal: City of Noise." "Les petits lieux sont des endroits où on développe la culture dans les quartiers et c'est très important qu'ils puissent demeurer où ils sont. On parle de La Casa Del Popolo, Le Divan Orange, je les verrais mal déménager, je ne sais pas si ils seraient capables de survivre un déménagement parce que souvent on n'a pas d'aide financière pour ça. C'est donc très important de travailler à encrer ces lieux là dans leurs communautés. Et une des seules façons d'encrer ces lieux la, c'est de s'assurer que ces gens là qui sont locataires puissent avoir accès à la propriété. Et ça, il n'y rien encore pour s'assurer de ça. Ces lieux là développent toute une infrastructure, toute une vie qui se regroupe autour de ces lieux là, et ils sont tellement fragilisés par l'ensemble des réglementations, des lois. Ils sont surtout fragilisés par le fait qu'on n'est pas soutenu financièrement d'aucune façon."

58 Croteau, "Montreal: City of Noise." "Est-ce-que les propriétaires d'établissement on le temps d'aller à chaque fois contester en cours municipale?"

59 Croteau, "Montreal: City of Noise." "Est-ce que les gens comme Alexandre, qui font de l'administration, du bar, du booking, qui passe la mop, on le temps de participer ou de faire ce genre de chose là? C'est vraiment pas evident."

60 Elisabeth Faure, "Making the Grade? Merchants, Residents and Elected Officials Assess Projet Montréal's First Year Running the Plateau Borough," *The Mirror* (Montreal), 25 November 2010, http://www.montrealmirror.com/wp/2010/11/25/news/cover-making-the-grade/.

CHAPTER SEVEN

1 Hamilton, *Undervoiced Voices*, 3.
2 Jenkins, *Convergence Culture*, 215.

3 Piano, "Resisting Subjects," 254.
4 Ibid.
5 Ignite the Americas, *Policy Primer*, 1.
6 Straw, *Cultural Scenes*, 412.
7 Oakley, "Include Us Out," 261–2.
8 Ibid., 262.
9 DECODE, *Next Generation*, 22–3.
10 *Foundations & Pipelines*, 2.
11 Risa Dickens, interview with the author, April 2009.
12 Ibid.
13 *Foundations & Pipelines*, 4.
14 Walcott cited in Fix and Sivak, "The Growing Case," 148.
15 Sokoloski, *So Much Things to Say*, 6.
16 Ibid., 7.
17 Hamilton, *Undervoiced Voices*, 17.
18 Ibid., 24, 28.
19 Albright, *Creative Spaces*, 2.
20 Ibid., 5.
21 Ibid., 6.
22 DECODE, *Next Generation*, 25.
23 Ibid., 8.
24 Hamilton, *Undervoiced Voices*, 8–9.
25 DECODE, *Next Generation*, 25.
26 Ibid., 55.
27 Ibid., 54.
28 Hamilton, *Undervoiced Voices*, 8.
29 Ibid., 10.
30 Leadbeater and Oakley, *The Independents*, 29.
31 DECODE, *Next Generation*, 10.
32 Ibid., 19.
33 Sokoloski, *So Much Things to Say*, 7.
34 Ibid.
35 Ibid., 8.

CHAPTER EIGHT

1 Ignite the Americas, *Ignite the Americas Youth Arts Policy Forum*, 4.
2 Michaëlle Jean, "Speech on the Occasion of the Youth Arts Policy Forum: Ignite the Americas" (speech, Ignite the Americas Conference, Toronto, 16 September 2008).
3 Ignite the Americas, *Ignite the Americas Youth Arts Policy Forum*, 12.

4 Ignite the Americas, "About Ignite the Americas," accessed 8 September 2009, http://www.ignitetheamericas.ca/content/abouts.

5 Ignite the Americas, *Policy Primer*, 2.

6 Ignite the Americas, "About Ignite the Americas." http://www.ignitethe americas.ca/content/abouts.

7 Ignite the Americas, *Ignite the Americas Youth Arts Policy Forum*, 3.

8 Che Kothari, "Ignite Speech Made at the Fourth Ministerial Meeting of Cultural Ministers and Highest Appropriate Authorities" (speech, Bridgetown, Barbados, 21 November 2008).

9 Canadian Conference of the Arts, *Towards a National Advocacy Strategy*, 11.

10 DECODE, *Next Generation*, 68.

11 Hamilton, *Undervoiced Voices*, 8, 10.

12 Ignite the Americas, *Policy Primer*, 4.

13 Ignite the Americas, *Ignite the Americas Youth Arts Policy Forum*, 7.

14 Ibid., 12–13.

15 Upchurch, "Linking Cultural Policy," 239.

16 Andrew and Gattinger, Introduction, 2.

17 Regent Park Focus Youth Media Arts Centre, "About Us," accessed 18 November 2012, http://www.catchdaflava.com/content/aboutus.html.

18 Warner, *Youth on Youth*, 32.

19 Low, "Says Who?" 45–6.

20 Ibid., 46.

21 Warner, *Youth on Youth*, 28. Phrases in square brackets are Warner's additions.

22 Ibid., 33.

23 The Remix Project, "Remix Refresh."

24 Warner, *Youth on Youth*, 33.

25 Ibid.

26 Ibid.

27 Wright, John, and Sheel, *Edmonton Arts*, 11.

28 DECODE, *Next Generation*, 6.

29 The Remix Project, accessed 9 September 2009, http://theremixproject.ca/site/.

30 Ibid.

31 The Remix Project, "Remix Refresh."

32 Ibid.

33 Gavin Sheppard, interview with the author, November 2010.

34 I.C. Visions, "Bio," MySpace, accessed 18 November 2012, http://www.myspace.com/icvisions.

35 Sheppard, interview.

36 The Remix Project, http://theremixproject.ca/site/.
37 The Remix Project, "The Remix Project – Investing in Talent."
38 The Remix Project, "Remix Refresh." .
39 The Remix Project, "The Remix Project – A New Home."
40 The Remix Project, "The Remix Project – What's Up Next?"
41 Sheppard, interview.
42 The Remix Project, "Remix Refresh."
43 Ibid.
44 Sheppard, interview.

CONCLUSION

1 *Almost Famous*, dir. Crowe.
2 Gaudet, *Emerging Adulthood*, 7.
3 Zemans, "Where Is Here," 10.
4 Ibid.
5 Jeffrey, *Youth Policy*.
6 Franke, *Current Realities*, 18.
7 Franke, *Current Realities*; Zemans and Coles, "One Hundred Musicians."
8 Secréteriat à la Jeunesse, *Investing in Youth*, 4.
9 Secréteriat à la Jeunesse, *Bringing Youth*, 13.
10 Zemans and Coles, "One Hundred Musicians," 12.
11 Cited in Jeffrey, *Youth Policy*, 9.
12 Jeffrey, *Youth Policy*, 13.
13 Piper, "An 'Independent' View," 425.
14 Jeffrey, *Youth Policy*, 4.
15 *Foundations & Pipelines*, 1.
16 Gaudet, *Emerging Adulthood*, 19.
17 Franke, *Current Realities*, 48.
18 Ministère de l'Éducation, du Loisir et du Sport, *Teacher Training*, 201.
19 Ibid., 204.
20 Noah Bick, interview with the author, June 2009.
21 August to December is the length of a CEGEP semester. In the province of Quebec, CEGEP is a post-secondary institution that prepares students for university or technical careers.
22 Meyer Billurcu, interview with the author, July 2009.
23 Noah Bick, interview the author, October 2010.
24 Meyer Billurcu, interview with the author, October 2010.
25 Bick, interview, October 2010.
26 Hesmondhalgh, "Indie: The Institutional Politics," 42.

27 Billurcu, interview, October 2010.
28 Bick, interview, October 2010.
29 Billurcu, interview, October 2010.

Bibliography

Albright, Linda. *Creative Spaces of Children and Youth: Submission to the Government of Canada's Ministry of Finance Stimulus Package 2009 Federal Budget.* Toronto: Arts Network for Children & Youth, 2008.

Almost Famous. Directed by Cameron Crowe. 2000. Los Angeles, CA: Colombia Pictures, 2005. DVD.

Andrew, Caroline, and Monica Gattinger. Introduction to *Accounting for Culture: Thinking through Cultural Citizenship,* edited by Caroline Andrew, Monica Gattinger, M. Sharon Jeannotte, and Will Straw, 1–6. Ottawa: University of Ottawa Press, 2005.

Arnett, Jeffrey. "Emerging Adulthood: A Theory of Development from the Late Teens through the Twenties." *American Psychologist* 55, no. 5 (2000): 469–80.

Arnold, Matthew. "Sweetness and Light." 1869. In *A Cultural Studies Reader: History, Theory, Practice,* edited by Jessica Munns and Gita Rajan, 20–32. London: Longman, 1995.

Atkinson, Robert. *The Life Story Interview.* London: Sage, 1998.

Baeker, Greg. "Back to the Future: The Colloquium in Context: The Democratization of Culture and Cultural Democracy." In *Accounting for Culture: Thinking through Cultural Citizenship,* edited by Caroline Andrew, Monica Gattinger, M. Sharon Jeannotte, and Will Straw, 279–86. Ottawa: University of Ottawa Press, 2005.

Banks, Mark, and David Hesmondhalgh. "Looking for Work in Creative Industries Policy." *International Journal of Cultural Policy* 15, no. 4 (2009): 415–30.

Banks, Mark, and Justin O'Connor. "After the Creative Industries." *International Journal of Cultural Policy* 15, no. 4 (2009): 365–73.

Beaujot, Roderic, and Don Kerr. *Emerging Youth Transition Patterns in Canada: Opportunities and Risks*. Ottawa: Policy Research Initiative, Government of Canada, 2007.

Bennett, Tony. "Putting Policy into Cultural Studies." In *Cultural Studies*, edited by Lawrence Grossberg, Cary Nelson, and Paula Treichler, 23–33. London: Routledge, 1992.

Bertaux, Daniel, ed. *Biography and Society: The Life History Approach in the Social Sciences*. Beverly Hills, CA: Sage, 1981.

Booth, Timothy A., and Wendy Booth. *Growing up with Parents Who Have Learning Difficulties*. London: Routledge, 1998.

Bourdieu, Pierre. *The Field of Cultural Production: Essays on Art and Literature*. Edited by Randal Johnson. Cambridge, UK: Polity Press, 1993.

– *The Rules of Art: Genesis and Structure of the Literary Field*. 1992. Translated by Susan Emanuel. Cambridge, UK: Polity Press, 1996.

Bradford, Neil. *Creative Cities Structure Policy Dialogue Backgrounder*. Ottawa: Canadian Policy Research Networks, 2004.

Buckingham, David. *Media Education: Literacy, Learning, and Contemporary Culture*. Cambridge, UK: Polity Press, 2003.

Canadian Conference of the Arts. *ABC on the Status of the Artist*. Ottawa: Canadian Conference of the Arts, 2008.

– *A Canadian Cultural Policy: A Study in First Principles*. Ottawa: Canadian Conference of the Arts, 2006.

– "CCA Bulletin 03/09 – The 2009/2010 Federal Stimulus Budget and Culture: More Status Quo than Economic Stimulus." *Canadian Conference for the Arts.ca*, 27 January 2009. http://ccarts.ca/federal-policies-investments/the-2009-2010-federal-stimulus-budget-and-culture-more-status-quo-than-economic-stimulus/.

– "CCA Bulletin 04/09 – More Budget Details: Where Is the $335 Million Going?" *Canadian Conference of the Arts.ca*, 9 February 2009. http://ccarts.ca/federal-policies-investments/more-budget-details-where-is-the-335-million-going/.

– "CCA Bulletin 49/08 – The Economic Meltdown: Arts Organizations Feel the Heat and Finance Minister Flaherty Seeks Ideas for Economic Stimulation." *Canadian Conference for the Arts.ca*, 25 November 2008. http://ccarts.ca/federal-policies-investments/the-economic-meltdown-arts-organizations-feel-the-heat-and-finance-minister-flaherty-seeks-ideas-for-economic-stimulation/.

– "CCA Bulletin 52/08 – The Cultural Sector: Part of the Solution for an Economic Stimulus." *Canadian Conference of the Arts.ca*, 18 December

2008. http://ccarts.ca/federal-policies-investments/the-cultural-sector-
%E2%80%93-part-of-the-solution-for-economic-stimulus/.

– *Final Report of the Working Group on Cultural Policy for the 21st
Century.* Ottawa: Canadian Conference of the Arts, 1998.

– *Towards a National Advocacy Strategy: If There's a Will, There's a Way:
Report on the 2008 CCA Regional Forums.* Ottawa: Canadian Conference of the Arts, 2009.

Canadian Youth Arts Network. *The Final Report of the Canadian Youth
Arts Forum Des Arts De La Jeunesse Canadienne.* Toronto: Canadian
Youth Arts Network, 2008.

Caves, Richard. *Creative Industries: Contracts between Art and Commerce.*
Cambridge, MA: Harvard University Press, 2000.

Chamberlayne, Prue, Joanna Bornat, and Tom Wengraf, eds. *The Turn to
Biographical Methods in Social Science: Comparative Issues and
Examples.* London: Routledge, 2000.

Clarke, John, Stuart Hall, Tony Jefferson, and Brian Roberts. "Subcultures,
Cultures, and Class." In *Resistance through Rituals: Youth Subcultures
in Post-War Britain*, edited by Stuart Hall and Tony Jefferson, 3–59.
London: Routledge, 2006.

Clough, Peter. *Narratives and Fictions in Educational Research.* Buckingham:
Open University Press, 2002.

Coles, Amanda. *Focus on Youth: Canadian Youth Arts Programming and
Policy.* Ottawa: Canadian Cultural Observatory, Department of
Canadian Heritage, 2007.

Coles, Bob. "The Transformation of Youth Labour Markets in the UK."
Youth & Policy 100 (2008): 119–28.

COLLE. "Legal Information Sheet," http://collemontreal.org/wp-content/
uploads/2010/05/LegalInformationSheet.pdf.

Conference Board of Canada. *Valuing Culture: Measuring and Understanding Canada's Creative Economy.* Ottawa: Conference Board of
Canada, 2008.

Creative City Network of Canada. *Making the Case for Culture: Personal
and Social Development of Children and Youth.* Vancouver: Creative
City Network of Canada, 2005.

Creative Skillset. *Strategic Skills Assessment for the Creative Industries.*
London: Creative Skillset, 2010.

Cunningham, Stuart. "The Creative Industries after Cultural Policy: A
Genealogy and Some Possible Preferred Futures." *International Journal
of Cultural Studies* 7, no. 1 (2004): 105–15.

DECODE. *Next Generation of Artistic Leaders and Arts Audience Dialogues.*
    Ottawa: Canada Council for the Arts, 2007.
Department for Culture, Media and Sport. *Creative Britain: New Talents
    for the New Economy.* London, UK: Department of Culture, Media and
    Sport, 2008.
Department of Finance Canada. *Canada's Economic Action Plan: Budget
    2009.* Ottawa: Government of Canada, 2009.
Department of Justice Canada. "Arts and Recreation Sector Round
    Table on Youth Justice Renewal 13 December 1999." *Justice.gc.ca.*
    http://www.justice.gc.ca/eng/pi/yj-jj/prt/ars.html.
– *Status of the Artist Act,* S.C. 1992, c. 33, Ottawa: Government of
    Canada, 1992.
Denzin, Norman K., and Yvonna S. Lincoln, eds. *Handbook of Qualitative
    Research.* Thousand Oaks, CA: Sage, 1994.
– *The Landscape of Qualitative Research.* Thousand Oaks, CA: Sage,
    1998.
Donald, Betsy, and Douglas Morrow, with Andrew Athanasiu. *Competing
    for Talent: Implications for Social and Cultural Policy in Canadian City-
    Regions.* Ottawa: Strategic Research and Analysis (SRA), Strategic Plan-
    ning and Policy, Department of Canadian Heritage, 2003.
Dubinsky, Lon. "In Praise of Small Cities: Cultural life in Kamloops, BC."
    Canadian Journal of Communication 31, no.1 (2006): 85–106.
Duxbury, Nancy. *Creative Cities: Principles and Practices.* Ottawa:
    Canadian Policy Research Networks, 2004.
– ed. *Under Construction: The State of Cultural Infrastructure in Canada.*
    Vancouver: Centre for Expertise on Culture and Communities, 2008.
Erben, Michael, ed. *Biography and Education.* London: Falmer, 1998.
Fix, Elizabeth, and Nadine Sivak. "The Growing Case for Youth Engage-
    ment through Culture." *Our Diverse Cities: Ontario* 4 (2007): 145–51.
Florida, Richard. *The Rise of the Creative Class: And How It's Transform-
    ing Work, Leisure, Community, and Everyday Life.* New York: Basic
    Books, 2002.
Foote, John A. *Federal Cultural Policy in Canada.* Ottawa: Strategic
    Research and Analysis Division (SRA), Strategic Policy and Research,
    Department of Canadian Heritage, 2003.
*Foundations & Pipelines: Building Social Infrastructure to Foster Youth
    Organizing.* Toronto: Funders Alliance for Children Youth and Families
    and the Laidlaw Foundation.
Franke, Sandra. *Current Realities and Emerging Issues Facing Youth in
    Canada: An Analytical Framework for Public Policy Research,*

Development, and Evaluation. Ottawa: Policy Research Initiative, Government of Canada, 2010.

Galloway, Susan, and Stewart Dunlop. "A Critique of Definitions of the Cultural and Creative Industries in Public Policy." *International Journal of Cultural Policy* 13, no.1 (2007): 17–31.

Gattinger, Monica, and Diane Saint-Pierre. "Can National Cultural Policy Approaches Be Used for Sub-National Comparisons? An Analysis of the Québec and Ontario Experiences in Canada." *International Journal of Cultural Policy* 14, no. 3 (2008): 335–54.

Gaudet, Stéphanie. *Emerging Adulthood: A New Stage in the Life Course.* Ottawa: Policy Research Initiative, Government of Canada, 2007.

Gaztambide-Fernandez, Ruben. "The Artist in Society: Understandings, Expectations, and Curriculum Implications." *Curriculum Inquiry* 38, no. 3 (2008): 233–65.

Gertler, Meric S. *Creative Cities: What Are They For, How Do They Work, and How Do We Build Them?* Ottawa: Canadian Policy Research Networks, 2004.

Gertler, Meric S., Richard Florida, Gary Gates, and Tara Vinodrai. *Competing on Creativity: Placing Ontario's Cities in North American Context.* Toronto: Ontario Ministry of Enterprise, Opportunity and Innovation and the Institute for Competitiveness and Prosperity, 2002.

Giroux, Henry. *Fugitive Cultures: Race, Violence, and Youth.* New York: Routledge, 1996.

Gollmitzer, Mirjam, and Catherine Murray. *From Economy to Ecology: A Policy Framework for Creative Labour.* Ottawa: Canadian Conference for the Arts, 2008.

Goodley, Dan. *Self-Advocacy in the Lives of People with Learning Disabilities: The Politics of Resilience.* Buckingham: Open University Press, 2000.

Goodley, Dan, Rebecca Lawthom, Peter Clough, and Michele Moore, eds. *Researching Life Stories: Method, Theory and Analyses in a Biographical Age.* London: Routledge, 2004.

Government of Canada. "Protecting Canada's Future." Speech from the Throne. Ottawa. 19 September 2008.

Gregg, Allan. "Reframing the Case for Culture." In *Accounting for Culture: Thinking through Cultural Citizenship,* edited by Caroline Andrew, Monica Gattinger, M. Sharon Jeannotte, and Will Straw, 74–81. Ottawa: University of Ottawa Press, 2005.

Hamilton, Dale. *Undervoiced Voices: Strategies for Participation.* Toronto: Arts Network for Children & Youth, 2006.

Haraway, Donna. "Situated Knowledges: The Science Question in Feminism and the Privilege of Partial Perspective." In *The Blackwell Reader in Contemporary Social Theory*, edited by Anthony Elliot, 287–99. London: Blackwell, 1999.

Hebdige, Dick. *Hiding in the Light: On Images and Things*. London: Routledge, 1988.

Henighan, Tom. *The Presumption of Culture: Structure, Strategy, and Survival in the Canadian Cultural Landscape*. Vancouver: Raincoast Books, 1996.

Hesmondhalgh, David. "Bourdieu, the Media and Cultural Production." *Media, Culture & Society* 28, no. 2 (2006): 211–31.

– "The British Dance Music Industry: A Case Study in Independent Cultural Production." *British Journal of Sociology* 49, no. 2 (1998): 234–51.

– *The Cultural Industries*. London: Sage, 2002.

– "Indie: The Institutional Politics and Aesthetics of a Popular Music Genre." *Cultural Studies* 13, no. 1 (1999): 34–61.

– "Post-Punk's Attempt to Democratise the Music Industry: The Success and Failure of Rough Trade." *Popular Music* 16, no. 3 (1997): 255–74.

Hesmondhalgh, David, and Andy Pratt. "Cultural Industries and Cultural Policy." *International Journal of Cultural Policy* 11, no. 1 (2005): 1–13.

Hill Strategies Research Inc. *New Report Reveals 10 Key Facts About the Working Lives of Artists in Canada*. Hamilton: Hill Strategies, 2008.

Higgs, Peter, Stuart Cunningham, and Hasan Bakhshi. *Beyond the Creative Industries: Mapping the Creative Economy in the United Kingdom*. London: Nesta, 2008.

Hoechsmann, Michael, and Bronwen Low. *Reading Youth Writing: New Literacies, Cultural Studies, and Education*. New York: Peter Lang, 2008.

Huq, Rupa. *Beyond Subculture: Youth and Pop in a Multi-Ethnic World*. London: Routledge, 2005.

Ignite the Americas. *Ignite the Americas Youth Arts Policy Forum: Post Forum Report*. Toronto: Ignite the Americas, 2009.

– *Policy Primer*. Toronto: Ignite the Americas, 2008.

Jeannotte, M. Sharon, and Will Straw. "Reflections on the Cultural and Political Implications of Cultural Citizenship." In *Accounting for Culture: Thinking through Cultural Citizenship*, edited by Caroline Andrew, Monica Gattinger, M. Sharon Jeannotte, and Will Straw, 273–8. Ottawa: University of Ottawa Press, 2005.

Jeffrey, Kamara. *Youth Policy: What Works and What Doesn't*. Toronto: United Way, 2008.

Jenkins, Henry. *Confronting the Challenges of Participatory Culture: Media Education for the 21st Century*. Chicago: MacArthur Foundation, 2006.

– *Convergence Culture: Where Old and New Media Collide*. New York: New York University Press, 2006.

L'APLAS. *Quand L'Affichage Devient Sauvage!* Montreal: L'APLAS, 2010.

Leadbeater, Charles, and Kate Oakley. *The Independents: Britain's New Cultural Entrepreneur*. London: Demos, 1999.

Levine, Peter. "A Public Voice for Youth: The Audience Problem in Digital Media and Civic Education." In *Civic Life Online: Learning How Digital Media Can Engage Youth*, edited by W. Lance Bennett, 119–38. Cambridge, MA: MIT Press, 2007.

Lloyd, Richard. *Neo-Bohemia: Art and Commerce in the Postindustrial City*. New York: Routledge, 2006.

Low, Bronwen. "Says Who? Video, Voice, and Youth Self-Representation." In *Reading Youth Writing: New Literacies, Cultural Studies, and Education*, by Michael Hoechsmann and Bronwen Low. New York: Peter Lang, 2008.

Maxwell, Joseph. "Designing a Qualitative Study." In *Handbook of Applied Social Research Methods*, edited by Leonard Bickman and Debra J. Rog, 69–100. Thousand Oaks, CA: Sage, 1998.

Maxwell, Rachel. *The Place of Arts and Culture in Canada's Foreign Policy*. Ottawa: Canadian Conference of the Arts, 2007.

McGuigan, Jim. "Doing a Florida Thing: The Creative Class Thesis and Cultural Policy." *International Journal of Cultural Policy* 15, no. 3 (2009): 291–300.

McRobbie, Angela. *British Fashion Design: Rag Trade or Image Industry?* London: Routledge, 1998.

– "Clubs to Companies: Notes on the Decline of Political Culture in Speeded up Creative Worlds." *Culture Studies* 16, no.4 (2002): 516–31.

– *Feminism and Youth Culture*. London: Routledge, 2000.

– "From Holloway to Hollywood: Happiness at Work in the New Cultural Economy." In *Cultural Economy: Cultural Analysis and Commercial Life*, edited by Paul du Gay and Michael Pryke, 97–114. London: Sage, 2002.

– *In the Culture Society: Art, Fashion, and Popular Music*. London: Routledge, 1999.

– "Making a Living in London's Small-Scale Creative Sector." In *Cultural Industries and the Production of Culture*, edited by Dominic Power and Allen J. Scott, 130–43. London: Routledge, 2004.

– *Postmodernism and Popular Culture*. London: Routledge, 1994.

- "Second-hand Dresses and the Role of the Ragmarket." In *Zoot Suits and Second-Hand Dresses: An Anthology of Fashion and Music*, edited by Angela McRobbie, 23–49. London: MacMillan, 1989.

Meisel, John. "The Chameleon-like Complexion of Cultural Policy: Re-educating an Octogenarian." In *Accounting for Culture: Thinking through Cultural Citizenship*, edited by Caroline Andrew, Monica Gattinger, M. Sharon Jeannotte, and Will Straw, 54–73. Ottawa: University of Ottawa Press, 2005.

Mercer, Colin. "From Indicators to Governance to the Mainstream: Tools for Cultural Policy and Citizenship." In *Accounting for Culture: Thinking through Cultural Citizenship*, edited by Caroline Andrew, Monica Gattinger, M. Sharon Jeannotte, and Will Straw, 9–20. Ottawa: University of Ottawa Press, 2005.

Miller, Robert L. *Researching Life Stories and Family Histories*. London: Sage, 2000.

Ministère de l'Éducation, du Loisir et du Sport. *Quebec Education Program: Secondary School Education, Cycle One*. Quebec: Government of Quebec, 2004.

- *Teacher Training: Orientations, Professional Competencies*. Quebec: Government of Quebec, 2001.

Molgat, Marc, and Katharine Larose-Hébert. *The Values of Youth in Canada*. Ottawa: Policy Research Initiative, Government of Canada, 2010.

Muggleton, David, and Rupert Weinzierl. "What is 'Post-subcultural Studies' Anyway?" In *The Post-Subcultures Reader*, edited by David Muggleton and Rupert Weinzierl, 3–23. Oxford: Berg, 2003.

Murray, Catherine. "Cultural Participation: A Fuzzy Cultural Policy Paradigm." In *Accounting for Culture: Thinking through Cultural Citizenship*, edited by Caroline Andrew, Monica Gattinger, M. Sharon Jeannotte, and Will Straw, 32–54. Ottawa: University of Ottawa Press, 2005.

Neil, Garry. *The Status of Status: Update on Initiatives to Improve the Socio-Economic Status of Canadian Artists*. Toronto: Neil Craig Associates, 2007.

Oakley, Kate. "The Disappearing Arts: Creativity and Innovation after the Creative Industries." *International Journal of Cultural Policy* 15 (2009): 403–13.

- "Include Us Out: Economic Development and Social Policy in the Creative Industries." *Cultural Trends* 15, no. 4 (2006): 255–73.

- "Not So Cool Britannia: The Role of the Creative Industries in Economic Development." *International Journal of Cultural Studies* 7, no. 1 (2004): 67–77.

Parker, Tony. *Life after Life: Interviews with Twelve Murderers*. London: Secker & Warburg, 1990.

Piano, Doreen. "Resisting Subjects: DIY Feminism and the Politics of Style in Subcultural Formations." In *The Post-Subcultures Reader*, edited by David Muggleton and Rupert Weinzierl, 253–65. Oxford: Berg, 2003.

Pied Carré. *Mémoire sur les Quartiers Culturels*. Présenté à la Commission sur la Culture, le Patrimoine et les Sports. Montréal: Pied Carré, 2011.

Piper, Tina. "An 'Independent' View of Bill C-32's Copyright Reform." In *From "Radical Extremism" To "Balanced Copyright": Canadian Copyright and the Digital Agenda*, edited by Michael Geist, 423–46. Toronto: Irwin Law, 2010.

Plummer, Kenneth. *Documents of Life: An Introduction to the Problems and Literature of a Humanistic Method*. London: George Allen & Unwin, 1983.

Potts, Jason, and Stuart Cunningham. "Four Models of the Creative Industries." *International Journal of Cultural Policy* 14, no. 3 (2008): 233–47.

Q. CBC Radio. "Jian Ghomeshi Interviews The Bitter End." 3 December 2009. http://podcast.cbc.ca/mp3/qpodcast_ 20091203_23990.mp3.

Reddington, Helen. "'Lady' Punks in Bands: A Subculturette?" In *The Post-subcultures Reader*, edited by David Muggleton and Rupert Weinzierl, 239–51. Oxford: Berg, 2003.

"The Remix Project – A New Home." YouTube. Uploaded 25 May 2010. http://www.youtube.com/user/theremixproject#p/c/323FB8C409DA2 FoF/4/FKRZ8ZyLtxo.

"The Remix Project – Investing in Talent." YouTube. Uploaded 25 May 2010. http://www.youtube.com/user/theremixproject#p/a/323FB8C409 DA2FoF/o/4Zbn3If2oiw.

"The Remix Project – What's Up Next?" YouTube. Uploaded 25 May 2010. http://www.youtube.com/user/theremixproject#p/a/323FB8C409 DA2FoFo/4Zbn3If2oiw.

The Remix Project. "Remix Refresh." YouTube. Uploaded 30 June 2010. http://www.youtube.com/user/theremixproject#p/a/u/1/WknFSeaElrI.

Riessman, Catherine Kohler. *Narrative Analysis*. London: Sage, 1993.

Robertson, Clive. *Policy Matters: Administrations of Art and Culture*. Toronto: YYZ Books, 2006.

Schafer, D. Paul, and André Fortier. *Review of the Federal Policies for the Arts in Canada 1944–1988*. Ottawa: Canadian Conference of the Arts, 1989.

Secrétariat à la Jeunesse. *Bringing Youth into Québec's Mainstream*. Quebec: Government of Quebec, 2001.

– *Investing in Youth: Empowering Québec's Future*. Quebec: Government of Quebec, 2009.
– *Young People Fully Involved in Their Own Success*. Quebec: Government of Quebec, 2006.
Sefton-Green, Julian. "Introduction: Evaluating Creativity." In *Evaluating Creativity: Making and Learning by Young People*, edited by Julian Sefton-Green and Rebecca Sinker, 1–15. London: Routledge, 2000.
– ed. *Young People, Creativity, and New Technologies: The Challenge of Digital Arts*. London: Routledge, 1999.
Sefton-Green, Julian, and Vivienne Reiss. "Multimedia Literacies: Developing the Creative Uses of New Technology with Young People." In *Young People, Creativity, and New Technologies: The Challenge of Digital Arts*, edited by Julian Sefton-Green, 1–11. London: Routledge, 1999.
Slaby, Alexandra. *Making a Single Case for the Arts: An International Perspective*. Ottawa: Canadian Conference of the Arts, 2008.
Smith, Jonathan A, Rom Harré, and Luk Van Langenhove, eds. *Rethinking Methods in Psychology*. London: Sage, 1995.
Sokoloski, Robin. *So Much Things to Say: Report II*. Toronto: Canadian Youth Arts Network and Manifesto, 2008.
Soulja Boy. *Souljaboytellem.com*. Interscope, 2007.
"Soulja Boy Response to Ice-T." YouTube. Uploaded 20 June 2008. http://www.youtube.com/watch?v=OYsytJvYJzw.
Spencer, Amy. DIY: *The Rise of Lo-Fi Culture*. London: Marion Byars, 2005.
Stahl, Geoff. "Musicmaking and the City: Making Sense of the Montreal Scene." In *Sound and the City*, edited by Dietrich Helms and Thomas Phleps, 141–60. Bielfeld, DE: Transcript Verlag, 2007.
– "Tracing out an Anglo-Bohemia: Musicmaking and Myth in Montreal." *Public* 22/23, (2001): 99–121.
Standing Committee on Canadian Heritage. *A Sense of Place, A Sense of Being*. Ottawa: Department of Canadian Heritage, 1999.
Stanley, Dick. "Introduction: The Social Effects of Culture." *Canadian Journal of Communication* 31, no.1 (2006): 7–15.
Statistics Canada. *Industry – North American Industry Classification System 2002 (433), Class of Worker (6) and Sex (3) for the Labour Force 15 Years and over of Canada, Provinces, Territories, Census Metropolitan Areas and Census Agglomerations, 2006 Census – 20% Sample Data*. Ottawa: Industry Canada, 2008. Catalogue no. 97-559-XWE2006009. http://www5.statcan.gc.ca/bsolc/olc-cel/olc-cel?catno=97-559-XWE2006009&lang=eng.

– *Occupation – 2001 National Occupational Classification for Statistics (720a), Selected Labour Force, Demographic, Cultural, Educational and Income Characteristics (258) and Sex (3) for Population 15 Years and over, for Canada, Provinces, Territories, Census Metropolitan Areas and Census Agglomerations, 2001 Census – 20% Sample Data.* Ottawa: Industry Canada, 2003. Catalogue No. 97F0012XIE2001050. http://www5.statcan.gc.ca/bsolc/olc-cel/olc-cel?catno=97F0012XIE2001050&lang=eng.

Stolarick, Kevin, Richard Florida, and Lou Musante. *Montréal's Capacity for Creative Connectivity: Outlook & Opportunities.* Montreal: Culture Montreal, 2005.

Straw, Will. "Cultural Scenes." *Society and Leisure* 27, no. 2 (2004): 411–22.

– "Pathways of Cultural Movement." In *Accounting for Culture: Thinking through Cultural Citizenship,* edited by Caroline Andrew, Monica Gattinger, M. Sharon Jeannotte, and Will Straw, 183–97. Ottawa: University of Ottawa Press, 2005.

– "Scenes and Sensibilities." *Public* 22/23 (2002): 245–57.

Sutherland, Richard, and Will Straw. "The Canadian Music Industry at a Crossroads." In *How Canadian Communicate II: Media, Globalization, and Identity,* edited by David Taras, Maria Bakardjieva, and Frits Pannekoek, 141–65. Calgary: University of Calgary Press, 2007.

Thornton, Sarah. "The Social Logic of Subcultural Capital." In *The Subcultures Reader,* edited by Ken Gelder and Sarah Thornton, 200–9. London: Routledge, 2005.

Throsby, David. "Modelling the Cultural Industries." *International Journal of Cultural Policy* 14, no. 3 (2008): 217–32.

Towse, Ruth, ed. *Cultural Economics.* Cheltenham: Edward Elgar, 1997.

– *A Handbook of Cultural Economics.* Cheltenham: Edward Elgar, 2003.

Upchurch, Anna. "Linking Cultural Policy from Great Britain to Canada." *International Journal of Cultural Policy* 13, no. 3 (2007): 239–54.

Van Manen, Max. *Researching Lived Experience: Human Science for an Action Sensitive Pedagogy.* London, ON: Althouse Press, 2006.

Ville de Montréal. *Cultural Quarters.* Document presented to the Commission sur la Culture, le Patrimoine et les Sports. Montreal: Ville de Montréal, 2011.

– *Plan D'Action 2007–2017 – Montréal, Metropole Culturelle.* Montreal: Ville de Montréal, 2007.

Volkerling, Michael. "From Cool Britannia to Hot Nation: 'Creative Industries' Policies in Europe, Canada, and New Zealand." *Cultural Policy* 7, no. 3 (2001): 437–55.

Warner, Remi, in conjunction with the Grassroots Youth Collaborative. *Youth on Youth: Grassroots Youth Collaborative on Youth Led Organizing in the City of Toronto*. Toronto: Ontario Region of the Department of Canadian Heritage, 2005.

Williams, Raymond. *Culture*. London: Fontana, 1981.

Willis, Paul. *Common Culture: Symbolic Work at Play in the Everyday Cultures of the Young*. Boulder, CO: Westview Press, 1990.

Wright, Robin, Lindsay John, and Julia Sheel. *Edmonton Arts and Youth Feasibility Study*. Ottawa: Department of Justice Canada – Youth Justice Policy, 2005.

Zemans, Joyce. "Where Is Here? Canadian Culture in a Globalized Environment." Tenth Annual Robarts Lecture, York University, Toronto, 13 March 1996.

Zemans, Joyce, and Amanda Coles. "One Hundred Musicians! Youth Arts Policies in Canada." In *Art Programs for Positive Youth Development in Low-Income Communities*, edited by Robin Wright and Lindsay John. Waterloo, ON: Wilfrid Laurier University Press, forthcoming.

Index